ב"ה

TORAH STUDIES

Torah Studies

Season Two 5779

Student Textbook

The ROHR JEWISH LEARNING INSTITUTE
gratefully acknowledges
the pioneering support of

George & Pamela Rohr

Since its inception,
the JLI has been
a beneficiary of the vision,
generosity, care, and concern
of the Rohr family.

In the merit of
the tens of thousands of hours
of Torah study
by JLI students worldwide,
may they be blessed with health,
Yiddishe nachas from all their loved ones,
and extraordinary success
in all their endeavors.

DEDICATED TO

Mrs. Frumeth Polasky

*With deep appreciation for her partnership with JLI
in bringing Torah study to all corners of the world.*

෴

*In the merit of the Torah study by thousands of
students worldwide, may she be blessed with
good health, happiness, nachas from her loved
ones, and success in all her endeavors.*

לאורך ימים ושנים טובות.

Contents

Bo

Breaking Norms

Challenging Yourself to Touch Another

*Dedicated in loving memory of **Henoch Ephraim Ben Hershel** on the occasion of his yahrtzeit, 20 Teves*

לעילוי נשמת העניך אפרים בן הרשל ע"ה

PARSHA OVERVIEW
Bo

The last three of the Ten Plagues are visited on Egypt: a swarm of locusts devours all the crops and greenery; a thick, palpable darkness envelops the land; and all the firstborn of Egypt are killed at the stroke of midnight of the fifteenth day of the month of Nisan.

G-d commands the first mitzvah to be given to the people of Israel: to establish a calendar based on the monthly rebirth of the moon. The Israelites are also instructed to bring a "Passover offering" to G-d: a lamb or kid is to be slaughtered, and its blood sprinkled on the doorposts and lintels of every Israelite home, so that G-d should pass over these homes when He comes to kill the Egyptian firstborn. The roasted meat of the offering is to be eaten that night together with matzah (unleavened bread) and bitter herbs.

The death of the firstborn finally breaks Pharaoh's resistance, and he literally drives the Children of Israel from his land. So hastily do they depart that there is no time for their dough to rise, so the only provisions they take along are unleavened. Before they go, they ask their Egyptian neighbors for gold, silver, and garments—*fulfilling the promise made to Abraham that his descendants would leave Egypt with great wealth.*

The Children of Israel are commanded to consecrate all firstborn, and to observe the anniversary of the Exodus each year by removing all leaven from their possession for seven days, eating matzah, and telling the story of their redemption to their children. They are also commanded to wear tefilin *on the arm and head as a reminder of the Exodus and their resultant commitment to G-d.*

Origins of the Haggadah

A Text of Many Versions

TEXT 1

Shemot (Exodus) 13:3–8

וַיֹּאמֶר מֹשֶׁה אֶל הָעָם זָכוֹר אֶת הַיּוֹם הַזֶּה אֲשֶׁר יְצָאתֶם מִמִּצְרַיִם מִבֵּית עֲבָדִים כִּי בְּחֹזֶק יָד הוֹצִיא ה' אֶתְכֶם מִזֶּה וְלֹא יֵאָכֵל חָמֵץ: הַיּוֹם אַתֶּם יֹצְאִים בְּחֹדֶשׁ הָאָבִיב: וְהָיָה כִי יְבִיאֲךָ ה' אֶל אֶרֶץ הַכְּנַעֲנִי וְהַחִתִּי וְהָאֱמֹרִי וְהַחִוִּי וְהַיְבוּסִי אֲשֶׁר נִשְׁבַּע לַאֲבֹתֶיךָ לָתֶת לָךְ אֶרֶץ זָבַת חָלָב וּדְבָשׁ וְעָבַדְתָּ אֶת הָעֲבֹדָה הַזֹּאת בַּחֹדֶשׁ הַזֶּה: שִׁבְעַת יָמִים תֹּאכַל מַצֹּת וּבַיּוֹם הַשְּׁבִיעִי חַג לַה': מַצּוֹת יֵאָכֵל אֵת שִׁבְעַת הַיָּמִים וְלֹא יֵרָאֶה לְךָ חָמֵץ וְלֹא יֵרָאֶה לְךָ שְׂאֹר בְּכָל גְּבֻלֶךָ: וְהִגַּדְתָּ לְבִנְךָ בַּיּוֹם הַהוּא לֵאמֹר בַּעֲבוּר זֶה עָשָׂה ה' לִי בְּצֵאתִי מִמִּצְרָיִם.

Moses said to the people, "Remember this day, when you went out of Egypt, out of the house of bondage, for, with a mighty hand, G-d took you out of here, and [therefore] no leaven shall be eaten.

"Today you are going out, in the month of spring.

"And it will come to pass that G-d will bring you into the land of the Canaanites, the Hittites, the Amorites, the Hivvites, and the Jebusites, which He swore to your forefathers to give you a land flowing with milk and honey, and you shall perform this service in this month.

"For seven days you shall eat unleavened cakes, and on the seventh day, there is a festival for G-d.

"Unleavened cakes shall be eaten during the seven days, and no leaven shall be seen of yours [in your possession], and no leavening shall be seen of yours throughout all of your borders.

"And you shall tell your son on that day, saying, 'Because of this, G-d did [this] for me when I went out of Egypt.'"

An Obligation to Retell

TEXT 2

Maimonides, Mishneh Torah, Hilchot Chametz U'matzah, 7:1–2

Rabbi Moshe ben Maimon
(Maimonides, Rambam)
1135–1204

Halachist, philosopher, author, and physician. Maimonides was born in Córdoba, Spain. After the conquest of Córdoba by the Almohads, he fled Spain and eventually settled in Cairo, Egypt. There, he became the leader of the Jewish community and served as court physician to the vizier of Egypt. He is most noted for authoring the *Mishneh Torah*, an encyclopedic arrangement of Jewish law, and for his philosophical work, *Guide for the Perplexed*. His rulings on Jewish law are integral to the formation of halachic consensus.

מצות עשה של תורה לספר בנסים ונפלאות שנעשו לאבותינו במצרים בליל חמשה עשר בניסן שנאמר זכור את היום הזה אשר יצאתם ממצרים כמו שנאמר זכור את יום השבת. ומנין שבליל חמשה עשר תלמוד לומר והגדת לבנך ביום ההוא לאמר בעבור זה בשעה שיש מצה ומרור מונחים לפניך. ואף על פי שאין לו בן. אפילו חכמים גדולים חייבים לספר ביציאת מצרים וכל המאריך בדברים שאירעו ושהיו הרי זה משובח. מצוה להודיע לבנים ואפילו לא שאלו שנאמר והגדת לבנך.

It is a positive commandment of the Torah to relate the miracles and wonders wrought for our ancestors in Egypt on the night of the fifteenth of Nisan, as the verse states, "Remember this day, when you went out of Egypt," just as the verse states, "Remember the Sabbath day." From where [is it derived that this mitzvah is to be fulfilled on] the night of the fifteenth? The Torah teaches, "And you shall tell your son on that day, saying, 'Because of this . . . [implying that the mitzvah is to be fulfilled] when matzah and maror are placed before you. [The mitzvah applies] even though one does not have a son. Even great sages are obligated to tell about the Exodus from Egypt.

*Whoever elaborates concerning the events which oc-
curred and took place is worthy of praise.*

*It is a mitzvah to inform one's sons even though they do
not ask, as Exodus 13:8 states: "You shall tell your son."*

The Four Sons

TEXT 3

Passover Haggadah

כְּנֶגֶד אַרְבָּעָה בָנִים דִּבְּרָה תוֹרָה. אֶחָד חָכָם, וְאֶחָד רָשָׁע, וְאֶחָד תָּם,
וְאֶחָד שֶׁאֵינוֹ יוֹדֵעַ לִשְׁאוֹל.

חָכָם מָה הוּא אוֹמֵר? מַה הָעֵדוֹת וְהַחֻקִּים וְהַמִּשְׁפָּטִים אֲשֶׁר צִוָּה יְיָ
אֱלֹהֵינוּ אֶתְכֶם? וְאַף אַתָּה אֱמָר לוֹ כְּהִלְכוֹת הַפֶּסַח: אֵין מַפְטִירִין אַחַר
הַפֶּסַח אֲפִיקוֹמָן.

רָשָׁע מָה הוּא אוֹמֵר? מָה הָעֲבוֹדָה הַזֹּאת לָכֶם? לָכֶם - וְלֹא לוֹ. וּלְפִי
שֶׁהוֹצִיא אֶת עַצְמוֹ מִן הַכְּלָל כָּפַר בְּעִקָּר. וְאַף אַתָּה הַקְהֵה אֶת שִׁנָּיו
וֶאֱמָר לוֹ: בַּעֲבוּר זֶה עָשָׂה יְיָ לִי בְּצֵאתִי מִמִּצְרָיִם. לִי - וְלֹא לוֹ. אִילוּ
הָיָה שָׁם, לֹא הָיָה נִגְאָל.

תָּם מָה הוּא אוֹמֵר? מַה זֹּאת? וְאָמַרְתָּ אֵלָיו: בְּחֹזֶק יָד הוֹצִיאָנוּ יְיָ
מִמִּצְרַיִם, מִבֵּית עֲבָדִים.

וְשֶׁאֵינוֹ יוֹדֵעַ לִשְׁאוֹל - אַתְּ פְּתַח לוֹ, שֶׁנֶּאֱמַר: וְהִגַּדְתָּ לְבִנְךָ בַּיּוֹם הַהוּא
לֵאמֹר, בַּעֲבוּר זֶה עָשָׂה יְיָ לִי בְּצֵאתִי מִמִּצְרָיִם.

Passover *Haggadah*
The Passover *Haggadah* was
compiled during the Talmudic
era. It incorporates verses
from the Torah and Talmudic
exegesis to tell the story of the
Exodus. The *Haggadah*, which
also establishes the structure
of the *seder*, has been printed
in thousands of editions and
has spawned thousands of
commentaries, making it one
of the most popular books
in the history of literature.

*The Torah speaks of four children: One is wise, one
is wicked, one is simple, and one does not know how
to ask.*

The wise one, what does he say? "What are the testi-monies, the statutes, and the laws which the L-rd, our G-d, has commanded you?" You, in turn, shall instruct him in the laws of Passover, [up to] "One is not to eat any dessert after the Passover lamb."

The wicked one, what does he say? "What is this service to you?!" He says "to you," but not to him! By thus excluding himself from the community he has denied that which is fundamental. You therefore blunt his teeth and say to him, "It is because of this that the L-rd did for me when I left Egypt"; "for me"—but not for him! If he had been there, he would not have been redeemed!

The simpleton, what does he say? "What is this?" Thus you shall say to him, "With a strong hand the L-rd took us out of Egypt, from the house of slaves."

As for the one who does not know how to ask, you must initiate him, as it is said, "You shall tell your child on that day, 'It is because of this that the L-rd did for me when I left Egypt.'"

1. The Wicked Son

TEXT 4A

Shemot (Exodus) 12:26

וְהָיָה כִּי יֹאמְרוּ אֲלֵיכֶם בְּנֵיכֶם מָה הָעֲבֹדָה הַזֹּאת לָכֶם:

And it will come to pass if your children say to you, "What is this service to you?"

TEXT 4B

Rashi to Shemot (Exodus) 13:5

נאמר והיה כי יאמרו אליכם בניכם מה העבודה הזאת לכם בבן רשע הכתוב מדבר שהוציא את עצמו מן הכלל.

It is stated, "And it will come to pass if your children say to you, 'What is this service to you?'" That verse refers to a wicked son, who excludes himself from the community [by saying "to you"].

Rabbi Shlomo Yitzchaki (Rashi)
1040–1105
Most noted biblical and Talmudic commentator. Born in Troyes, France, Rashi studied in the famed *yeshivot* of Mainz and Worms. His commentaries on the Pentateuch and the Talmud, which focus on the straightforward meaning of the text, appear in virtually every edition of the Talmud and Bible.

2. The Simple Son

TEXT 5A

Shemot (Exodus) 13:14

וְהָיָה כִּי יִשְׁאָלְךָ בִנְךָ מָחָר לֵאמֹר מַה זֹּאת וְאָמַרְתָּ אֵלָיו בְּחֹזֶק יָד
הוֹצִיאָנוּ ה' מִמִּצְרַיִם מִבֵּית עֲבָדִים:

And it will come to pass if your son asks you in the future, saying, "What is this?" you shall say to him, "With a mighty hand did the L-rd take us out of Egypt, out of the house of bondage."

TEXT 5B

Rashi, ad loc.

"מַה זֹּאת." זֶה תִּנוֹק טִפֵּשׁ שֶׁאֵינוֹ יוֹדֵעַ לְהַעֲמִיק שְׁאֵלָתוֹ וְסוֹתֵם
וְשׁוֹאֵל מַה זֹּאת.

[And it will come to pass if your son asks you in the future, saying,] "What is this?" ["What is this"] is the question of the simple child, who does not know how to pose his question in depth, and asks a general question, "What is this?"

3. The Son Who Does Not Know How to Ask

TEXT 6A

Shemot (Exodus) 13:8

וְהִגַּדְתָּ לְבִנְךָ בַּיּוֹם הַהוּא לֵאמֹר בַּעֲבוּר זֶה עָשָׂה ה' לִי בְּצֵאתִי מִמִּצְרָיִם:

And you shall tell your son on that day, saying, "Because of this, G-d did [this] for me when I went out of Egypt."

TEXT 6B

Rashi to Shemot (Exodus) 13:5

וכאן והגדת לבנך בבן שאינו יודע לשאול והכתוב מלמדך שתפתח לו אתה בדברי אגדה המושכין את הלב.

"And you shall tell your son," refers to a son who does not know to ask. Scripture teaches that you yourself should initiate the discourse for him with words of the Agadah, which draw his interest.

4. The Wise Son

TEXT 7A

Devarim (Deuteronomy) 6:20–24

כִּי יִשְׁאָלְךָ בִנְךָ מָחָר לֵאמֹר מָה הָעֵדֹת וְהַחֻקִּים וְהַמִּשְׁפָּטִים אֲשֶׁר צִוָּה ה' אֱ-לֹהֵינוּ אֶתְכֶם:

וְאָמַרְתָּ לְבִנְךָ עֲבָדִים הָיִינוּ לְפַרְעֹה בְּמִצְרָיִם וַיּוֹצִיאֵנוּ ה' מִמִּצְרַיִם בְּיָד חֲזָקָה:

וַיִּתֵּן ה' אוֹתֹת וּמֹפְתִים גְּדֹלִים וְרָעִים בְּמִצְרַיִם בְּפַרְעֹה וּבְכָל בֵּיתוֹ לְעֵינֵינוּ:

וְאוֹתָנוּ הוֹצִיא מִשָּׁם לְמַעַן הָבִיא אֹתָנוּ לָתֶת לָנוּ אֶת הָאָרֶץ אֲשֶׁר נִשְׁבַּע לַאֲבֹתֵינוּ:

וַיְצַוֵּנוּ ה' לַעֲשׂוֹת אֶת כָּל הַחֻקִּים הָאֵלֶּה לְיִרְאָה אֶת ה' אֱ-לֹהֵינוּ לְטוֹב לָנוּ כָּל הַיָּמִים לְחַיֹּתֵנוּ כְּהַיּוֹם הַזֶּה:

If your son asks you in time to come, saying, "What are the testimonies, the statutes, and the ordinances which the L-rd our G-d has commanded you?"

You shall say to your son, "We were slaves to Pharaoh in Egypt, and the L-rd took us out of Egypt with a strong hand.

"And G-d gave signs and wonders, great and terrible, upon Egypt, upon Pharaoh, and upon all his household, before our eyes.

"And he brought us out of there in order that He might bring us and give us the land which He swore to our fathers.

"And G-d commanded us to perform all these statutes, to fear the L-rd, our G-d, for our good all the days, to keep us alive, as of this day."

TEXT 7B

Rashi to Shemot (Exodus) 13:14

ובמקום אחר הוא אומר מה העדות והחקים והמשפטים וגו' הרי זאת שאלת בן חכם.

Elsewhere it says: "What are the testimonies, the statutes, and the ordinances. . . ?" so it follows that here is the question of the wise son.

Piquing the Children's Interest

Dipping Vegetables in Salt Water

TEXT 8

Rabbi Shneur Zalman of Liadi, Shulchan Aruch HaRav, Orach Chayim, 473:14

Rabbi Shneur Zalman of Liadi
(Alter Rebbe)
1745–1812

Chasidic rebbe, halachic authority, and founder of the Chabad movement. The Alter Rebbe was born in Liozna, Belarus, and was among the principal students of the Magid of Mezeritch. His numerous works include the *Tanya,* an early classic containing the fundamentals of Chabad Chasidism, and *Shulchan Aruch HaRav,* an expanded and reworked code of Jewish law.

אחר ששתו כוס ראשון צריך כל אחד ואחד לאכול מעט ירקות בטיבול, דהיינו שיטבלנו בחומץ או במי מלח או בשאר מיני טיבולים, ואם אין לו יטבלנו בחרוסת.

ולמה תקנו חכמים דבר זה?

כדי להתמי' את התינוקות שיראו שינוי שאוכלין ירקות בטיבול שאין דרך לאכלם קודם הסעודה בכל ימות השנה וישאלו על שינוי זה, שאמירת ההגדה מצותה לאמרה דרך תשובה על שאלות ששאלוהו שנאמר כי ישאלך בנך וגו' ואמרת לבנך עבדים היינו וגו'".

After drinking the first cup [of wine], each and every person must eat a small amount of dipped vegetables, i.e., they should dip [the vegetable] in vinegar or salt-water or other dips. If one has no other dip, he may dip it in the charoset.

Why did the rabbis ordain this practice?

To make the children wonder, so that when they see everyone eating dipped vegetables, something that is not usually done throughout the year, they will ask about it. For the Haggadah *must be recited as an answer to questions, as the verse states, "If your son asks you . . . You shall say to your son, 'We were slaves. . . .'"*

Handing Out Nuts

TEXT 9

Ibid. 472:31

מצוה לחלק לתינוקות קליות ואגוזים בליל פסח קודם עשיית הסדר
כדי שיראו שינוי וישאלו מה נשתנה הלילה הזה מכל הלילות.
ואף על פי שעל שאלה זו אין לנו מה להשיב להם, מכל מקום על
ידי שיראו שינוי זה ויתעוררו לשאול עליו, יתעוררו גם כן לשאול
על שינויים אחרים דהיינו שאוכלין מצה ומרור ויושבין בהסיבה,
וישיבו להם עבדים היינו וכו'".

It is a mitzvah to distribute roasted seeds and nuts to children on Passover night before carrying out the seder *so that the children will notice the change and ask: Why is this night different than all other nights?*

Although we do not have an answer for them [concerning this matter], since they will see this change and be curious to ask about it, they will be motivated to ask about the other changes [that take place], e.g., that matzah and maror *are eaten, that we sit reclining, [etc]. And [then,] we will answer them, "We were slaves to Pharaoh in Egypt. . . ."*

Removing the Table

TEXT 10A

Rabbi Shneur Zalman of Liadi, ibid., 473:38

בימי חכמי הגמרא שהיו להם שולחנות קטנים לפני כל אחד ואחד
מהמסובין, הצריכו חכמים לעקור מלפני מי שאומר ההגדה את
השולחן הקטן שלפניו עם המצות המונחות עליו ולהניחם בזוית
אחרת כדי שיראו התינוקות וישאלו למה מסירין המצות ועדיין לא
אכלנו, ועל ידי כן יתעוררו לשאול גם כן שאר השאלות מה נשתנה
כו' כמו שיתבאר.

ובדורות האחרונים שכל המסובין אוכלין על שולחן אחד גדול ויש
טורח גדול בעקירתו, נהגו לעקור הקערה שבה המצות מלפני בעל
הבית האומר ההגדה ולהניחו בסוף השלחן, כאלו כבר אכלו כדי
שישאלו התינוקות.

In the sages of the Talmud's time, when it was customary for every person partaking of the meal to dine at his own small table, the sages mandated to remove from the person reciting the Haggadah his small table with the matzah upon it and to place it in another corner, so that the children will see and ask, "Why are the matzot being removed if we haven't yet eaten?" This will prompt them to also ask the rest of the questions, "Why is this night different?" etc. . . .

In later generations, when everyone partaking in a meal eats at one large table, and removing it would be difficult, it became customary to remove the seder plate which holds the matzot from before the person reciting the Haggadah and to place it at the edge of the table, as if everyone had already eaten, so that the children will ask.

Pouring the Second Cup of Wine

TEXT 10B

Ibid. 473:40

וְאַף עַל פִּי שֶׁאֵין צָרִיךְ לֶאֱחֹז הַכּוֹס בְּיָדוֹ עַד שֶׁיַּגִּיעַ לִלְפִיכָךְ כְּמוֹ שֶׁיִּתְבָּאֵר, אַף עַל פִּי כֵן צָרִיךְ לִמְזֹג מִיָּד קֹדֶם הַתְחָלַת אֲמִירַת הַהַגָּדָה כְּדֵי שֶׁיִּשְׁאֲלוּ הַתִּינוֹקוֹת לָמָּה שׁוֹתִין כּוֹס שֵׁנִי קֹדֶם הַסְּעוּדָה שֶׁאֵין דֶּרֶךְ לִשְׁתּוֹת כֵּן בְּכָל יְמוֹת הַשָּׁנָה, וְעַל יְדֵי כָךְ יִתְעוֹרְרוּ לִשְׁאֹל גַּם כֵּן שְׁאָר הַשְּׁאֵלוֹת מַה נִּשְׁתַּנָּה וְכוּ', לְקַיֵּם מַה שֶּׁנֶּאֱמַר כִּי יִשְׁאָלְךָ בִנְךָ מָחָר לֵאמֹר מָה הָעֵדוֹת וְהַחֻקִּים וְהַמִּשְׁפָּטִים וְגוֹ' וְאָמַרְתָּ לְבִנְךָ עֲבָדִים הָיִינוּ וְכוּ'".

Though it is not necessary to hold the [second] cup [of wine] until one reaches the passage "lefichach," we still pour the second cup immediately before beginning to recite the Haggadah so that the children will ask why we are drinking a second cup before eating the meal—something not done every other day of the year. They will thereby be prompted to ask the rest of the questions, "Why is this night different?" etc., so that one can fulfill for his children the verse, "If your son asks you in time to come, saying, 'What are the testimonies, the statutes, and the ordinances,' etc. you shall say to your son, 'We were slaves.'"

Change

Mutual Responsibility

TEXT 11

The Rebbe, Rabbi Menachem Mendel Schneerson,
Igrot Kodesh, vol. 3, letter 749

Rabbi Menachem Mendel Schneerson
1902–1994

The towering Jewish leader of the 20th century, known as "the Lubavitcher Rebbe," or simply as "the Rebbe." Born in southern Ukraine, the Rebbe escaped Nazi-occupied Europe, arriving in the U.S. in June 1941. The Rebbe inspired and guided the revival of traditional Judaism after the European devastation, impacting virtually every Jewish community the world over. The Rebbe often emphasized that the performance of just one additional good deed could usher in the era of Mashiach. The Rebbe's scholarly talks and writings have been printed in more than 200 volumes.

ב"ה, ח"י אלול, השי"ת

ברוקלין,

אל אחינו ואחיותינו, בני ובנות ישראל, די בכל אתר ואתר,

ה' עליהם יחיו

שלום וברכה!

. . והנה האדם, כמו כל הנבראים ואפילו מלאכי עליון, בעל גוף ונפש הוא, וכמו שיש עני בגוף וצרכי הגוף, כך יש עני בנפש וצרכי הנפש, לכן גם בצדקה - ישנה צדקה בגשם וצדקה ברוח וכמרז"ל (תדב"א רבה פכ"ז) כי תראה ערום וכסיתו כיצד אלא אם ראית אדם שאין בו דברי תורה הכניסהו לביתך ולמדהו קריאת שמע ותפלה ולמדהו כו' וזרזהו במצות.

וכמו שבקשת כל אחד ואחת מאתנו היא לכתיבה וחתימה טובה בגשמיות וברוחניות, כך על כל אחד ואחת מאתנו להשתדל בצדקה הגשמית וצדקה הרוחניית גם יחד, ובפרט בימי אלול ותשרי.

ובבואנו בימים האלו לפני מלך מלכי המלכים הקדוש ברוך הוא יהי' בידי כל אחד ואחת מאתנו כולנו - חשבון גדול, גדול לפי מאודו שלו, של צדקה שעעשה להושיע את העני בגשם, ושל צדקה שעעשה להושיע את העני ברוח.

וכמו שבצדקה בגשם גם עני בגשם מחוייב בה, כי אין לך עני שאינו יכול למצוא אופן איך לעזור לעני חברו, כך בצדקה ברוח שגם העני ברוח מחוייב בה, כי אין לך איש ואשה בישראל שאינו יכול להשפיע על בני ובנות ישראל לקרבם ליראת שמים תורה ומצות.

By the Grace of G-d

18 Elul, 5710 [August 31, 1950]

Brooklyn, N.Y.

To our brothers and sisters, the sons and daughters of Israel, wherever they may be:

Greeting and Blessing:

The human being, like all creatures (including the supernal angels), possesses both a body and a soul. Just as there are those who are poor in body and bodily needs, so, too, are there paupers in spirit and spiritual needs. Thus, the mitzvah of charity includes both physical charity and spiritual charity. In the words of our sages, "[It is written:] 'If you see a naked person, you should cover him.' What is the meaning of this? If you see a person who is naked of the words of Torah, take him into your home, teach him to read the Shema and pray, teach him . . . and enjoin him regarding the mitzvot. . . ."

Just as every one of us wishes to be inscribed and sealed for material and spiritual good, so too must each and every one of us exert ourselves in both material and spiritual charity, specifically in the period of Elul and Tishrei.

As we come in these days before G-d, the King of Kings, blessed is He, may each of us have a large count of charitable deeds to help save those who are poor materially and those who are poor spiritually.

Regarding material charity, the law is that the material pauper is also obligated [to give], for even the most impoverished person can find a way to help his fellow pauper. The same applies to spiritual charity. There is no man or woman in Israel who cannot, in some way, influence his or her fellow Jews and bring them closer to the fear of Heaven, the Torah, and the mitzvot.

Changing the Routine

TEXT 12

The Rebbe, Rabbi Menachem Mendel Schneerson,
Igrot Kodesh, vol. 5, letter 1,477

ימי חג הפסח מתקרבים ובאים.

כל ענין שבעולם מלמד את האדם המתבונן חכמה והוראה...ונקל ביותר, על ידי עיון המתאים, למצוא הוראות כאלו בעיני התורה... ומצותי׳. ובפרט בענינים הכלליים אשר בה.

והנה אחד המיוחד שבענינים אלו הוא – זכרון יציאת מצרים, שהוא יסוד גדול ועמוד חזק בתורתנו ובאמונתנו, ונשתנה מכל הנסים שהוזהרנו להזכירו (וגם קריעת ים סוף) בכל יום. ובתוספות יותר נצטוינו על זה בהתחלת חג הפסח – בליל התקדש חג.

כמה וכמה דברים יש ללמוד הן מעצם ענין זה...ובאתי בזה להדגיש רק נקודה אחת...הוראה למעשה בחיינו, ולא רק בימי החג, אלא בכל השנה כולה....כי הנה התחלת דיני ומנהגי החג, מיד כשתחשך, הוא ה"סדר". ותיכף להתחלת הסדר ומעיקריו, הוא: והגדת לבנך משנים כמה דברים ומחדשים כמה דברים כדי לעורר את התינוקות. ולא עוד, אלא שחיוב זה הוא לא רק בנוגע לבנים חכמים, כי אם – אחד חכם ואחד רשע ואחד תם ואחד שאינו יודע לשאול. את כולם צריך לקבץ לסדר של פסח, ולפי דעתו ויכולת הבנתו של בן – אביו מלמדו...עלינו להשתדל בכל עוז ומרץ לחפש דרכים עצות ותחבולות (אף אם על ידי זה מוכרח יהי׳ לשנות מהטבע וההרגל שלו, ובל–) לכבוש את הדור הצעיר, ולקרב את כל בני ובנות ישראל, אחד חכם ואחד רשע ואחד תם ואחד שאינו יודע לשאול, לתורה ומצוות.

Everything in this world has a lesson for the thinking person. . . . It is very easy, with the proper effort, to find such lessons in the Torah . . . and its mitzvot, specifically in the broader topics found in the Torah.

One such topic is the obligation to recall the Exodus from Egypt, which is a tremendous foundation and strong pillar of our Torah and our faith. It is different from all other miracles in that we are required to remember it (and the splitting of the sea) daily. We are obligated to remember it further at the beginning of Passover.

There are many things we can learn from this. . . . I will focus on one point . . . a practical lesson for our lives, not only for the days of Passover but for all year long. . . . At the very beginning of the holiday, as soon as it gets dark, is the seder. At the seder's start, we change some standard customs, and introduce some new customs, in order to provoke the children's curiosity.

This obligation applies not only to wise children, but to the wise son, the wicked son, the simple son, and the one who doesn't know how to ask. We must gather them all at the Passover seder, and, according to the abilities of each son, his father teaches. . . . One must exhaust every effort to find ways and tricks (even if it means one must change his nature and habit) to win over the young generation, and to draw all the sons and daughters of Israel—whether they are smart, wicked, simple, or don't even know how to ask—to the Torah and mitzvot.

An Example from Yeshiva Students

TEXT 13

Ibid., vol. 6, letter 1,675

ב"ה, ב' תמוז, תשי"ב

שואל הוא כוונתי במכתבי לחג הפסח בהתיבות "אף אם על ידי זה
מוכרח יהי' לשנות מהטבע וההרגל שלו".

הנה צריך עיון במה נתקשה, כי כוונתי כפשוטה, שבני הישיבות
הורגלו בענין דתלמוד גדול, ובמילא חדש בעיניהם הדרך להקדיש
חלק מזמנם שיכולים לשגשג בתורה ותחת זה להשתמש בו לקרב
הסביבה שלו בענינים פשוטים, כמו שמירת שבת, לימוד אל"ף
בי"ת, עברי וכו' וכו'.

וכמה מבני הישיבות מטעימים זה לעצמם, שזהו מצד היראת
שמים, שכיון שפסקו רז"ל שמצוה שאפשר לעשותה על ידי
אחרים, הרי אין מבטלין תלמוד תורה בשביל זה...הרי אין להם
להפרד ח"ו מן התורה אפילו לרגע, ועל הקדוש ברוך הוא להבטיח
את החינוך הכשר של בני ובנות ישראל העומדים בסכנת טמיעה
וכפירה היה לא תהיה, אבל באמת אין זה מצד היראת שמים, כי
מצוה עוברת היא ואין די אחרים העושים אותה.

ובענין זה יש להזהר בפרט מהסתות היצר הרע, כיון שאצל בני
הישיבות זהו הטבע שלהם.

(וכידוע שאלו השוקדים בתורה בילדותם (היינו קודם שמבינים
בשכל גודל ערך התורה) הרי הוא שקדנים בטבע, ואינם להוטים
כל כך אחרי עניני שחוק וקלות ראש) וההרגל שלהם, כי אפילו
אלו שנכנסו להישיבה לא ברצון עצמם אלא על פי הכרח הורים
ומורים, אף שזה היפך טבעם, הנה אחרי שהורגלו בחיי הישיבה
וסדרה, קשה להם לפרוש מזה, וכידוע מאמר החכם אשר הרגל
נעשה טבע שני.

In response to your question as to the meaning in my pre-Passover letter of the words, "even if it means one must change his nature and habit."

Your question is unclear, for my intent was simple—that yeshiva students are accustomed to Torah study alone, and therefore the practice of dedicating of their time to teach those around them of simple Jewish matters such as keeping Shabbat, the aleph-bet, Hebrew, etc. is new to them.

Some students may try to excuse themselves by quoting Jewish law which states that one must not pause from Torah study for the sake of a mitzvah which can be performed by others. . . . As such, they believe, they need not pause their studies for even a second, and it is G-d's responsibility to ensure a proper Jewish education for the Jewish boys and girls at risk of assimilation or abandonment of the Jewish faith, G-d forbid. In truth, this reasoning is not rooted in fear of Heaven; this is not a mitzvah which can be performed by others because the efforts currently being invested in it are not enough. . . .

In this matter one must beware of the evil inclination's tactics, for such is the nature of yeshiva students (as it is known, those yeshiva students who studied diligently in their youth [before they were old enough to understand the great value of the Torah] are diligent by nature; they are not much drawn to jesting and frivolity) and such is their habit. Even those students who were enrolled in yeshiva not by choice but at the will of their parents and teachers, though the yeshiva atmosphere runs contrary to their nature, after getting used to yeshiva life, it is difficult for them to leave it, as the saying of the wise goes, "Habit becomes second nature."

Even One Letter

TEXT 14

The Rebbe, Rabbi Menachem Mendel Schneerson,
Sichot Kodesh 5739, vol. 2, p. 720

עס זיינען דא אזוינע וואס טענה'ן—ווי אזוי זאגט מען אים ער זאל
גיין טאן אין "מבצע תורה", בשעת ער ווייסט אז ער האט א שייכות
מערניט ווי צו א "פרק אחד", מערניט ווי צו אן "אות אחת", און
מער האט ער ניט קיין הבנה...זאגט מען אים: הער זיך איין, ס'איז
ניטא קיין צייט! אט קומט משיח! איז לויף ארויס אין גאס און לערן
תורה מיט א אידן! דו קענסט מערניט ווי "פרק אחד"—לערן מיט
אים " פרק אחד"!

נאכמער: אפילו אויב דו ווייסט מערניט ווי "דיבור אחד, או אפילו
אוה אחת", מ'האט דיר געלערנט אל"ף בי"ת, און דו ווייסט צורת
האות פון אן אל"ף, איז גיי ארויס אין גאס און שריי אל"ף! דו
וועסט טרעפן א אידן וואס ווייסט ניט וואס אן אל"ף איז, וועסטו
דאס אים מסביר זיין!

טענה'ט ער אבער—נו, וואס וועט שוין זיין אז ער וועט וויסן וואס
אן אל"ף איז?!

זאָגט מען אים—נ״ין! דו וועסט טאַקע אָנהויבן מיט אַן אַל״ף, און
דערנאָך קען אפילו ז״ין אַז דו וועסט פון אים אַוועקגיין—אָבער
וו״באַלד אַז דאָס איז אַן "אות אחת" פון תורה , איז דאָס ניט ק״ין
"אות אחת בלבד", נאָר דערפון וועט אויסוואַקסן אַ "פרק אחד",
ביז צו אַ ריבוי עניינים אין תורה.

*Some people claim, "How can you tell me to get in-
volved in spreading Torah when I myself am only capable of learning 'one chapter' or 'one letter,' and have
no understanding of anything more than that. . . ." We
tell such a person, "Listen, there's no time! Mashiach
is coming any minute! So run in the street and study
Torah with another Jew! You only know 'one chapter'?
So study with him 'one chapter'!*

*"Furthermore: Even if you only know 'one saying, or
even one letter,' i.e., you were taught* aleph-bet, *and
you know what an* aleph *looks like, so go in the street
and scream* aleph! *You'll meet a Jew who doesn't yet
know* aleph, *and you'll teach it to him!"*

*He may respond, "Nu, what will happen already if this
person will know what an* aleph *is?"*

We tell him, "No! True, you'll start with aleph, *and
maybe you won't see him again—but because this is
'one letter' of the Torah, it's not just 'one letter.' From
this letter will grow 'one chapter,' until, eventually, this
person will acquire a broad knowledge of the Torah."*

2

BESHALACH

Wet Behind the Ears

Balancing Enthusiasm with Maturity

*Dedicated by **Moshe** and **Rebecca Bolinsky** in loving memory
of **Nachum Chaim** ben **Menachem Mendel** on the occasion of his yahrtzeit, 28 Teves*

PARSHA OVERVIEW
Beshalach

Soon after allowing the Children of Israel to depart from Egypt, Pharaoh chases after them to force their return, and the Israelites find themselves trapped between Pharaoh's armies and the sea. G-d tells Moses to raise his staff over the water; the sea splits to allow the Israelites to pass through, and then closes over the pursuing Egyptians. Moses and the Children of Israel sing a song of praise and gratitude to G-d.

In the desert, the people suffer thirst and hunger. They repeatedly complain to Moses and Aaron. G-d miraculously sweetens the bitter waters of Marah, and later has Moses bring forth water from a rock by striking it with his staff. G-d causes manna to rain down from the heavens before dawn each morning, and quails to appear in the Israelite camp each evening.

The Children of Israel are instructed to gather a double portion of manna on Friday, as none will descend on Shabbat, the divinely decreed day of rest. Some disobey and go to gather manna on the seventh day, but find nothing. Aaron preserves a small quantity of manna in a jar, as a testimony for future generations.

In Rephidim, the people are attacked by the Amalekites, who are defeated by Moses's prayers and an army raised by Joshua.

Crisis at Sea

Who Goes First?

TEXT 1

Talmud Tractate Sotah, 36b

Babylonian Talmud

A literary work of monumental proportions that draws upon the legal, spiritual, intellectual, ethical, and historical traditions of Judaism. The 37 tractates of the Babylonian Talmud contain the teachings of the Jewish sages from the period after the destruction of the 2nd Temple through the 5th century CE. It has served as the primary vehicle for the transmission of the Oral Law and the education of Jews over the centuries; it is the entry point for all subsequent legal, ethical, and theological Jewish scholarship.

היה רבי מאיר אומר כשעמדו ישראל על הים היו שבטים מנצחים
זה עם זה זה אומר אני יורד תחלה לים וזה אומר אני יורד תחלה
לים. קפץ שבטו של בנימין וירד לים תחילה שנאמר "שם בנימין
צעיר רודם"—אל תקרי רודם אלא רד ים, והיו שרי יהודה רוגמים
אותם שנאמר "שרי יהודה רגמתם". לפיכך זכה בנימין הצדיק
ונעשה אושפיזכן לגבורה שנאמר "ובין כתפיו שכן".
אמר לו רבי יהודה לא כך היה מעשה אלא זה אומר אין אני יורד
תחילה לים וזה אומר אין אני יורד תחילה לים קפץ נחשון בן
עמינדב וירד לים תחילה.

Rabbi Meir said: When the Israelites stood by the sea, the tribes argued with one another [each wishing to descend into the sea first]. The tribe of Benjamin took the initiative and descended first into the sea, as it is stated, "There is little Benjamin their ruler"—read not "rodem" [their ruler], but "red yam" [descended into the sea].

Thereupon, the princes of Judah hurled stones at them, as it is stated, "The princes of Judah their council [rigmatam]." [The word can also be translated as "stoned them."]

For that reason, the righteous Benjamin was worthy to become the host of the All-Powerful, as it is said, "G-d dwells between his shoulders."

Rabbi Judah said to [Rabbi Meir]: That is not what happened, but each tribe was unwilling to be the first to enter the sea. Then sprang forward Nahshon the son of Amminadab.

TEXT 2

Rashi to Tehilim (Psalms) 68:28

"שרי יהודה רגמתם". מתקנאים בהם וזורקין בהם אבנים.

[The princes of Judah] were jealous of [the tribe of Benjamin], and so they threw stones.

Rabbi Shlomo Yitzchaki (Rashi)
1040–1105
Most noted biblical and Talmudic commentator. Born in Troyes, France, Rashi studied in the famed *yeshivot* of Mainz and Worms. His commentaries on the Pentateuch and the Talmud, which focus on the straightforward meaning of the text, appear in virtually every edition of the Talmud and Bible.

TEXT 3

Baraita, cited in Tosafot to Sotah, ad loc., s.v. Vehayu

Tosafot

A collection of French and German Talmudic commentaries written during the 12th and 13th centuries. Among the most famous authors of *Tosafot* are Rabbi Yaakov Tam, Rabbi Shimshon ben Avraham of Sens, and Rabbi Yitzchak ("the Ri"). Printed in almost all editions of the Talmud, these commentaries are fundamental to basic Talmudic study.

ומה שכר נטלו שבטו של יהודה זכה למלכות שנאמר שרי יהודה
רגמתם אין רגמתם אלא מלכות שנאמר באדין אמר בלשצר
והלבישו לדניאל ארגוונא.

What reward did the tribe of Judah receive? . . . [They] merited kingship [over the other tribes], as it is stated, "The princes of Judah their council [rigmatam]." The word rigmatam is associated with royalty, as it is stated, "Then Belshazzar ordered, and they attired Daniel with purple [and the golden chain on his neck, and they announced about him that he should rule over a third of the kingdom]."

Maturity vs. Eagerness

A Tale of Two Princes

TEXT 4

Tosafot, ibid.

כך שנויה ברייתא: משל למה הדבר דומה, למלך בשר ודם שהיו לו
שני בנים אחד גדול ואחד קטן. אמר לקטן העמידני עם הנץ החמה.
אמר לגדול העמידני בג' שעות. בא הקטן להעמידו עם הנץ החמה
ולא הניחו גדול, אמר לו לא אמר לי אלא עד ג' שעות, והקטן אמר
לא אמר לי אלא עד הנץ החמה. מתוך שהיו עומדים צהובין (כלומר
רבים ומתווכחים ביניהם) ננער אביהן, אמר להן: בניי, מכל מקום
שניכם לא כיוונתם אלא לכבודי, אף אני לא אקפח את שכרכם.
מה שכר נטלו שבטו של בנימין שירד תחילה לים, ששרתה שכינה
בחלקו שנאמר וכו'. ומה שכר נטלו שבטו של יהודה, זכה למלכות
וכו'. עד כאן לשונו

*[The argument between the tribe of Benjamin and the
tribe of Judah] is analogous to a king who had two sons.
The king told his younger son, "Wake me at sunrise,"
and [then] told his older son, "Wake me at three hours
[after sunrise]." The younger son came to awaken [the
king] at sunrise and the older son prevented him from
doing so, explaining, "[Father] told me to wake him in
three hours [from now]." But the younger son insisted,
"[Father] told me to wake him [now,] at sunrise." As*

they were arguing, their father awoke, and he said to them, "My children, you both only intended to honor me [by your actions], so I will bestow [each of] you with a reward."

[The parable relates to the story at the sea:] What reward did the tribe of Benjamin receive for entering the sea first? The divine presence dwelled in their territory [when the Holy Temple was built]. What reward did the tribe of Judah receive? They merited kingship, etc.

A Royal Wakeup

TEXT 5

Talmud Tractate Berachot, 9b

מאימתי קורין את שמע בשחרית משיכיר בין תכלת ללבן רבי
אליעזר אומר בין תכלת לכרתי וגומרה עד הנץ החמה רבי יהושע
אומר עד שלש שעות שכן דרך בני מלכים לעמוד בשלש שעות.

From what time may one recite the Shema in the morning? From the time that one can distinguish between blue and white. Rabbi Eliezer says: Between blue and green; and he has time to finish until sunrise. Rabbi Yehoshua says that one may recite the Shema [from dawn] until three hours [after sunrise,] because kings typically arise three hours [after sunrise].

Miraculous Messages

TEXT 6

The Rebbe, Rabbi Menachem Mendel Schneerson,
Likutei Sichot, vol. 3, p. 886

און דאָס איז דער ביאור פון דעם וואָס דורך דער עבודה פון ויסעו
טוט זיך אויף קריעת ים סוף בנפשו: יעדער איד בפנימיות נפשו
האָט דעם ביטול צום רצון העליון.... איז בשעת ער גייט אַוועק
פון זיין מצרים אַלץ ווייטער, ער רעכנט זיך ניט מיט זיינע אייגענע
ענינים און איז זיך מבטל צום רצון העליון – ווערט דאָן נתגלה
פנימיות נפשו [קריעת ים סוף בנפשו].

When one serves G-d by heeding His command to "journey on," one can split the spiritual "sea" that exists within the soul. All Jews possess the desire to fulfill G-d's will. . . . The farther one leaves his spiritual "Egypt," the less involved one is with personal considerations and the more devoted one is to G-d's will: at that point, the innermost desire of one's soul is revealed [the sea is now split].

Rabbi Menachem Mendel Schneerson
1902–1994

The towering Jewish leader of the 20th century, known as "the Lubavitcher Rebbe," or simply as "the Rebbe." Born in southern Ukraine, the Rebbe escaped Nazi-occupied Europe, arriving in the U.S. in June 1941. The Rebbe inspired and guided the revival of traditional Judaism after the European devastation, impacting virtually every Jewish community the world over. The Rebbe often emphasized that the performance of just one additional good deed could usher in the era of Mashiach. The Rebbe's scholarly talks and writings have been printed in more than 200 volumes.

Judah the Mature, Benjamin the Eager

TEXT 7

Shemot (Exodus) 14:4

וְחִזַּקְתִּי אֶת לֵב פַּרְעֹה וְרָדַף אַחֲרֵיהֶם וְאִכָּבְדָה בְּפַרְעֹה וּבְכָל חֵילוֹ
וְיָדְעוּ מִצְרַיִם כִּי אֲנִי ה' וַיַּעֲשׂוּ כֵן:

I will become glorified [at the Sea of Reeds] through Pharaoh and his entire army, and the Egyptians shall know that I am G-d.

Stone the Desecrators!

TEXT 8

I Melachim (I Kings) 19:10

וַיֹּאמֶר קַנֹּא קִנֵּאתִי לַה' אֱלֹקֵי צְבָאוֹת כִּי עָזְבוּ בְרִיתְךָ בְּנֵי יִשְׂרָאֵל אֶת
מִזְבְּחֹתֶיךָ הָרָסוּ וְאֶת נְבִיאֶיךָ הָרְגוּ בֶחָרֶב וָאִוָּתֵר אֲנִי לְבַדִּי וַיְבַקְשׁוּ אֶת
נַפְשִׁי לְקַחְתָּהּ:

And Elijah said, "I have been zealous for the L-rd, the G-d of Hosts, for the Children of Israel have forsaken Your covenant. They have torn down Your altars, and they have killed Your prophets by the sword, and I have remained alone, and they seek my life to take it.

Travel Plans

TEXT 9A

Rashi to Bereishit (Genesis) 50:13

"וישאו אתו בניו: ולא בני בניו"... וקבע להם מקום, שלשה למזרח
וכן לארבע רוחות, וכסדרן למסע מחנה של דגלים נקבעו כאן. לוי
לא ישא שהוא עתיד לשאת את הארון, ויוסף לא ישא שהוא שהוא מלך,
מנשה ואפרים יהיו תחתיהם, וזהו "איש על דגלו באותות"—באות
שמסר להם אביהם לישא מטתו.

*"And his sons carried him." . . . He designated a posi-
tion for his children [by his coffin], [so that] three [of
them would carry] on the east, and so on for [all] four
directions. [This was] similar to their arrangement in
the traveling of the camp [in the desert] of the group-
ings [of the tribes as] they were designated here. [He
also ordered,] "Levi shall not carry it because his tribe
is destined to carry the ark. Joseph shall not carry it
because he is a king. Manasseh and Ephraim shall
carry it instead of them." That is the meaning of [the
verse later in Bamidbar (Numbers) which states that
the tribes traveled in the desert,] "Each one according
to his group with signs," according to the sign that their
father gave them to carry his coffin.*

TEXT 9B

Bamidbar (Numbers) 2:2

אִישׁ עַל דִּגְלוֹ בְאֹתֹת לְבֵית אֲבֹתָם יַחֲנוּ בְּנֵי יִשְׂרָאֵל מִנֶּגֶד סָבִיב לְאֹהֶל מוֹעֵד יַחֲנוּ:

The Children of Israel shall encamp, each man by his division with the flagstaff of their fathers' house; some distance from the Tent of Meeting they shall encamp.

TEXT 9C

Rashi, ad loc.

דבר אחר באותות לבית אבותם באות שמסר להם יעקב אביהם כשנשאוהו ממצרים, שנאמר "ויעשו לו בניו כן כאשר צום", יהודה ויששכר וזבולן ישאוהו מן המזרח, וראובן ושמעון וגד מן הדרום וכו', כדאיתא בתנחומא בפרשה זו.

Another explanation: "With the signs [the literal translation of בְאֹתֹת] of their fathers' house"—according to the sign their father Jacob gave them when they carried him out of Egypt, as it says, "His sons did for him just as he had commanded them," [which was that] Judah, Issachar, and Zebulun should bear him [his body] from the east; Reuben, Simeon, and Gad from the south, etc., as it states in the [Midrash] Tanchuma on this section.

Judah and Benjamin in Our Lives

Two Sides of the Coin

TEXT 10

Talmud Tractate Gitin, 62a

רב הונא ורב חסדא הוו יתבי חליף ואזיל גניבא אמר לי' חד לחבריה
ניקום מקמיה דבר אוריין הוא אמר לו ומקמי פלגאה ניקום אדהכי
אתא איהו
לגבייהו אמר להו שלמא עלייכו מלכי שלמא עלייכו מלכי אמרו
ליה מנא לך דרבנן איקרו מלכים אמר להו דכתיב בי מלכים
ימלוכו וגו'.

Rav Huna and Rav Chisda were once sitting when the sage Geneiva passed by alongside them. One of them said to the other, "We should stand before him, in his honor, for he is a son of Torah." The other one said to him, "But should we stand before an argumentative person?" In the meantime, Geneiva approached them and said to them, "Peace be upon you, kings, peace be upon you, kings." They said to him, "From where do you know that the sages are called kings?" He said to them, "As it is written with regard to the Torah in the book of Mishlei (Proverbs), 'Through Me kings rule.'"

TEXT 11

Rabbi Shneur Zalman of Liadi, Torah Or, 27b

Rabbi Shneur Zalman of Liadi (Alter Rebbe) 1745–1812

Chasidic rebbe, halachic authority, and founder of the Chabad movement. The Alter Rebbe was born in Liozna, Belarus, and was among the principal students of the Magid of Mezeritch. His numerous works include the *Tanya*, an early classic containing the fundamentals of Chabad Chasidism, and *Shulchan Aruch HaRav*, an expanded and reworked code of Jewish law.

כי דבר ה' זו הלכה היא היא הנגלית בו והיא המדברת מתוך גרונו. ולכן נאמר על התורה בי מלכים ימלוכו. ואמרינן מאן מלכי רבנן. ומתניתא מלכתא. כי להיותו בביטול אל דבר ה' ורצונו וחכמתו ואינו תופס מקום מצד עצמו כלל, הנה דבר המלך הוא השלטון והיא בחינת מלך שגוזר ואומר שאם יטעון ראובן כך כו' יהיה הפסק כך.

G-d's words are the halachic rulings. [When a sage speaks words of Torah,] he is literally expressing the word of G-d. That is the why the Torah is described as . . . royalty . . . because [the sage] is utterly effaced before the word of G-d and His will and wisdom. To the extent that [the sage] negates his ego entirely, then the "words of the King reign," and [the sage] expresses the King's (i.e., G-d's) decrees. He is then empowered to hand down a halachic ruling that if Reuven claims such and such, etc., the ruling is such and such.

3

YITRO

Life Is Art

*Human Flaws Are the Brushstrokes
of Divine Beauty*

*In tribute to the **Lubavitcher Rebbe**, whose leadership, beginning on 10 Shevat, 5711 (1951)
continues to bring the world closer to the age of Mashiach. And marking the yahrtzeit of the **Previous
Rebbe**, 10 Shevat, 5710 (1950). Dedicated by **Rabbi Ari Laine**, Panama City, Panama*

PARSHA OVERVIEW
Yisro

Moses's father-in-law, Jethro, hears of the great miracles that G-d performed for the people of Israel, and comes from Midian to the Israelite camp, bringing with him Moses's wife and her two sons. Jethro advises Moses to appoint a hierarchy of magistrates and judges to assist him in the task of governing and administering justice to the people.

The Children of Israel camp opposite Mount Sinai, where they are told that G-d has chosen them to be His "kingdom of priests" and "holy nation." The people respond by proclaiming, "All that G-d has spoken, we shall do."

On the sixth day of the third month (Sivan), seven weeks after the Exodus, the entire nation of Israel assembles at the foot of Mount Sinai. G-d descends on the mountain amidst thunder, lightning, billows of smoke, and the blast of the shofar, and summons Moses to ascend.

G-d proclaims the Ten Commandments, commanding the people of Israel to believe in G-d, not to worship idols or take G-d's name in vain, to keep the Shabbat, to honor their parents, not to murder, not to commit adultery, not to steal, and not to bear false witness or covet another's property. The people cry out to Moses that the revelation is too intense for them to bear, begging him to receive the Torah from G-d and convey it to them.

The Prelude to Sinai

Moses's Father-in-Law

TEXT 1

Shemot (Exodus) 18:1–11

וַיִּשְׁמַע יִתְרוֹ כֹהֵן מִדְיָן חֹתֵן מֹשֶׁה אֵת כָּל אֲשֶׁר עָשָׂה אֱלֹקִים לְמֹשֶׁה
וּלְיִשְׂרָאֵל עַמּוֹ כִּי הוֹצִיא ה' אֶת יִשְׂרָאֵל מִמִּצְרָיִם:
וַיִּקַּח יִתְרוֹ חֹתֵן מֹשֶׁה אֶת צִפֹּרָה אֵשֶׁת מֹשֶׁה אַחַר שִׁלּוּחֶיהָ:
וְאֵת שְׁנֵי בָנֶיהָ אֲשֶׁר שֵׁם הָאֶחָד גֵּרְשֹׁם כִּי אָמַר גֵּר הָיִיתִי בְּאֶרֶץ נָכְרִיָּה:
וְשֵׁם הָאֶחָד אֱלִיעֶזֶר כִּי אֱלֹהֵי אָבִי בְּעֶזְרִי וַיַּצִּלֵנִי מֵחֶרֶב פַּרְעֹה:
וַיָּבֹא יִתְרוֹ חֹתֵן מֹשֶׁה וּבָנָיו וְאִשְׁתּוֹ אֶל מֹשֶׁה אֶל הַמִּדְבָּר אֲשֶׁר הוּא
חֹנֶה שָׁם הַר הָאֱלֹקִים:
וַיֹּאמֶר אֶל מֹשֶׁה אֲנִי חֹתֶנְךָ יִתְרוֹ בָּא אֵלֶיךָ וְאִשְׁתְּךָ וּשְׁנֵי בָנֶיהָ עִמָּהּ:
וַיֵּצֵא מֹשֶׁה לִקְרַאת חֹתְנוֹ וַיִּשְׁתַּחוּ וַיִּשַּׁק לוֹ וַיִּשְׁאֲלוּ אִישׁ לְרֵעֵהוּ
לְשָׁלוֹם וַיָּבֹאוּ הָאֹהֱלָה:
וַיְסַפֵּר מֹשֶׁה לְחֹתְנוֹ אֵת כָּל אֲשֶׁר עָשָׂה ה' לְפַרְעֹה וּלְמִצְרַיִם עַל אוֹדֹת
יִשְׂרָאֵל אֵת כָּל הַתְּלָאָה אֲשֶׁר מְצָאָתַם בַּדֶּרֶךְ וַיַּצִּלֵם ה':
וַיִּחַדְּ יִתְרוֹ עַל כָּל הַטּוֹבָה אֲשֶׁר עָשָׂה ה' לְיִשְׂרָאֵל אֲשֶׁר הִצִּילוֹ
מִיַּד מִצְרָיִם:
וַיֹּאמֶר יִתְרוֹ בָּרוּךְ ה' אֲשֶׁר הִצִּיל אֶתְכֶם מִיַּד מִצְרַיִם וּמִיַּד פַּרְעֹה אֲשֶׁר
הִצִּיל אֶת הָעָם מִתַּחַת יַד מִצְרָיִם:
עַתָּה יָדַעְתִּי כִּי גָדוֹל ה' מִכָּל הָאֱלֹהִים כִּי בַדָּבָר אֲשֶׁר זָדוּ עֲלֵיהֶם:

Now, Moses's father-in-law, Jethro, the chieftain of Midian, heard all that G-d had done for Moses and for Israel, His people, that G-d had taken Israel out of Egypt.

So Moses's father-in-law, Jethro, took Zipporah, Moses's wife, after she had been sent away.

And her two sons, one of whom was named Gershom, because he [Moses] said, "I was a stranger in a foreign land."

And one who was named Eliezer, because [Moses said,] "The G-d of my father came to my aid and rescued me from Pharaoh's sword."

Now Moses's father-in-law, Jethro, and his [Moses's] sons and his wife came to Moses, to the desert where he was encamped, to the mountain of G-d.

And he said to Moses, "I, Jethro, your father-in-law, am coming to you, and [so is] your wife and her two sons with her."

So Moses went out toward Jethro, prostrated himself and kissed him, and they greeted one another, and they entered the tent.

Moses told his father-in-law [about] all that G-d had done to Pharaoh and to the Egyptians on account of Israel, [and about] all the hardships that had befallen them on the way, and [that] G-d had saved them.

Jethro was happy about all the good that G-d had done for Israel, that He had rescued them from the hands of the Egyptians.

[Thereupon,] Jethro said, "Blessed is G-d, Who has rescued you from the hands of the Egyptians and from

the hand of Pharaoh, Who has rescued the people from beneath the hand of the Egyptians.

"Now I know that G-d is greater than all the deities, for with the thing that the Egyptians plotted, [He came] upon them."

An Ennobling Visit

TEXT 2

Rabbi Avraham Ibn Ezra on Shemot (Exodus) 18:1

Rabbi Avraham ibn Ezra
1092–1167

Biblical commentator, linguist, and poet. Ibn Ezra was born in Toledo, Spain and fled the Almohad regime to other parts of Europe. It is believed that he was living in London at the time of his death. Ibn Ezra is best known for his literalistic commentary on the Pentateuch. He also wrote works of poetry, philosophy, medicine, astronomy, and other topics.

"וישמע יתרו". הזכיר למעלה דבר עמלק כי לרפידים בא. והיתה ראויה פרשת בחדש השלישי להיותה כתובה אחר דבר עמלק. כי שם כתוב ויסעו מרפידים ויבאו מדבר סיני. אם כן למה נכנס דברי יתרו בין שתי הפרשיות...ועתה אפרש למה נכנסה פרשת יתרו במקום הזה.

בעבור שהזכיר למעלה הרעה שעשה עמלק לישראל הזכיר כנגדו הטובה שעשה יתרו לישראל. וכתוב ויחד יתרו על כל הטובה. ונתן להם עצה טובה ונכונה למשה ולישראל.

"And Jethro heard." It was mentioned earlier in the Torah about Amalek arriving at Refidim. The next matter in the Torah should theoretically be the arrival at Mount Sinai, since the story of Amalek ends with, "And they traveled from Refidim and arrived in the Sinai desert." So why is the story of Jethro inserted here?

Because the evil that Amalek did to the Children of Israel is mentioned earlier, the good that Jethro did to Israel is mentioned to counter it, "And Jethro rejoiced over all the kindness. . . ." He gave good and correct counsel to Moses and Israel.

TEXT 3

Rashi to Shemot (Exodus) 18:11

"מכל האלהים". מלמד שהיה מכיר בכל עבודה זרה שבעולם שלא הניח עבודה זרה שלא עבדה.

"Than all the deities." This teaches us that Jethro was knowledgeable about every type of idolatry in the world, and there was no pagan deity that he did not worship.

Rabbi Shlomo Yitzchaki (Rashi)
1040–1105

Most noted biblical and Talmudic commentator. Born in Troyes, France, Rashi studied in the famed *yeshivot* of Mainz and Worms. His commentaries on the Pentateuch and the Talmud, which focus on the straightforward meaning of the text, appear in virtually every edition of the Talmud and Bible.

The Necessary Imperfection

A Priest of Midian

TEXT 4

Shemot (Exodus) 2:16–17

וּלְכֹהֵן מִדְיָן שֶׁבַע בָּנוֹת וַתָּבֹאנָה וַתִּדְלֶנָה וַתְּמַלֶּאנָה אֶת הָרְהָטִים
לְהַשְׁקוֹת צֹאן אֲבִיהֶן:
וַיָּבֹאוּ הָרֹעִים וַיְגָרְשׁוּם וַיָּקָם מֹשֶׁה וַיּוֹשִׁעָן וַיַּשְׁקְ אֶת צֹאנָם:

Now, the priest of Midian had seven daughters, and they came and drew [water], and they filled the troughs to water their father's flocks.

But the shepherds came and drove them away; so Moses arose and rescued them and watered their flocks.

TEXT 5

Talmud Tractate Sotah, 11a

אמר רבי חייא בר אבא אמר רבי סימאי שלשה היו באותה עצה
בלעם ואיוב ויתרו.

*Rabbi Chiya bar Abba said in the name of Rabbi Simai:
Three advisors were present when Pharaoh was delib-
erating what to do with the Jewish people—Bilaam,
Iyov, and Jethro.*

Babylonian Talmud

A literary work of monumental
proportions that draws upon
the legal, spiritual, intellectual,
ethical, and historical
traditions of Judaism. The 37
tractates of the Babylonian
Talmud contain the teachings
of the Jewish sages from the
period after the destruction of
the 2nd Temple through the
5th century CE. It has served
as the primary vehicle for the
transmission of the Oral Law
and the education of Jews
over the centuries; it is the
entry point for all subsequent
legal, ethical, and theological
Jewish scholarship.

TEXT 6

Rashi to Shemot (Exodus) 2:16

"וְלכהן מדין". רַב שֶׁבָּהֶן; וּפָרַשׁ לוֹ מעבודה זרה וְנִדוּהוּ מֵאֶצְלָם.

*"Now, the priest of Midian." Jethro was the most
prominent among them. He had abandoned idolatry,
so they banned him from [living with] them.*

The Conflicted Convert

TEXT 7A

Shemot (Exodus) 18:8–10

וַיְסַפֵּר מֹשֶׁה לְחֹתְנוֹ אֵת כָּל אֲשֶׁר עָשָׂה ה' לְפַרְעֹה וּלְמִצְרַיִם עַל אוֹדֹת
יִשְׂרָאֵל אֵת כָּל הַתְּלָאָה אֲשֶׁר מְצָאָתַם בַּדֶּרֶךְ וַיַּצִּלֵם ה':
וַיִּחַדְּ יִתְרוֹ עַל כָּל הַטּוֹבָה אֲשֶׁר עָשָׂה ה' לְיִשְׂרָאֵל אֲשֶׁר הִצִּילוֹ
מִיַּד מִצְרָיִם:
וַיֹּאמֶר יִתְרוֹ בָּרוּךְ ה' אֲשֶׁר הִצִּיל אֶתְכֶם מִיַּד מִצְרַיִם וּמִיַּד פַּרְעֹה אֲשֶׁר
הִצִּיל אֶת הָעָם מִתַּחַת יַד מִצְרָיִם:

Moses told his father-in-law [about] all that G-d had done to Pharaoh and to the Egyptians on account of Israel, [and about] all the hardships that had befallen them on the way, and [that] G-d had saved them.

Jethro was happy about all the good that G-d had done for Israel, that He had rescued them from the hands of the Egyptians.

[Thereupon,] Jethro said, "Blessed is the L-rd, Who has rescued you from the hands of the Egyptians and from the hand of Pharaoh, Who has rescued the people from beneath the hands of the Egyptians.

TEXT 7B

Rashi, ad loc.

"וַיִּחַד יתרו." וישמח יתרו, זהו פשוטו ומדרשו נעשה בשרו חדודין
חדודין, מיצר על איבוד מצרים, היינו דאמרי אינשי גיורא עד עשרה
דרי לא תבזי ארמאה באפיה.

*"Jethro was happy." The Hebrew word "vayichad" is
conventionally translated as, "and Jethro rejoiced."
The Agadic Midrash, however, [explains that] his
flesh became prickly [i.e., gooseflesh (chidudin chidudin)] [because] he was upset about the destruction of
the Egyptians.*

*This is [the source of] the popular saying: Do not dis-
grace a gentile in the presence of a convert, [even] up
to the tenth generation [after the conversion].*

TEXT 8

Talmud Tractate Sanhedrin, 94a

"ויחד יתרו." רב ושמואל רב אמר שהעביר חרב חדה על בשרו
ושמואל אמר שנעשה חדודים חדודים כל בשרו.

"Jethro was happy." Rav and Samuel debated the meaning of this phrase.

Rav said that he was so overjoyed, he passed a sharp blade over his flesh to circumcise himself and join the Jewish people.

Samuel said that Jethro felt so much pain, it was as if he had cuts prickling all his flesh.

Yitro's Epiphany about Judgment

TEXT 9

Shemot (Exodus) 18:13–22

וַיְהִי מִמָּחֳרָת וַיֵּשֶׁב מֹשֶׁה לִשְׁפֹּט אֶת הָעָם וַיַּעֲמֹד הָעָם עַל מֹשֶׁה מִן הַבֹּקֶר עַד הָעָרֶב:

וַיַּרְא חֹתֵן מֹשֶׁה אֵת כָּל אֲשֶׁר הוּא עֹשֶׂה לָעָם וַיֹּאמֶר מָה הַדָּבָר הַזֶּה אֲשֶׁר אַתָּה עֹשֶׂה לָעָם מַדּוּעַ אַתָּה יוֹשֵׁב לְבַדֶּךָ וְכָל הָעָם נִצָּב עָלֶיךָ מִן בֹּקֶר עַד עָרֶב:

וַיֹּאמֶר מֹשֶׁה לְחֹתְנוֹ כִּי יָבֹא אֵלַי הָעָם לִדְרֹשׁ אֱלֹקִים:

כִּי יִהְיֶה לָהֶם דָּבָר בָּא אֵלַי וְשָׁפַטְתִּי בֵּין אִישׁ וּבֵין רֵעֵהוּ וְהוֹדַעְתִּי אֶת חֻקֵּי הָאֱלֹקִים וְאֶת תּוֹרֹתָיו:

וַיֹּאמֶר חֹתֵן מֹשֶׁה אֵלָיו לֹא טוֹב הַדָּבָר אֲשֶׁר אַתָּה עֹשֶׂה:

נָבֹל תִּבֹּל גַּם אַתָּה גַּם הָעָם הַזֶּה אֲשֶׁר עִמָּךְ כִּי כָבֵד מִמְּךָ הַדָּבָר לֹא תוּכַל עֲשֹׂהוּ לְבַדֶּךָ:

עַתָּה שְׁמַע בְּקֹלִי אִיעָצְךָ וִיהִי אֱלֹהִים עִמָּךְ הֱיֵה אַתָּה לָעָם מוּל הָאֱלֹהִים וְהֵבֵאתָ אַתָּה אֶת הַדְּבָרִים אֶל הָאֱלֹהִים:

וְהִזְהַרְתָּה אֶתְהֶם אֶת הַחֻקִּים וְאֶת הַתּוֹרֹת וְהוֹדַעְתָּ לָהֶם אֶת הַדֶּרֶךְ יֵלְכוּ בָהּ וְאֶת הַמַּעֲשֶׂה אֲשֶׁר יַעֲשׂוּן:

וְאַתָּה תֶחֱזֶה מִכָּל הָעָם אַנְשֵׁי חַיִל יִרְאֵי אֱלֹהִים אַנְשֵׁי אֱמֶת שֹׂנְאֵי בָצַע וְשַׂמְתָּ עֲלֵהֶם שָׂרֵי אֲלָפִים שָׂרֵי מֵאוֹת שָׂרֵי חֲמִשִּׁים וְשָׂרֵי עֲשָׂרֹת:

וְשָׁפְטוּ אֶת הָעָם בְּכָל עֵת וְהָיָה כָּל הַדָּבָר הַגָּדֹל יָבִיאוּ אֵלֶיךָ וְכָל הַדָּבָר הַקָּטֹן יִשְׁפְּטוּ הֵם וְהָקֵל מֵעָלֶיךָ וְנָשְׂאוּ אִתָּךְ:

It came about on the next day that Moses sat down to judge the people, and the people stood before Moses from the morning until the evening.

When Moses's father-in-law saw what he was doing to the people, he said, "What is this thing that you are doing to the people? Why do you sit by yourself while all the people stand before you from morning until evening?"

Moses said to his father-in-law, "For the people come to me to seek G-d.

"If any of them has a case, he comes to me, and I judge between a man and his neighbor, and I make known the statutes of G-d and His teachings."

Moses's father-in-law said to him, "The thing you are doing is not good.

"You will surely wear yourself out, both you and these people who are with you, for the matter is too heavy for you; you cannot do it alone.

"Now listen to me. I will advise you, and may G-d be with you. [You] represent the people before G-d, and you shall bring the matters to G-d.

"And you shall admonish them concerning the statutes and the teachings, and you shall make known to them the way they shall go and the deed[s] they shall do.

"But you shall choose out of the entire nation men of substance, G-d fearers, men of truth, who hate monetary gain, and you shall appoint over them [Israel]

leaders over thousands, leaders over hundreds, leaders over fifties, and leaders over tens.

"And they shall judge the people at all times, and it shall be that any major matter they shall bring to you, and they themselves shall judge every minor matter, thereby making it easier for you, and they shall bear [the burden] with you."

TEXT 10

Talmud Tractate Yoma, 72b

אמר רבי יוחנן שלשה זירים הן של מזבח ושל ארון ושל שלחן. של
מזבח, זכה אהרן ונטלו. של שלחן, זכה דוד ונטלו. של ארון, עדיין
מונח הוא כל הרוצה ליקח יבא ויקח.

Rabbi Yohanan said: There were three crowns in the Temple, corresponding to the three crowns of the Jewish people: the crown of the altar, the crown of the ark, and the crown of the table.

The crown of the altar, symbolizing the priesthood, Aaron earned and took.

The crown of the table, symbolizing the kingship, David earned and took.

The crown of the ark, symbolizing Torah, still rests upon the ark, waiting to be earned. Whoever wishes to take it may come and take it.

Lessons from Yitro

Adding to Perfection

TEXT 11

Zohar, vol. 2, 68a

אָתָא יִתְרוֹ, כּוֹמָרָא עִלָּאָה וְרַבְרְבָא, רַב מְמָנָא (דכל ממנא) דְּכָל טַעֲוָון
אַחֲרָנִין, וְאוֹדֵי לֵיהּ לְקוּדְשָׁא בְּרִיךְ הוּא, וְאָמַר עַתָּה יָדַעְתִּי כִּי גָדוֹל
ה' מִכָּל הָאֱלֹקִים, כְּדֵין אִסְתַּלָּק וְאִתְיְיקָר קוּדְשָׁא בְּרִיךְ הוּא בִּיקָרֵיהּ
עֵילָא וְתַתָּא, וּלְבָתַר יְהַב אוֹרַיְיתָא בִּשְׁלִימוּ, דְּשָׁלְטָנוּ עַל כֹּלָּא.

Zohar
The seminal work of kabbalah, Jewish mysticism. The *Zohar* is a mystical commentary on the Torah, written in Aramaic and Hebrew. According to the Arizal, the *Zohar* contains the teachings of Rabbi Shimon bar Yochai, who lived in the Land of Israel during the 2nd century. The *Zohar* has become one of the indispensable texts of traditional Judaism, alongside and nearly equal in stature to the Mishnah and Talmud.

Jethro arrived. He was a great and superior priest, the great chosen one among all other idols. And he then acknowledged G-d by saying, "Now I know that G-d is greater than any other power." Through this acknowledgement, G-d was exalted and honored in his full glory above and below, and he was then able to give the Torah in a state of completion, of complete dominion over all the earth.

TEXT 12

Talmud Tractate Shabbat, 88b

אמר רבי יהושע בן לוי: בשעה שעלה משה למרום אמרו מלאכי
השרת לפני הקדוש ברוך הוא: רבונו של עולם, מה לילוד אשה
ביננו? אמר להן: לקבל תורה בא.

אמרו לפניו: חמודה גנוזה שגנוזה לך תשע מאות ושבעים וארבעה
דורות קודם שנברא העולם, אתה מבקש ליתנה לבשר ודם? "מה
אנוש כי תזכרנו ובן אדם כי תפקדנו"! "ה' אדנינו מה אדיר שמך
בכל הארץ אשר תנה הודך על השמים"!

אמר לו הקדוש ברוך הוא למשה: החזיר להן תשובה!

אמר לפניו: רבונו של עולם... תורה שאתה נותן לי מה כתיב בה
"אנכי ה' אלהיך אשר הוצאתיך מארץ מצרים." אמר להן: למצרים
ירדתם? לפרעה השתעבדתם? תורה למה תהא לכם? שוב מה כתיב
בה "לא יהיה לך אלהים אחרים" בין הגויים אתם שרויין שעובדין
עבודה זרה? שוב מה כתיב בה "זכור את יום השבת לקדשו" כלום
אתם עושים מלאכה שאתם צריכין שבות? שוב מה כתיב בה "לא
תשא", משא ומתן יש ביניכם? שוב מה כתיב בה "כבד את אביך
ואת אמך" אב ואם יש לכם?

שוב מה כתיב בה "לא תרצח לא תנאף לא תגנב", קנאה יש ביניכם,
יצר הרע יש ביניכם?

מיד הודו לו להקדוש ברוך הוא.

Rabbi Joshua ben Levi also said: When Moses ascended on high, the ministering angels spoke before the Holy One, blessed be He, asking, "Master of the Universe! What business has one born of woman amongst us?"

"He has come to receive the Torah," answered He to them.

Said they to Him, "That secret treasure, that You have hidden for 974 generations before the world was created, You desire to give to flesh and blood! What is man, that You are mindful of him, and the son of man, that You visit him?! O L-rd, our G-d, how excellent is Your name in all the earth! Who hast set thy glory [the Torah] upon the heavens!"

"Answer them," bade the Holy One, blessed be He, to Moses.

"Master of the Universe," replied Moses . . . "The Torah that You give me, what is written therein? 'I am the L-rd your G-d, Who took you out of the Land of Egypt.'" Moses said to the angels, "Did you go down to Egypt? Were you enslaved to Pharaoh? Why, then, should the Torah be yours?

"Again, what is written therein? 'You shall have no other gods.' Do you dwell among peoples that engage in idol worship?

"Again, what is written therein? 'Remember the Sabbath day, to keep it holy.' Do you then perform work, that you need to rest?

"Again, what is written therein? 'You shall not take [the name . . . in vain].' Is there any business dealing among you?

"Again, what is written therein? 'Honor your father and mother.' Have you fathers and mothers?

"Again, what is written therein? 'You shall not murder. You shall not commit adultery. You shall not steal.' Is there jealousy among you? Is the evil tempter among you?"

Straightaway, the angels conceded to the Holy One, blessed be He [to give the Torah to humanity].

The Solution for Apathy

TEXT 13

The Rebbe, Rabbi Menachem Mendel Schneerson,
Likutei Sichot, vol. 2, pp. 388–389

Rabbi Menachem Mendel Schneerson
1902–1994

The towering Jewish leader of the 20th century, known as "the Lubavitcher Rebbe," or simply as "the Rebbe." Born in southern Ukraine, the Rebbe escaped Nazi-occupied Europe, arriving in the U.S. in June 1941. The Rebbe inspired and guided the revival of traditional Judaism after the European devastation, impacting virtually every Jewish community the world over. The Rebbe often emphasized that the performance of just one additional good deed could usher in the era of Mashiach. The Rebbe's scholarly talks and writings have been printed in more than 200 volumes.

דער ענין פון עמלק אין רוחניות איז, אשר קרך בדרך, וואס ער מאכט קאלט... אין דעם דרך פון תורה ומצוות. און אנטקעגן דער קרירות פון עמלק'ן דארף מען מלחמה האלטן יעדן טאג.

The spiritual notion of Amalek is alluded to in the verse, "That they encountered (korcha) on the way." The Hebrew word "korcha" is etymologically related to the word "kar—cold," in this context, the notion of being indifferent and apathetic to a life of Torah and mitzvot. We must battle this apathy of Amalek every day.

4

MISHPATIM

Making Tough Choices

Grabbing On to the Reins of Life

*Dedicated in loving memory of **Rabbi Ariel Rav-Noy**, a dear shliach, on the occasion of his yahrtzeit, 8 Shevat*

לעילוי נשמת השליח הרב אריאל רב-נוי ע״ה בן יבלחט״א ר׳ שאלתיאל זאב שליט״א, נפטר ח׳ שבט, תשע״ה

PARSHA OVERVIEW
Mishpatim

Following the revelation at Sinai, G-d legislates a series of laws for the people of Israel. These include the laws of the indentured servant; the penalties for murder, kidnapping, assault, and theft; civil laws pertaining to redress of damages, the granting of loans, and the responsibilities of the "four guardians"; and the rules governing the conduct of courts of law in administering justice.

Also included are laws warning against mistreatment of foreigners, the observance of the seasonal festivals and the agricultural gifts that are to be brought to the Holy Temple in Jerusalem, the prohibition against cooking meat with milk, and the mitzvah of prayer. Altogether, the parsha *of Mishpatim contains fifty-three* mitzvot: *twenty-three imperative commandments and thirty prohibitions.*

G-d promises to bring the people of Israel to the Holy Land and warns them against assuming the pagan ways of its current inhabitants.

The people of Israel proclaim, "We will do and we will hear all that G-d commands us." Leaving Aaron and

Hur in charge in the Israelite camp, Moses ascends Mount Sinai and remains there for forty days and forty nights to receive the Torah from G-d.

The Pierced Slave

Logical Principles

TEXT 1

Shemot (Exodus) 21:1–6

וְאֵלֶּה הַמִּשְׁפָּטִים אֲשֶׁר תָּשִׂים לִפְנֵיהֶם:

כִּי תִקְנֶה עֶבֶד עִבְרִי שֵׁשׁ שָׁנִים יַעֲבֹד וּבַשְּׁבִעִת יֵצֵא לַחָפְשִׁי חִנָּם:

אִם בְּגַפּוֹ יָבֹא בְּגַפּוֹ יֵצֵא אִם בַּעַל אִשָּׁה הוּא וְיָצְאָה אִשְׁתּוֹ עִמּוֹ:

אִם אֲדֹנָיו יִתֶּן לוֹ אִשָּׁה וְיָלְדָה לוֹ בָנִים אוֹ בָנוֹת הָאִשָּׁה וִילָדֶיהָ תִּהְיֶה לַאדֹנֶיהָ וְהוּא יֵצֵא בְגַפּוֹ:

וְאִם אָמֹר יֹאמַר הָעֶבֶד אָהַבְתִּי אֶת אֲדֹנִי אֶת אִשְׁתִּי וְאֶת בָּנָי לֹא אֵצֵא חָפְשִׁי:

וְהִגִּישׁוֹ אֲדֹנָיו אֶל הָאֱלֹהִים וְהִגִּישׁוֹ אֶל הַדֶּלֶת אוֹ אֶל הַמְּזוּזָה וְרָצַע אֲדֹנָיו אֶת אָזְנוֹ בַּמַּרְצֵעַ וַעֲבָדוֹ לְעֹלָם:

And these are the ordinances that you shall set before them.

Should you buy a Hebrew slave, he shall work [for] six years, and in the seventh [year], he shall go out to freedom without charge.

If he comes [in] alone, he shall go out alone; if he is a married man, his wife shall go out with him.

If his master gives him a wife and she bears him sons or daughters, the woman and her children shall belong to her master, and he shall go out alone.

But if the slave says, "I love my master, my wife, and my children. I will not go free," his master shall bring him to the judges, and he shall bring him to the door or to the doorpost, and his master shall bore his ear with an awl, and he shall serve him forever.

Slave to G-d, Slave to Man

TEXT 2A

Shemot (Exodus) 20:2–3

אָנֹכִי ה' אֱלֹקֶיךָ אֲשֶׁר הוֹצֵאתִיךָ מֵאֶרֶץ מִצְרַיִם מִבֵּית עֲבָדִים לֹא יִהְיֶה
לְךָ אֱלֹקִים אֲחֵרִים עַל פָּנָי:

"I am the L-rd, your G-d, Who took you out of the land of Egypt, out of the house of bondage. You shall not have the gods of others in My presence."

TEXT 2B

Rashi, ad loc.

Rabbi Shlomo Yitzchaki (Rashi)
1040–1105
Most noted biblical and Talmudic commentator. Born in Troyes, France, Rashi studied in the famed *yeshivot* of Mainz and Worms. His commentaries on the Pentateuch and the Talmud, which focus on the straightforward meaning of the text, appear in virtually every edition of the Talmud and Bible.

"אֲשֶׁר הוֹצֵאתִיךָ מֵאֶרֶץ מִצְרָיִם". כְּדַאי הִיא הַהוֹצָאָה שֶׁתִּהְיוּ מְשׁוּעְבָּדִים לִי.

"Who took you out of the land of Egypt." Taking [you] out [of Egypt] is sufficient reason for you to be subservient to Me.

TEXT 3A

Maimonides, Mishneh Torah, Laws of Slaves, 1:1

Rabbi Moshe ben Maimon (Maimonides, Rambam)
1135–1204
Halachist, philosopher, author, and physician. Maimonides was born in Córdoba, Spain. After the conquest of Córdoba by the Almohads, he fled Spain and eventually settled in Cairo, Egypt. There, he became the leader of the Jewish community and served as court physician to the vizier of Egypt. He is most noted for authoring the *Mishneh Torah*, an encyclopedic arrangement of Jewish law, and for his philosophical work, *Guide for the Perplexed*. His rulings on Jewish law are integral to the formation of halachic consensus.

עֶבֶד עִבְרִי הָאָמוּר בַּתּוֹרָה זֶה הַיִּשְׂרְאֵלִי שֶׁמְּכָרוּהוּ בֵּית דִּין עַל כָּרְחוֹ, אוֹ הַמּוֹכֵר עַצְמוֹ לִרְצוֹנוֹ. כֵּיצַד: גָּנַב, וְאֵין לוֹ לְשַׁלֵּם אֶת הַקֶּרֶן בֵּית דִּין מוֹכְרִין אוֹתוֹ כְּמוֹ שֶׁבֵּיאַרְנוּ בְּהִלְכוֹת גְּנֵיבָה... מוֹכֵר עַצְמוֹ כֵּיצַד: יִשְׂרָאֵל שֶׁהֶעֱנִי בְּיוֹתֵר נָתְנָה לוֹ תּוֹרָה רְשׁוּת לִמְכּוֹר אֶת עַצְמוֹ, שֶׁנֶּאֱמַר: וְכִי יָמוּךְ אָחִיךָ עִמָּךְ, וְנִמְכַּר לָךְ. וְאֵינוֹ רַשַּׁאי לִמְכּוֹר אֶת עַצְמוֹ וּלְהַצְנִיעַ דָּמָיו, אוֹ לִקְנוֹת בָּהֶם סְחוֹרָה אוֹ כֵּלִים, אוֹ לִיתְּנָם לְבַעַל חוֹבוֹ, אֶלָּא אִם כֵּן צָרִיךְ לְאוֹכְלָן בִּלְבַד. וְאֵין אָדָם רַשַּׁאי לִמְכּוֹר אֶת עַצְמוֹ עַד שֶׁלֹּא יִשָּׁאֵר לוֹ כְּלוּם, וַאֲפִילוּ כְּסוּת לֹא תִשָּׁאֵר לוֹ; וְאַחַר כָּךְ יִמְכּוֹר עַצְמוֹ.

The term "Hebrew servant" used in the Torah refers to a Jew whom the court sells by compulsion, or a person who sells himself willingly.

What is implied? When a person steals and does not have the resources to repay the principal, the court sells him, as we have explained in the laws concerning thievery.

To what does the term "a person who sells himself" refer? When a Jew becomes sorely impoverished, the Torah gives him permission to sell himself as a servant, as Vayikra (Leviticus) 25:39 states, "When your brother will become impoverished and be sold to you."

A person is not allowed to sell himself as a servant and stash away the money, use it to buy merchandise or utensils, or give it to his creditor. He may sell himself only when he needs the money for his very livelihood. A person is not permitted to sell himself unless he has no property remaining at all—i.e., even his clothing no longer remains. Only in such a situation may he sell himself.

TEXT 3B

Ibid., 3:4

אֵין עֶבֶד עִבְרִי מוּתָּר בְּשִׁפְחָה כְנַעֲנִית, עַד שֶׁתְּהְיֶה לוֹ אִשָּׁה יִשְׂרְאֵלִית
וּבָנִים, אֲבָל אִם אֵין לוֹ אִשָּׁה וּבָנִים, אֵין רַבּוֹ מוֹסֵר לוֹ שִׁפְחָה כְנַעֲנִית;
וְדָבָר זֶה, קַבָּלָה הוּא.

A Hebrew servant is not permitted to marry a Ca-
naanite maidservant unless he already has a Jewish
wife and children. If, however, he does not have a
Jewish wife and children, his master may not give him
a Canaanite maidservant. This concept is part of the
Oral Tradition.

Piercing, a Punishment?

TEXT 4A

Devarim (Deuteronomy) 15:16

וְהָיָה כִּי יֹאמַר אֵלֶיךָ לֹא אֵצֵא מֵעִמָּךְ כִּי אֲהֵבְךָ וְאֶת בֵּיתֶךָ כִּי טוֹב
לוֹ עִמָּךְ:

And it will be, if he says to you, "I will not leave you,"
because he loves you and your household, for it is good
for him with you.

TEXT 4B

Talmud Tractate Kidushin, 20a

תנו רבנן "כי טוב לו עמך" עמך במאכל עמך במשתה שלא תהא
אתה אוכל פת נקיה והוא אוכל פת קיבר אתה שותה יין ישן והוא
שותה יין חדש אתה ישן על גבי מוכין והוא ישן על גבי תבן מכאן
אמרו כל הקונה עבד עברי כקונה אדון לעצמו.

Babylonian Talmud

A literary work of monumental proportions that draws upon the legal, spiritual, intellectual, ethical, and historical traditions of Judaism. The 37 tractates of the Babylonian Talmud contain the teachings of the Jewish sages from the period after the destruction of the Second Temple through the 5th century CE. It has served as the primary vehicle for the transmission of the Oral Law and the education of Jews over the centuries; it is the entry point for all subsequent legal, ethical, and theological Jewish scholarship.

The sages taught, "For it is good for him with you"— the slave is truly with you; your equal in food, your equal in drink. You may not eat fine bread while he eats inferior bread. You may not drink aged wine while he drinks new wine. You may not sleep on soft sheets while he sleeps on straw.

From here the sages taught: Anyone who acquires a Hebrew slave, it as if he acquired a master for himself, since he is responsible for giving the slave everything equal to his own.

TEXT 5

Rashi to Shemot (Exodus) 21:2

"ורצע אדניו את אזנו במרצע"... ומה ראה אזן להרצע מכל שאר אברים שבגוף (מכילתא) אמר ר' יוחנן בן זכאי אזן זאת ששמעה על הר סיני לא תגנוב והלך וגנב תרצע ואם מוכר עצמו אזן ששמעה על הר סיני כי לי בני ישראל עבדים והלך וקנה אדון לעצמו תרצע.

Why was the ear chosen to be bored out of all the organs of the body? Rabbi Yochanan ben Zakkai said: The ear that heard on Mount Sinai, "You shall not steal" and [then] went and stole shall be pierced. And if [the text is referring to] one who sold himself [into servitude, the reason is that] the ear that heard, "For the children of Israel are slaves to Me" and [then] went and acquired a master for himself, [this ear] shall be pierced.

Compassionate Law

Do Not Shame the Thief

TEXT 6

Mishlei (Proverbs) 6:30

לֹא יָבוּזוּ לַגַּנָּב, כִּי יִגְנוֹב לְמַלֵּא נַפְשׁוֹ כִּי יִרְעָב:

They will not despise a thief if he steals to satisfy his appetite, for he is hungry.

TEXT 7

Talmud Tractate Eiruvin, 41b

ג' דברים מעבירין את האדם על דעתו ועל דעת קונו ... ודקדוקי
עניות. למאי נפקא מינה? למיבעי רחמי עלייהו.

Three things cause a person to act against his will and the will of his Creator, and one of them is extreme poverty. What are the practical ramifications of this idea? It allows us to request mercy for those people acting against their will.

The Pain of the Slave

TEXT 8

Rabbi Dovber of Lubavitch, Derech Chayim, ch. 2

Rabbi Dovber of Lubavitch
(Miteler Rebbe)
1773–1827

Rabbi Dovber was the eldest son of and successor to Rabbi Shneur Zalman of Liadi and greatly expanded upon and developed his father's groundbreaking teachings. He was the first Chabad rebbe to live in the village of Lubavitch. Dedicated to the welfare of Russian Jewry, at that time confined to the Pale of Settlement, he established Jewish agricultural colonies. His most notable works on Chasidic thought include *Shaar Hayichud, Torat Chayim,* and *Imrei Binah.*

שהדמעות שלו מיד נובעין ממילא בזכרו על מעשיו ומחשבותיו
בלבו רק רע כו' שזהוא אמיתות הכנעת הלב והשפלתו בעצם כמו
שיכנע הלב על פי הטבע כשנזכר העני ואביון על רוב דוחקו בעוני
ויסורין בבני חיי ומזוני שיבכה במר נפשו תכף כו' כך כמו טבע בנפש
זו החוטאת הבכי' זאת על חטאיו בשפלות והכנעה עצומה שנקרא
לב נשבר ונדכה תמיד כעני זה שלבו בשפלות והכנעה גדולה תמיד.

The sinner will immediately and automatically weep upon recalling the evil actions and thoughts of his heart, which were "only evil, all the day." This constitutes the true chastening and humbling of the heart itself.

The heart of the poor and impoverished man is chastened by the straits of his destitution and his suffering in matters of children, health, and wealth, and he will cry out with a bitter soul at the immediate thought of his situation.

So, too, should the soul of the sinner cry over his sins in humility and absolute contrition, with the constantly "broken and forsaken heart," like a poor man who is always humble and contrite.

TEXT 9

Talmud Tractate Shabbat, 152b

אמר רב כהנא מאי דכתיב "כי הוא אמר ויהי"? –זו אשה. "הוא צוה
ויעמוד" –אלו בנים.

Rabbi Kahana said: What does the verse refer to when it says, "For He spoke and it was, He commanded and it stood"?

"He spoke and it was"—this is a wife.

"He commanded and it stood"—this is children.

The Slave's Growth

A Hard Life

TEXT 10

Shemot (Exodus) 22:24

אִם כֶּסֶף תַּלְוֶה אֶת עַמִּי אֶת הֶעָנִי עִמָּךְ לֹא תִהְיֶה לוֹ כְּנֹשֶׁה לֹא
תְשִׂימוּן עָלָיו נֶשֶׁךְ:

When you lend money to My people, to the poor person [who is] with you, you shall not behave toward him as a lender; you shall not impose interest upon him.

TEXT 11

Mechilta to Shemot (Exodus), ad loc.

Mechilta
A halachic Midrash to Exodus. Midrash is the designation of a particular genre of rabbinic literature usually forming a running commentary on specific books of the Bible. The name *"Mechilta"* means "rule" and was given to this Midrash because its comments and explanations are based on fixed rules of exegesis. This work is often attributed to Rabbi Yishmael ben Elisha, a contemporary of Rabbi Akiva, though there are some references to later sages in this work.

"אִם כֶּסֶף תַּלְוֶה אֶת עַמִּי". רבי ישמעאל אומר, כל אם ואם שבתורה
רשות, חוץ מזה ועוד שנים . . . עַנִיֶּיךָ וַעֲנִיֵּי עִירְךָ עֲנִיֵּי קוֹדְמִין לַעֲנִיֵּי
עִירְךָ. עֲנִיֵּי עִירְךָ וַעֲנִיֵּי עִיר אַחֶרֶת עֲנִיֵּי עִירְךָ קוֹדְמִין שֶׁנֶּאֱמַר אֶת
הֶעָנִי עִמָּךְ.

"When you lend money to My people." Rabbi Yishmael said: Every "im" [the first word in our verse] in the Torah is understood to be optional ["if"], except for this one and two others, which are commands [i.e., it is compulsory to lend money to the poor, not

optional]. . . . *If you are faced with the poor of your family and the poor of your city, the poor of your family take precedence; if you are faced with the poor of your city and the poor of a different city, the poor of your city take precedence, since the verse says, "the poor person with you."*

TEXT 12

Mishlei (Proverbs) 22:7

עָשִׁיר בְּרָשִׁים יִמְשׁוֹל וְעֶבֶד לֹוֶה לְאִישׁ מַלְוֶה:

A rich man will rule over the poor, and a borrower is a slave to a lender.

The Test of Time

TEXT 13

The Rebbe, Rabbi Menachem Mendel Schneerson,
Likutei Sichot, vol. 21, p. 93

Rabbi Menachem Mendel Schneerson
1902–1994

The towering Jewish leader of the 20th century, known as "the Lubavitcher Rebbe," or simply as "the Rebbe." Born in southern Ukraine, the Rebbe escaped Nazi-occupied Europe, arriving in the U.S. in June 1941. The Rebbe inspired and guided the revival of traditional Judaism after the European devastation, impacting virtually every Jewish community the world over. The Rebbe often emphasized that the performance of just one additional good deed could usher in the era of Mashiach. The Rebbe's scholarly talks and writings have been printed in more than 200 volumes.

בשעת מעשה אין להענישו ברציעה מכיון דאנוס הוא מצד דחקו;
אבל באם אחרי זה טוען "אהבתי את אדוני וגו'" ואינו רוצה לצאת
לחפשי הרי מוכיח בזה שאין ענין זה – להיות עבד – חמור אצלו,
וכשמכר את עצמו לכתחלה לא הי' רק מצד אונס דחקו אלא שלא
איכפת לו להיות עבד.

– ולכן עם היות שעל רצונו עכשיו להשאר אצל אדונו אין ענשו
בעונש דרציעה שהרי (במקצת על כל פנים) אנוס הוא מצד אהבתו
הטבעית אל אשתו ובניו כנ"ל – מכל מקום מובן מטענתו "אהבתי
את אדוני" שלא איכפת לי' (כל כך) להיות עבד ומוכיח סופו על
תחלתו שלא מכר את עצמו מלכתחלה מצד אונס דחקו אלא
מרצונו הטוב, ולכן נרצע על ש"הלך וקנה אדון לעצמו."

When first becoming a slave, we do not punish the man by piercing his ear, since he is compelled by difficult circumstances. However, if, after six years of slavery, he claims, "I love my master" and does not seek his freedom, this proves that he does not view slavery as a necessary evil. Rather, when he sold himself to begin with, it was not because he lacked any other choice, but simply because he doesn't mind being a slave.

It may be true that his current wish to remain with his master is not necessarily punishable with ear piercing, inasmuch as he is compelled (at least to some extent) by his natural love of his wife and children. However, when he now states, "I love my master," we know that he truly does not mind being a slave. This proves that his initial act of selling himself into slavery was not out of duress but rather his true wish. And so, we punish him for the initial act of "actively seeking out a master."

To Truly Live

TEXT 14

The Rebbe, Rabbi Menachem Mendel Schneerson,
Torat Menachem 5772, vol. 2, p. 250

הגם שיארצייט הוא היום שבו היה הסתלקות הנשמה מן הגוף,
העלם והסתר על הגילוי דנפש מישראל, "חלק אלוק ממעל ממש",
בהגוף – שזהו ההעלם הכי גדול שיכול להיות רחמנא ליצלן – הרי,
הכוונה בכך היא (כמו בכל ירידה) שזה יפעל אחר כך עלי' יותר
גדולה... הן עלי' בהנשמה, והן באלה שנמצאים נשמות בגופים
למטה (שהי' להם קשר עם הנשמה), שניתוסף להם באריכות ימים
ושנים טובות, מלאים בתורה ומצוות ובמעשים טובים.

A yahrtzeit *is the day commemorating the moment
when the soul departed from the body—a sad moment
for the body, a moment when it was deprived from the
expression of a pure, holy Jewish soul. Certainly, the
intent of this sad moment—like any "dip"—is to spur
greater growth . . . both with regard to the soul that
has departed as well as those left behind who were
connected with that soul. The intent is that they should
be blessed with added life, full of Torah and* mitzvot.

5

TERUMAH

The Aroma of Acrimony

Why You Should Never Give Up

*Dedicated in loving memory of **Rabbi Yehoshua B. Gordon**, a dear shliach and teacher, on the occasion of his yahrtzeit, 29 Shevat*

PARSHA OVERVIEW
Terumah

The people of Israel are called upon to contribute thirteen materials—gold, silver, and copper; blue-, purple-, and red-dyed wool; flax, goat hair, animal skins, wood, olive oil, spices, and gems—out of which, G-d says to Moses, "They shall make for Me a Sanctuary, and I shall dwell amidst them."

On the summit of Mount Sinai, Moses is given detailed instructions on how to construct this dwelling for G-d so that it could be readily dismantled, transported, and reassembled as the people journeyed in the desert.

In the Sanctuary's inner chamber, behind an artistically woven curtain, was the ark containing the tablets of testimony engraved with the Ten Commandments; on the ark's cover stood two winged cherubim hammered out of pure gold. In the outer chamber stood the seven-branched menorah and the table upon which the "showbread" was arranged.

The Sanctuary's three walls were fitted together from forty-eight upright wooden boards, each of which was overlaid with gold and held up by a pair of silver foundation sockets. The roof was formed of three layers of coverings: (a) tapestries of multicolored wool and linen; (b) a covering made of goat hair; and (c) a covering of ram and tachash skins. Across the front of the Sanctuary was an embroidered screen held up by five posts.

Surrounding the Sanctuary and the copper-plated altar which stood before it was an enclosure of linen hangings, supported by sixty wooden posts with silver hooks and trimmings, and reinforced by copper stakes.

Do You Know the Best Way to Serve G-d?

Description of the Mishkan

TEXT 1

Shemot (Exodus) 25:1–9

וַיְדַבֵּר ה' אֶל מֹשֶׁה לֵּאמֹר:

דַּבֵּר אֶל בְּנֵי יִשְׂרָאֵל וְיִקְחוּ לִי תְּרוּמָה מֵאֵת כָּל אִישׁ אֲשֶׁר יִדְּבֶנּוּ לִבּוֹ תִּקְחוּ אֶת תְּרוּמָתִי:

וְזֹאת הַתְּרוּמָה אֲשֶׁר תִּקְחוּ מֵאִתָּם זָהָב וָכֶסֶף וּנְחֹשֶׁת:

וּתְכֵלֶת וְאַרְגָּמָן וְתוֹלַעַת שָׁנִי וְשֵׁשׁ וְעִזִּים:

וְעֹרֹת אֵילִם מְאָדָּמִים וְעֹרֹת תְּחָשִׁים וַעֲצֵי שִׁטִּים:

שֶׁמֶן לַמָּאֹר בְּשָׂמִים לְשֶׁמֶן הַמִּשְׁחָה וְלִקְטֹרֶת הַסַּמִּים:

אַבְנֵי שֹׁהַם וְאַבְנֵי מִלֻּאִים לָאֵפֹד וְלַחֹשֶׁן:

וְעָשׂוּ לִי מִקְדָּשׁ וְשָׁכַנְתִּי בְּתוֹכָם:

כְּכֹל אֲשֶׁר אֲנִי מַרְאֶה אוֹתְךָ אֵת תַּבְנִית הַמִּשְׁכָּן וְאֵת תַּבְנִית כָּל כֵּלָיו וְכֵן תַּעֲשׂוּ:

G-d spoke to Moses saying:

"Speak to the children of Israel, and have them take for Me an offering; from every person whose heart inspires him to generosity, you shall take My offering.

And this is the offering that you shall take from them: gold, silver, and copper;

blue, purple, and crimson wool; linen and goat hair;

ram skins dyed red, tachash skins, and acacia wood;

oil for lighting, spices for the anointing oil and for the incense;

shoham *stones and filling stones for the ephod and for the* choshen.

And they shall make Me a sanctuary, and I will dwell in their midst

According to all that I show you, the pattern of the Mishkan and the pattern of all its vessels; and so shall you do."

Nachmanides—A Place to Deliver G-d's Word

TEXT 2

Nachmanides, Pirush Haramban to Shemot (Exodus) 25:2

Rabbi Moshe ben Nachman
(Nachmanides, Ramban)
1194–1270

Scholar, philosopher, author, and physician. Nachmanides was born in Spain and served as leader of Iberian Jewry. In 1263, he was summoned by King James of Aragon to a public disputation with Pablo Cristiani, a Jewish apostate. Though Nachmanides was the clear victor of the debate, he had to flee Spain because of the resulting persecution. He moved to Israel and helped reestablish communal life in Jerusalem. He authored a classic commentary on the Pentateuch and a commentary on the Talmud.

כאשר דבר השם עם ישראל פנים בפנים עשרת הדברות, וצוה אותם על ידי משה קצת מצות שהם כמו אבות למצותיה של תורה, כאשר הנהיגו רבותינו עם הגרים שבאים להתיהד, וישראל קבלו עליהם לעשות כל מה שיצום על ידו של משה, וכרת עמהם ברית על כל זה, מעתה הנה הם לו לעם והוא להם לאלהים... והנה הם קדושים ראוים שיהיה בהם מקדש להשרות שכינתו ביניהם. ולכן צוה תחלה על דבר המשכן שיהיה לו בית בתוכם מקודש לשמו, ושם ידבר עם משה ויצוה את בני ישראל. והנה עקר החפץ במשכן הוא מקום מנוחת השכינה שהוא הארון, כמו שאמר (להלן כה, כב) ונועדתי לך שם ודברתי אתך מעל הכפרת, על כן הקדים הארון והכפרת בכאן כי הוא מוקדם במעלה... וסוד המשכן הוא, שיהיה הכבוד אשר שכן על הר סיני שוכן עליו בנסתר... ובבא משה היה אליו הדבור אשר נדבר לו בהר סיני.

G-d personally told the Jews the Ten Commandments and transmitted through Moses additional mitzvot which are central to the Torah, as a rabbi would do with a prospective convert. The Jews then accepted upon themselves all they heard from Moses, and G-d formed a covenant with them; they were now "His nation," and He was "their G-d." Now, the time was ripe for a home to house His glory among them. Thus, He commanded them to build the Tabernacle, and there He would speak to Moses and relay His commands to the people.

Now, the primary object in the Tabernacle was the seat of His glory, the ark, as is written, "And I will arrange My meetings with you there, and I will speak with you from atop the ark cover." It is for this reason that the Torah first speaks of the ark and its cover, because it is the most important element of the Tabernacle.

This is the idea of the Tabernacle: a place where the glory that was present at Sinai would reside. . . . When Moses would come there, he would hear the same voice that he heard at Sinai.

Rambam—A House of Worship

TEXT 3

Maimonides, Mishneh Torah, Laws of the Temple, 1:1

מצות עשה לעשות בית לה׳ מוכן להיות מקריבים בו הקרבנות.

It is a positive commandment to construct a house for G-d, a place where the sacrifices will be offered.

Rabbi Moshe ben Maimon
(Maimonides, Rambam)
1135–1204

Halachist, philosopher, author, and physician. Maimonides was born in Córdoba, Spain. After the conquest of Córdoba by the Almohads, he fled Spain and eventually settled in Cairo, Egypt. There, he became the leader of the Jewish community and served as court physician to the vizier of Egypt. He is most noted for authoring the *Mishneh Torah*, an encyclopedic arrangement of Jewish law, and for his philosophical work, *Guide for the Perplexed*. His rulings on Jewish law are integral to the formation of halachic consensus.

What's with the Table?

TEXT 4

Shemot (Exodus) 25:23–24, 30

וְעָשִׂיתָ שֻׁלְחָן עֲצֵי שִׁטִּים אַמָּתַיִם אָרְכּוֹ וְאַמָּה רָחְבּוֹ וְאַמָּה וָחֵצִי קֹמָתוֹ:
וְצִפִּיתָ אֹתוֹ זָהָב טָהוֹר וְעָשִׂיתָ לוֹ זֵר זָהָב סָבִיב:
וְעָשִׂיתָ לוֹ מִסְגֶּרֶת טֹפַח סָבִיב וְעָשִׂיתָ זֵר זָהָב לְמִסְגַּרְתּוֹ סָבִיב:
וְעָשִׂיתָ לוֹ אַרְבַּע טַבְּעֹת זָהָב וְנָתַתָּ אֶת הַטַּבָּעֹת עַל אַרְבַּע הַפֵּאֹת
אֲשֶׁר לְאַרְבַּע רַגְלָיו:
לְעֻמַּת הַמִּסְגֶּרֶת תִּהְיֶיןָ הַטַּבָּעֹת לְבָתִּים לְבַדִּים לָשֵׂאת אֶת הַשֻּׁלְחָן:
וְעָשִׂיתָ אֶת הַבַּדִּים עֲצֵי שִׁטִּים וְצִפִּיתָ אֹתָם זָהָב וְנִשָּׂא בָם אֶת הַשֻּׁלְחָן:
וְעָשִׂיתָ קְּעָרֹתָיו וְכַפֹּתָיו וּקְשׂוֹתָיו וּמְנַקִּיֹּתָיו אֲשֶׁר יֻסַּךְ בָּהֵן זָהָב טָהוֹר
תַּעֲשֶׂה אֹתָם:
וְנָתַתָּ עַל הַשֻּׁלְחָן לֶחֶם פָּנִים לְפָנַי תָּמִיד:

And you shall make a table of acacia wood, two cubits its length, one cubit its width, and a cubit and a half its height.

And you shall overlay it with pure gold, and you shall make for it a golden crown all around.

And you shall make for it a frame a handbreadth [wide] all around, and you shall make a golden crown for its frame all around.

And you shall make for it four golden rings, and you shall place the rings on the four corners that are on its four legs.

The rings shall be opposite the frame as holders for the poles [with which] to carry the table.

And you shall make the poles of acacia wood, and you shall overlay them with gold, and the table shall be carried with them.

And you shall make its forms, its spoons, its half pipes, and its supports with which it will be covered; of pure gold you shall make them.

And you shall place on the table showbread before Me at all times.

TEXT 5

Maimonides, Laws of Maaseh Hakorbanot, 12:3;
Laws of Temidin U'Musafin, 5:4–5

לחם הפנים שעושין בכל שבת ואינו קרב לגבי המזבח אלא כולו נאכל לכהנים...

וכיצד מסדרין את הלחם ארבעה כהנים נכנסים, שנים בידן שני סדרין, ושנים בידם שני בזיכין, וארבעה מקדימין לפניהם שנים ליטול שני סדרים ושנים ליטול שני בזיכין שהיו שם על השולחן, הנכנסין עומדין בצפון ופניהם לדרום, והיוצאין עומדים בדרום ופניהם לצפון, אלו מושכין ואלו מניחין וטפחו של זה בתוך טפחו של זה שנאמר לפני תמיד.

יצאו ונתנו את הלחם שהוציאו על שולחן זהב אחר שהיה באולם והקטירו הבזיכין ואחר כך מחלקין החלות.

The showbread is brought every Shabbat. They are not offered on the altar, but instead are eaten entirely by the priests. . . .

How are the sets of the showbread arranged? Four priests enter the Sanctuary: two are holding the two sets [of bread] and two, the two dishes [of frankincense]. Four priests enter before them to remove the two sets of bread and the two dishes [of frankincense] that were on the table. The priests that enter stand in the north, facing the south, and those that depart stand in the south, facing the north. These remove [the showbread from the previous week] and these place down [the new breads]. . . .

When they departed, they would place the bread on a second golden table that would be placed in the Entrance Hall. They would offer [the incense in] the dishes on the pyre, and afterward the breads were divided [to be eaten by the priests].

Helping Is Holy

TEXT 6

Maimonides, Guide for the Perplexed, 3:45

> והצורך למזבח הקטורת ומזבח העולה וכליהם מבואר, אבל השלחן
> והיות עליו הלחם תמיד לא אדע בו סבה, ואיני יודע לאיזה דבר
> איחס אותו עד היום.

The use of the altar for incense and the altar for burnt-offerings and their vessels is obvious; but I do not know the object of the table with the bread upon it continually, and up to this day I have not been able to assign any reason to this commandment.

TEXT 7

Midrash Hagadol, cited in Torah Shleimah, Parshat Terumah §160

> ועשית שלחן השלחן זכר למן דכתיב תערך לפני שלחן נגד צוררי.

"And you shall make a table. . . ." The shulchan *is reminiscent of the manna, as it is stated, "You set a table before Me in the presence of My adversaries."*

Midrash Hagadol
A Midrashic work on the 5 books of the Pentateuch. Midrash is the designation of a particular genre of rabbinic literature usually forming a running commentary on specific books of the Bible. *Midrash Hagadol* quotes widely from Talmud and other earlier Midrashic works, serving as a valuable resource to reconstruct lost sections of Midrash. A traveler, Yaakov Sapir, first discovered the anonymous Midrash in Yemen in the middle of the 19th century. Some ascribe it to Rabbi Avraham, son of Maimonides.

TEXT 8

Rabbeinu Bachaye ben Asher ibn Chalawa, Shemot (Exodus) 25:23

Rabbeinu Bechaye ben Asher
c. 1265–1340
Biblical commentator.
Rabbeinu Bechaye lived in
Spain and was a disciple of
Rabbi Shlomo ben Aderet,
known as Rashba. He is best
known for his multifaceted
commentary on the Torah,
which interprets the text
on literal, Midrashic,
philosophical, and kabbalistic
levels. Rabbeinu Bechaye also
wrote *Kad Hakemach*, a work
on philosophy and ethics.

ועל דרך הפשט הוצרך השולחן בבית ה' בלחם אשר עליו להיות
שורש דבר שתחול הברכה בו. והלחם אשר עליו היה נאכל לכהנים
משרתי המקדש והיה מספיק לרבים מהם מעט ממנו, וכענין
שאמרו חז"ל (יומא לט.) כל כהן שהיה מגיעו כפול היה שבע, ועל
כן נקרא שולחן שהקדוש ברוך הוא שולח ברכתו בלחם שעליו
ומשם הברכה משתלח בכל המזונות ויבוא שובע לכל העולם.

Understood simply, the shulchan *was placed in the house of G-d in order to serve as a starting point that the blessing can attach itself to.*

The showbread was eaten by the priests who served in the Temple, and a small quantity of bread would satiate a large number of priests, as our sages stated, "Any priest who received even [a] pol [minuscule measurement] sized portion became satiated."

Thus, it was called the shulchan, *for G-d would send [shole'ach] His blessing through the bread placed upon it, and from there the blessing would be sent forth to all as sustenance for the entire world.*

Doing G-d's Work of Helping the World

TEXT 9

Chasidic aphorism, cited in Igrot Kodesh, vol. 13, p. 112

יענעמס גשמיות איז בא מיר רוחניות.

Another person's physical welfare is for me a spiritual matter.

Igrot Kodesh

A selection of Hebrew and Yiddish letters penned by the Rebbe. As of 2018, 32 volumes have been published in this series. The letters are published in chronological order, starting from 1925 and extending thus far to 1977. Only those letters that are of relevance to the public are published, and all personal information is excised. The letters cover a wide range of issues: communal activism, Chabad philosophy, Talmud, Jewish law, kabbalah, practical advice, and much more.

TEXT 10

Midrash Vayikra Rabah, 34:2

Vayikra Rabah

An early rabbinic commentary on the Book of Leviticus. This Midrash, written in Aramaic and Hebrew, provides textual exegeses and anecdotes, expounds upon the biblical narrative, and develops and illustrates moral principles. It was first printed in Constantinople in 1512 together with four other Midrashic works on the other four books of the Pentateuch.

דבר אחר וכי ימוך אחיך (עמך) הדא הוא דכתיב מלוה ה' חונן דל,
אר"א כתיב נותן לחם לכל בשר בא זה וחטף לו את המצוה אמר
הקב"ה עלי לשלם לו גמולו הדא הוא דכתיב וגמולו ישלם לו ר'
תנחומא אמר לה בשם ר' חייא בר אבא ר' נחמן אמר לה בשם
ר' יודן בר"ש ורבנן בשם רשב"ל אלמלא מקרא כתוב אי אפשר
לאומרו כביכול דרכו של לוה להיות עבד למלוה הדא הוא דכתיב
ועבד לוה לאיש מלוה.

Another exposition of the verse (Vayikra [Leviticus] 25:35), "If your brother becomes destitute and his hand falters beside you, you shall support him": It is written in Scripture (Mishlei [Proverbs] 19:17): "One who is generous to the poor makes a loan to G-d; He will repay what is due." Rabbi Eleazar said: It is written [elsewhere] (Tehilim [Psalms] 136:25), "[G-d is the One] who gives food to all flesh. . . ." Now, because this person comes and fulfills the commandment [before G-d can act], the blessed Holy One says, "I must compensate that person." Thus, it is written, ". . . He will repay what is due."

Rabbi Tanchuma taught in the name of Rabbi Chiya bar Abba . . . "If not for the verse, it would be impossible to say this: as it were, it is usual for a borrower [in this instance, G-d, so to speak] to become the servant of the lender, as it is written (Mishlei [Proverbs] 22:7), ". . . the borrower is a servant to the lender!"

Grounding

TEXT 11

Ethics of the Fathers, 1:2

שמעון הצדיק היה משירי כנסת הגדולה הוא היה אומר על שלשה
דברים העולם עומד על התורה ועל העבודה ועל גמילות חסדים.

Shimon the Righteous was among the last surviving members of the Great Assembly. He would say: The world stands on three things: Torah, the service of G-d, and deeds of kindness.

Ethics of the Fathers
(*Pirkei Avot*)
A six-chapter work on Jewish ethics that is studied widely by Jewish communities, especially during the summer. The first five chapters are from the Mishnah, tractate Avot. Avot differs from the rest of the Mishnah in that it does not focus on legal subjects; it is a collection of the sages' wisdom on topics related to character development, ethics, healthy living, piety, and the study of Torah.

Three Jews

TEXT 12

Talmud Tractate Berachot, 26b

Babylonian Talmud
A literary work of monumental
proportions that draws upon
the legal, spiritual, intellectual,
ethical, and historical
traditions of Judaism. The 37
tractates of the Babylonian
Talmud contain the teachings
of the Jewish sages from the
period after the destruction
of the Second Temple through
the 5th century CE. It has
served as the primary vehicle
for the transmission of the
Oral Law and the education
of Jews over the centuries;
it is the entry point for all
subsequent legal, ethical, and
theological Jewish scholarship.

רבי יהושע בן לוי אמר: תפלות כנגד תמידין תקנום...
ותניא כוותיה דרבי יהושע בן לוי: מפני מה אמרו תפלת השחר עד
חצות - שהרי תמיד של שחר קרב והולך עד חצות; ורבי יהודה
אומר: עד ארבע שעות, שהרי תמיד של שחר קרב והולך עד ארבע
שעות. ומפני מה אמרו תפלת המנחה עד הערב - שהרי תמיד של
בין הערבים קרב והולך עד הערב; רבי יהודה אומר: עד פלג המנחה,
שהרי תמיד של בין הערבים קרב והולך עד פלג המנחה. ומפני
מה אמרו תפלת הערב אין לה קבע - שהרי אברים ופדרים שלא
נתעכלו מבערב קרבים והולכים כל הלילה.

*Rabbi Yehoshua ben Levi says, "The prayers were
instituted to correspond to the daily sacrifices. . . ."*

*The following Tannaic statement supports Rabbi Ye-
hoshua ben Levi: Why did they say that the morning
prayer can be recited till midday? Because the regular
morning sacrifice could be offered up to midday. . . .*

*And why did they say that the afternoon prayer can
be recited up to the evening? Because the regular afternoon offering could be offered up to the evening. . . .*

*And why did they say that for the evening prayer
there is no limit? Because the limbs and the fat which
were not consumed [on the altar] by the evening could
be offered for the whole of the night.*

TEXT 13

Rabbi Yosef Yitzchak Schneersohn, Sefer Hasichot 5707, p. 87

Rabbi Yosef Yitschak Schneersohn
(Rayats, Frierdiker Rebbe, Previous Rebbe)
1880–1950

בא חסידים האט עבודת הלב אלעמאל פארנומען דעם גרעסטן
ארט. די עבודת המוח איז מער ניט ווי א הכנה צו עבודת הלב,
ווייל מוח שליט על הלב בתולדתו, אבער די עבודה עיקרית איז
עבודת הלב. וואס אזוי איז געווען [דער] סדר פנימי ביי חסידים, אז
מען האט פארבראכט, און דער חסידישער פארברייינגען האט זיך
אפגעשפיגעלט אין עבודת התפלה און אין תקון המדות.

Chasidic rebbe, prolific writer, and Jewish activist. Rabbi Yosef Yitschak, the sixth leader of the Chabad movement, actively promoted Jewish religious practice in Soviet Russia and was arrested for these activities. After his release from prison and exile, he settled in Warsaw, Poland, from where he fled Nazi occupation, and arrived in New York in 1940. Settling in Brooklyn, Rabbi Schneersohn worked to revitalize American Jewish life. His son-in-law, Rabbi Menachem Mendel Schneerson, succeeded him as the leader of the Chabad movement.

By Chasidim, working with the heart always took center stage position. Working with the intellect is merely a prelude to working with the heart, as the brain naturally controls the heart; but the primary service is with the heart.

That was the purposeful conduct of Chasidim: they would farbreng, *and the Chasidic* farbrengen *would reflect itself in laboring during prayer and refining the character.*

TEXT 14

Rabbi Shneur Zalman of Liadi, Tanya, Igeret Hakodesh, epistle 5

Rabbi Shneur Zalman of Liadi
(Alter Rebbe)
1745–1812

Chasidic rebbe, halachic authority, and founder of the Chabad movement. The Alter Rebbe was born in Liozna, Belarus, and was among the principal students of the Magid of Mezeritch. His numerous works include the *Tanya*, an early classic containing the fundamentals of Chabad Chasidism, and *Shulchan Aruch HaRav*, an expanded and reworked code of Jewish law.

מ"ש האריז"ל שיש ב' מיני נשמות בישראל נשמות ת"ח העוסקים בתורה כל ימיהם ונשמות בעלי מצות העוסקים בצדקה וגמ"ח.

This [is] what Rabbi Isaac Luria, the Arizal, of blessed memory, stated: that there are two kinds of souls among Israel: the souls of Torah scholars—who occupy themselves with the Torah all their lives, and the souls of those who perform the commandments—who occupy themselves with charity and the performance of kindness.

So Who's on Top?

TEXT 15A

Talmud Tractate Shabbat, 118b

אמר ליה רב יוסף לרב יוסף בריה דרבה: אבוך במאי זהיר טפי? אמר
ליה: בציצית. יומא חד הוה קא סליק בדרגא, איפסיק ליה חוטא -
ולא נחית ואתא כמה דלא רמיה.

Rabbi Joseph asked Rabbi Joseph the son of Rabah, "What was your father most careful with?" "Tzitzit," he replied. "One day he was ascending a ladder when a thread [of his tzitzit] snapped, and he would not descend until [another] was inserted."

TEXT 15B

Rabbi Shneur Zalman of Liadi, Tanya, Igeret Hakodesh, epistle 7

והנה אף שגילוי זה על ידי עסק התורה והמצות הוא שוה לכל
נפש מישראל בדרך כלל כי תורה אחת ומשפט א' לכולנו אף
על פי כן בדרך פרט אין כל הנפשות או הרוחות והנשמות שוות
בענין זה לפי עת וזמן גלגולם ובואם בעולם הזה וכמ"ארז"ל אבוך
במאי הוי זהיר טפי אמר ליה בציצית כו' וכן אין כל הדורות שוין
כי כמו שאברי האדם כל אבר יש לו פעולה פרטית ומיוחדת
העין לראות והאזן לשמוע כך בכל מצוה מאיר אור פרטי
ומיוחד מאור אין סוף ברוך הוא ואף שכל נפש מישראל צריכה
לבוא בגלגול לקיים כל תרי"ג מצות מכל מקום לא נצרכה אלא
להעדפה וזהירות וזריזות יתירה ביתר שאת ויתר עז כפולה
ומכופלת למעלה מעלה מזהירות שאר המצות. וזהו שאמר במאי
הוי זהיר טפי טפי דייקא.

*Though the G-dly revelation through the occupation
with Torah and the* mitzvot *is, generally, equal in
every one of Israel [for we all have one Torah and one
law], nevertheless, in a more specific way not all the
souls* (nefesh) *or spirits* (ruach) *and souls* (neshamah)
*are equal in this regard, depending on the occurrence
and time of their reincarnation and their coming into
this world; and as our sages, of blessed memory, said:
"'With what was your father more careful?' He answered him, 'With the* tzitzit. . . .'"*

*Likewise, not all the generations are the same. For just
as with the organs of man, where every organ has its*

own special and particular function, the eye to see and the ear to hear [etc.], so too, through every command- ment there radiates a special and particular light from G-d. And though every soul of Israel needs to be rein- carnated in order to fulfil all the 613 commandments, even so, this special care with a particular mitzvah is necessary only for the sake of an increase in prudence and additional zeal—with exceeding uplifting and strength, doubly and manifold, surpassing the zeal for the other commandments. And that is what he meant when he said, "With what was he more careful?" [the emphasis being on "more"].

6

Tᴇᴛᴢᴀᴠᴇʜ

Clothes Make the Person

Behavioral Mastery Is the Name of the Game

*Dedicated to **Elliot Brown** in appreciation of his friendship and partnership with JLI
and his dedication to bringing the light of Torah to communities across the globe.*

PARSHA OVERVIEW
Tetzaveh

G-d tells Moses to receive from the Children of Israel pure olive oil to feed the "everlasting flame" of the menorah, which Aaron is to kindle each day, "from evening till morning."

The priestly garments, to be worn by the kohanim (priests) while serving in the Sanctuary, are described. All kohanim *wore: 1) the* ketonet—*a full-length linen tunic; 2)* michnasayim—*linen breeches; 3)* mitznefet *or* migba'at—*a linen turban; 4)* avnet—*a long sash wound above the waist.*

In addition, the kohen gadol *(high priest) wore: 5) the* ephod—*an apron-like garment made of blue-, purple-, and red-dyed wool, linen, and gold thread; 6) the* choshen—*a breastplate containing twelve precious stones inscribed with the names of the twelve tribes of Israel; 7) the* me'il—*a cloak of blue wool, with gold bells and decorative pomegranates on its hem; 8) the* tzitz—*a golden plate worn on the forehead, bearing the inscription "Holy to G-d."*

Tetzaveh also includes G-d's detailed instructions for the seven-day initiation of Aaron and his four sons—Nadav, Avihu, Elazar and Itamar—into the priesthood, and for the making of the golden altar, on which the ketoret *(incense) was burned.*

PRIESTLY GARMENTS

Walk in to the Wardrobe

TEXT 1

Shemot (Exodus) 28:1–4, 40–43

וְאַתָּה הַקְרֵב אֵלֶיךָ אֶת אַהֲרֹן אָחִיךָ וְאֶת בָּנָיו אִתּוֹ מִתּוֹךְ בְּנֵי יִשְׂרָאֵל
לְכַהֲנוֹ לִי אַהֲרֹן נָדָב וַאֲבִיהוּא אֶלְעָזָר וְאִיתָמָר בְּנֵי אַהֲרֹן:
וְעָשִׂיתָ בִגְדֵי קֹדֶשׁ לְאַהֲרֹן אָחִיךָ לְכָבוֹד וּלְתִפְאָרֶת:
וְאַתָּה תְּדַבֵּר אֶל כָּל חַכְמֵי לֵב אֲשֶׁר מִלֵּאתִיו רוּחַ חָכְמָה וְעָשׂוּ אֶת
בִּגְדֵי אַהֲרֹן לְקַדְּשׁוֹ לְכַהֲנוֹ לִי:
וְאֵלֶּה הַבְּגָדִים אֲשֶׁר יַעֲשׂוּ חֹשֶׁן וְאֵפוֹד וּמְעִיל וּכְתֹנֶת תַּשְׁבֵּץ מִצְנֶפֶת
וְאַבְנֵט וְעָשׂוּ בִגְדֵי קֹדֶשׁ לְאַהֲרֹן אָחִיךָ וּלְבָנָיו לְכַהֲנוֹ לִי:...
וְלִבְנֵי אַהֲרֹן תַּעֲשֶׂה כֻתֳּנֹת וְעָשִׂיתָ לָהֶם אַבְנֵטִים וּמִגְבָּעוֹת תַּעֲשֶׂה
לָהֶם לְכָבוֹד וּלְתִפְאָרֶת:
וְהִלְבַּשְׁתָּ אֹתָם אֶת אַהֲרֹן אָחִיךָ וְאֶת בָּנָיו אִתּוֹ וּמָשַׁחְתָּ אֹתָם וּמִלֵּאתָ
אֶת יָדָם וְקִדַּשְׁתָּ אֹתָם וְכִהֲנוּ לִי:
וַעֲשֵׂה לָהֶם מִכְנְסֵי בָד לְכַסּוֹת בְּשַׂר עֶרְוָה מִמָּתְנַיִם וְעַד יְרֵכַיִם יִהְיוּ:
וְהָיוּ עַל אַהֲרֹן וְעַל בָּנָיו בְּבֹאָם אֶל אֹהֶל מוֹעֵד אוֹ בְגִשְׁתָּם אֶל הַמִּזְבֵּחַ
לְשָׁרֵת בַּקֹּדֶשׁ וְלֹא יִשְׂאוּ עָוֹן וָמֵתוּ חֻקַּת עוֹלָם לוֹ וּלְזַרְעוֹ אַחֲרָיו:

And you bring near to yourself your brother Aaron, and his sons with him, from among the Children of Israel to serve Me [as kohanim*]: Aaron, Nadab, and Abihu, Eleazar, and Ithamar, Aaron's sons.*

You shall make holy garments for your brother Aaron, for honor and for glory.

And you shall speak to all the wisehearted, whom I have filled with the spirit of wisdom, and they shall make Aaron's garments to sanctify him, [so] that he may serve Me [as a kohen].

And these are the garments that they shall make: a choshen, an ephod, a robe, a tunic of checker work, a cap, and a sash. They shall make holy garments for your brother Aaron and for his sons to serve Me [as kohanim]. . . .

For Aaron's sons you shall make tunics and make them sashes, and you shall make them high hats for honor and for glory.

With these you shall clothe Aaron, your brother, and his sons along with him, and you shall anoint them and invest them with full authority and sanctify them so that they may serve Me [as kohanim].

And make for them linen pants to cover the flesh of [their] nakedness; they shall reach from the waist down to the thighs.

They shall be worn by Aaron and by his sons when they enter the Tent of Meeting or when they approach the altar to serve in the Holy, so they will not bear iniquity and die. It shall be a perpetual statute for him and for his descendants after him.

Dressed to Impress

TEXT 2

Nachmanides, Pirush Haramban to Shemot (Exodus) 28:2

Rabbi Moshe ben Nachman
(Nachmanides, Ramban)
1194–1270
Scholar, philosopher, author, and physician. Nachmanides was born in Spain and served as leader of Iberian Jewry. In 1263, he was summoned by King James of Aragon to a public disputation with Pablo Cristiani, a Jewish apostate. Though Nachmanides was the clear victor of the debate, he had to flee Spain because of the resulting persecution. He moved to Israel and helped reestablish communal life in Jerusalem. He authored a classic commentary on the Pentateuch and a commentary on the Talmud.

"לכבוד ולתפארת". שיהיה נכבד ומפואר במלבושים נכבדים ומפוארים, כמו שאמר הכתוב כחתן יכהן פאר, כי אלה הבגדים לבושי מלכות הן, כדמותן ילבשו המלכים בזמן התורה. כמו שמצינו בכתנת ועשה לו כתנת פסים, שפירושו מרוקמת כדמות פסים והיא כתונת תשבץ כמו שפירשתי והלבישו כבן מלכי קדם...

והמצנפת ידועה גם היום למלכים ולשרים הגדולים... והאפוד והחשן לבוש מלכות.... והציץ נזר המלכים הוא...

על דרך האמת, לכבוד ולתפארת, יאמר שיעשו בגדי קדש לאהרן לשרת בהם לכבוד השם השוכן בתוכם ולתפארת עזם, כדכתיב "כי תפארת עזמו אתה" וכתיב "בית קדשנו ותפארתנו אשר הללוך אבותינו", וקדשנו הוא הכבוד ותפארתנו תפארת ישראל, ועוד נאמר "עוז ותפארת במקדשו", וכן "לפאר מקום מקדשי ומקום רגלי אכבד", שיהיה מקום המקדש מפואר בתפארת, ומקום רגליו, שהוא מקום בית המקדש, מכובד בכבוד השם.

"For honor and for glory": So that [Aaron] will be honorable and glorious, by wearing honorable and glorious clothing. So does the [prophet] speak of a "bridegroom dressing like a priest, in clothes of glory."

These garments [bring glory] because they are royal clothes; kings would dress in the fashion in the days of the Torah. So do we find that [Joseph's] fine tunic . . . which bore a similar pattern as the tunic worn in the

Temple, as I have explained, was worn by the kings of the East. . . .

The mitznefet—*hat [worn by the high priest is likewise] familiar today amongst the great kings and princes. . . . So too, the* ephod—*apron and* choshen—*breastplate are regal clothes . . . and the* tzitz—*showplate is a kind of crown worn by kings. . . .*

A deeper meaning of "honor and glory" is to say that these holy garments should be for Aaron to serve in them, in honor of G-d, who dwells amongst them, and who is the "glory of their might," as the verse states, "For You are the glory of their might."

It is also written of the Temple, "To glorify the place of My sanctuary, and the place of My feet I will honor," that the site of the Sanctuary should be glorified with beauty, and that the "place of my feet," which is the site of the Temple, should be with the honor of G-d.

TEXT 3

Rabbi Ovadiah Seforno, Seforno to Shemot (Exodus) 28:2

Rabbi Ovadiah Seforno
1475–1550

Biblical exegete, philosopher, and physician. Seforno was born in Cesena, Italy. After gaining a thorough knowledge of Talmud and the sciences, he moved to Rome, where he studied medicine and taught Hebrew to the German scholar Johannes Reuchlin. Seforno eventually settled in Bologna, where he founded and directed a yeshiva until his death. His magnum opus is a biblical commentary focused on the simple interpretation of the text, with an emphasis on philology and philosophy.

"לכבוד". לכבוד האל יתברך בהיותם בגדי קדש לעבודתו.

"לתפארת". שיהיה כהן מורה נורא על כל סביביו, שהם תלמידיו החקוקים על לבו וכתפיו.

"For honor." For the honor of G-d, since they are holy clothes, dedicated to serving Him.

"For glory." So that the kohen *should inspire all who surround him with awe, for they are his disciples, engraved on his heart and upon his shoulders.*

TEXT 4

Sefer Hachinuch, Mitzvah 69

Sefer Hachinuch
A work on the biblical
commandments. Four aspects
of every mitzvah are discussed
in this work: the definition of
the mitzvah; ethical lessons
that can be deduced from
the mitzvah; basic laws
pertaining to the observance
of the mitzvah; and who is
obligated to perform the
mitzvah, and when. The work
was composed in the 13th
century by an anonymous
author who refers to himself
as "the Levite of Barcelona."
It has been widely thought
that this referred to Rabbi
Aharon Halevi of Barcelona
(Re'ah); however, this view
has been contested.

משרשי המצוה, היסוד הקבוע לנו כי האדם נפעל לפי פעולותיו
ואחריהם מחשבותיו וכוונותיו, והשליח המכפר צריך להתפיס כל
מחשבתו וכוונתו אל העבודה, על כן ראוי להתלבש בגדים מיוחדים
אליה, שכשיסתכל בכל מקום שבגופו מיד יהיה נזכר ומתעורר
בלבו לפני מי הוא עובד.

וזה כעין תפילין שנצטוו הכל להניח בקצת הגוף שיהיה שיהיה לזכרון
מחשבת הכשר. ואף על פי שגם הכהן היה מניח תפילין, לגדל ענינו
היה צריך גם זה.

*The message of this mitzvah is the principle established
for us, namely that a person is impacted according to
his actions and pursuant to his thoughts and intentions.*

*The representative who atones [on behalf of his people]
(namely, the* kohen*) must attach all of his thoughts
and intentions to the [Divine] service. Therefore, it is
appropriate that he wears special clothes for it; as when
he stares at any place of his body, he will immediately
remember and be aroused in his heart to remember in
front of Whom he is serving.*

This is akin to the mitzvah of tefilin—*we are commanded to place it on a part of our body so that we
have a ready reminder to maintain proper thought.
Though the priest also wears* tefilin, *due to the greatness of his matter, he needs the priestly garments too.*

Seriously Sartorial

TEXT 5

Talmud Tractate Shabbat, 113a

Babylonian Talmud
A literary work of monumental proportions that draws upon the legal, spiritual, intellectual, ethical, and historical traditions of Judaism. The 37 tractates of the Babylonian Talmud contain the teachings of the Jewish sages from the period after the destruction of the 2nd Temple through the 5th century CE. It has served as the primary vehicle for the transmission of the Oral Law and the education of Jews over the centuries; it is the entry point for all subsequent legal, ethical, and theological Jewish scholarship.

רבי יוחנן קרי למאניה מכבדותי.

Rabbi Yochanan called his garments "my honor."

TEXT 6

Talmud Tractate Berachot, 62b

"ויקם דוד ויכרת את כנף המעיל אשר לשאול בלט". אמר רבי יוסי ברבי חנינא כל המבזה את הבגדים סוף אינו נהנה מהם שנאמר "והמלך דוד זקן בא בימים ויכסהו בבגדים ולא יחם לו".

"Then David arose and cut off the skirt of Saul's robe secretly."

Rabbi Yose son of Rabbi Chanina said: Whoever treats garments contemptuously will in the end derive no benefit from them, for it says, "Now King David was old and stricken in years; and they covered him with clothes, but he could get no heat."

TEXT 7

Midrash Lekach Tov, Shemot (Exodus) 6:6

הוצאתי אתכם, והצלתי אתכם, וגאלתי אתכם, ולקחתי אתכם, כנגד ד' זכיות שבידם, שלא שינו את לשונם, ולא חילפו את שמלותם, ולא גילו את סודם, דכתיב ושאלה אשה משכנתה, ולא בטלו ברית מילה.

Rabbi Tuvia ben Eliezer
1050—1108

Talmudist and poet. Born in Bulgaria in the early 11th century, Rabbi Tuvia ben Eliezer was the son of Eliezer ben Isaac Hagadol, thought to have been Rashi's teacher. His most famous and extensive work is the *Lekach Tov* or *Pesikta Zutarta*, a commentary on the Bible that includes both simple explanations as well as an agadic interpretation of the text.

"I will free you . . . and I will deliver you . . . and I will redeem you . . . and I will take you. . . ." [These four expressions of redemption, which G-d uses to foretell the Exodus to the Jewish people] correspond to four factors of merit:

[Throughout their slavery in Egypt,] the Jews did not alter their language, they did not change their mode of dress, they did not reveal the secret [that the Jews were going to leave Egypt and take its wealth with them]—as it is stated, [a full year before the Exodus, Moses told the Jewish people that] "Each woman shall borrow from her neighbor"—and they did not abandon the practice of circumcision.

Clothing in Jewish Law

The Habit Thy Purse Can Buy

TEXT 8A

Rabbi Shneur Zalman of Liadi, Shulchan Aruch HaRav, Orach Chayim 262:3

Rabbi Shneur Zalman of Liadi
(Alter Rebbe)
1745–1812
Chasidic rebbe, halachic authority, and founder of the Chabad movement. The Alter Rebbe was born in Liozna, Belarus, and was among the principal students of the Magid of Mezeritch. His numerous works include the *Tanya*, an early classic containing the fundamentals of Chabad Chasidism, and *Shulchan Aruch HaRav*, an expanded and reworked code of Jewish law.

חייב כל אדם להשתדל שיהיו לו בגדים נאים לשבת כפי יכולתו שצריך לכבד לכבוד השבת בכסות נקיה כמו שנתבאר בסימן רמ"ב. ובדברי קבלה נאמר "וכבדתו מעשות דרכיך", ודרשו חכמים "וכבדתו'—שלא יהא מלבושך של שבת כמלבושך של חול שיחליפנו באחר" (שהוא נאה ממנו) שהמלבוש נקרא כבוד שהוא מכבד את האדם כשבא למקום שאין מכירים אותו ורואים אותו לבוש בגדי חמודות אזי הם מכבדים אותו. ויש אנשי מעשה מדקדקים שלא ללבוש בשבת מכל מה שלבש בחול אפילו אזור ומכנסים וחלוק וטוב לילך בקצת בגדי שבת כל היום עד אחר הבדלה במוצאי שבת.

It is incumbent upon everyone to make an effort to obtain attractive garments for Shabbat, each one according to his or her capacity, for one must honor the Shabbat with fresh attire, as stated in sec. 242[:1].

Also, in the [prophetic] tradition, it is stated, "And you shall honor it [by refraining from] following your [ordinary] ways." Our sages interpreted [that phrase, stating]: "'You shall honor it'—[this implies that] your Shabbat garment should not be the same as your weekday garment." [Instead,] you should change to another (that is more attractive).

[The basis for this interpretation is that] a garment is called "one's honor" because it brings honor to a person. For when a person comes to a place where people do not know him, if they see him dressed in distinguished garments, they will honor him.

If it is possible for him, it is desirable that he have a second talit [for Shabbat prayer]. There are men [renowned for their good] deeds who are meticulous not to wear anything on Shabbat that they wore during the week, not even a belt, pants, or an undershirt. It is desirable to wear [at least] some of one's Shabbat clothing throughout the day until after Havdalah on Saturday night.

The same need to honor Shabbat with appropriate attire applies to the festivals, to an even greater degree.

TEXT 8B

Ibid., 529:7

וכן בגדי יום טוב צריכים להיות יותר טובים מבגדי שבת.

So, too, one's clothing for the festivals must be better than one's Shabbat clothes.

The Joys of Shopping

TEXT 9A

Rabbi Yosef Caro, Shulchan Aruch, Orach Chayim 223:3–6

Rabbi Yosef Caro
(Maran, *Beit Yosef*)
1488–1575
Halachic authority and author. Rabbi Caro was born in Spain but was forced to flee during the expulsion in 1492 and eventually settled in Safed, Israel. He authored many works including the *Beit Yosef*, *Kesef Mishneh*, and a mystical work, *Magid Meisharim*. Rabbi Caro's magnum opus, the Shulchan Aruch (Code of Jewish Law), has been universally accepted as the basis for modern Jewish law.

בנה בית חדש או קנה כלים חדשים אפילו היה לו כיוצא באלו תחלה או קנה וחזר וקנה מברך על כל פעם שהחיינו ולאו דוקא חדשים דהוא הדין לישנים אם הם חדשים לו שלא היו אלו שלו מעולם ולא אמרו חדשים אלא לאפוקי אם מכרן וחזר וקנאן... על דבר שאינו חשוב כל כך כגון חלוק או מנעלים ואנפלאות (פירוש נעלים קטנים שחופים רוב הרגל) אין לברך עליהם ואם הוא עני ושמח בהם יברך.

When one buys a new house or new utensils, even if one already owned a similar item or if it is a repeat purchase, the blessing of shehechiyanu *is recited each time. This applies even if the item isn't technically new, even if it is old, and is only new to [the purchaser], who has never owned it before. "New" is only meant to indicate that one did not sell, and then repurchase the item. . . .*

For something that is not especially notable, like a shirt or shoes or socks . . . the blessing need not be recited. If [the buyer] is poor, and does in fact celebrate [the purchase of this normally unimportant item], they should make the blessing.

TEXT 9B

Rabbi Moshe Isserlis, Glosses to the Shulchan Aruch, Orach Chayim 223:6

Rabbi Moshe Isserlis
(Rama)
1525–1572

Halachist. Rama served as rabbi in Krakow, Poland, and is considered the definitive authority on Jewish law among Ashkenazic Jewry. Rama authored glosses (known as the *Mapah*) on the Shulchan Aruch, and *Darchei Moshe*, a commentary on the halachic compendium *Arbaah Turim*.

הגה ויש אומרים דאפילו עני אינו מברך על חלוק ומנעלים וכדומה
וכן נוהגין.

המנהג לומר למי שלובש בגד חדש תבלה ותחדש. ויש מי שכתב
שאין לומר כן על מנעלים או בגדים הנעשים מעורות של בהמה
דאם כן היו צריכים להמית בהמה אחרת תחלה שיחדש ממנו בגד
אחר וכתיב ורחמיו על כל.

Note: Some say that even a pauper ought not to make this blessing on a shirt, shoes, or the like, and this is the prevailing custom.

It is customary to say to someone wearing a new item of clothing, "Wear it well and replace it!" However, someone has written not to say this of [leather] shoes, or some other item of clothing made from animal skin, since [buying the item anew] would mean killing another animal and using it for the replacement item of clothing, and it is written, "His mercy is on all His works."

TEXT 9C

Rabbi Shneur Zalman of Liadi, Seder Birchat Hanehenin, 12:5

ובמדינות אלו נוהגין שאפילו עני אינו מברך על חלוק ומנעלים
וכיוצא בהם.

In these lands, the custom is that even a poor person does not make the blessing over a shirt, shoes, or similar items.

Mixing and Matching

TEXT 10

Vayikra (Leviticus) 19:19

אֶת חֻקֹּתַי תִּשְׁמֹרוּ בְּהֶמְתְּךָ לֹא תַרְבִּיעַ כִּלְאַיִם שָׂדְךָ לֹא תִזְרַע כִּלְאָיִם
וּבֶגֶד כִּלְאַיִם שַׁעַטְנֵז לֹא יַעֲלֶה עָלֶיךָ:

You shall observe My statutes: You shall not crossbreed your livestock with different species. You shall not sow your field with a mixture of seeds, and a garment which has a mixture of shaatnez shall not come upon you.

Dressing Guidelines

TEXT 11A

Rabbi Shneur Zalman of Liadi, Shulchan
Aruch HaRav, Orach Chayim 2:2

וטוב לכל אדם לדקדק בחלוקו ללבשו כדרכו שלא יהפך הפנימי
לחוץ ויראו התפירות המגונות ויתגנה בעיני הבריות.

Everyone should be careful to put on his shirt prop-
erly—not inside out so as to show the unbecoming
stitches, lest people look down upon him.

TEXT 11B

Ibid., 2:3–4

וטוֹב שֶׁיִּשִׁים שְׁנֵי צִדֵּי הַמַּלְבּוּשׁ בְּיַד יְמִינוֹ וְיִלְבַּשׁ הַיָּמִין וְאַחַר־כָּךְ
הַשְּׂמֹאל, וְלִכְוֵן: כִּי הַכֹּל נִכְלָל בַּיָּמִין וּמִן הַיָּמִין בָּא לַשְּׂמֹאל. לְפִי
שֶׁמָּצִינוּ שֶׁהַיָּמִין הִיא חֲשׁוּבָה בְּכָל הַתּוֹרָה כּוּלָה לְעִנְיַן בֹּהֶן יַד וּבֹהֶן
רֶגֶל שֶׁל מִלּוּאִים וְשֶׁל מְצוֹרָע וְכֵן לְעִנְיַן חֲלִיצָה לָכֵן גַּם בַּנְּעִילַת
מִנְעָלִים צָרִיךְ לִיתֵּן חֲשִׁיבוּת לִימִין וְלִנְעוֹל שֶׁל יָמִין תְּחִלָּה

It is appropriate to hold both sides of a garment in one's right hand and to put on the right and then the left, keeping in mind that everything is included in the right side and from there proceeds to the left.

We find that the right side is preeminent throughout the Torah, [for example,] with regard to the right thumb and the right toe [of the kohanim*] in their initiation rites, with regard to [the purification of] a* metzora, *as well as in the* chalitzah *ceremony. Hence, when putting on shoes, too, one should also accord precedence to the right side by putting on the right shoe first.*

TEXT 11C

Ibid., 2:4–5

ולפי שמצינו שבקשירת תפילין חשובה יד שמאל שעליה קושרין
את התפילין לכן גם כאן בקשירת מנעלים צריך ליתן חשיבות
להשמאל ולכן לא יקשור את המנעל של ימין עד שינעול של
שמאל ויקשרנו ואחר כך יקשור של ימין ובמנעלים שלנו שאין
בהם קשירה ינעול של ימין תחלה מפני שאין נותנים חשיבות
להשמאל אלא אגבי קשירה בלבד דומיא דקשירת תפילין.
כשחולץ מנעליו – חולץ של שמאל תחלה, מפני שזהו כבודה
של ימין.

With regard to tying tefilin *we find that the left arm is granted prominence, for* tefilin *are bound upon it. Hence with regard to tying shoes as well, precedence should be accorded to the left, and one should not tie the right shoe until he has put on his left one and tied it; only then should he tie his right shoe.*

With regard to the shoes [worn in] our [time] that do not require tying, one should put on his right shoe first, for prominence is given to the left only with regard to tying, as with the tying of tefilin.

[Similarly,] when one takes off his shoes he should remove the left one first, thus showing deference to the right.

The Kabbalah of Clothing

The Soul's Power Suit

TEXT 12

Rabbi Shneur Zalman of Liadi, Tanya, ch. 4

ועוד יש לכל נפש אלקית שלשה לבושים שהם מחשבה דבור ומעשה של תרי"ג מצות התורה שכשהאדם מקיים במעשה כל מצות מעשיות ובדבור הוא עוסק בפירוש כל תרי"ג מצות והלכותיהן ובמחשבה הוא משיג כל מה שאפשר לו להשיג בפשט רמז דרוש סוד התורה הרי כללות תרי"ג אברי נפשו מלובשים בתרי"ג מצות התורה.

In addition, every divine soul (nefesh elokit) possesses three garments, viz., thought, speech, and action, [expressing themselves] in the 613 commandments of the Torah. For when a person actively fulfills all the precepts that require physical action, and with his power of speech he occupies himself in expounding all the 613 commandments and their practical application, and with his power of thought he comprehends all that is comprehensible to him in the pardes *of the Torah—then the totality of the 613 "organs" of his soul are "clothed" in the 613 commandments of the Torah.*

TEXT 13

Rabbi Shneur Zalman of Liadi, Likutei Torah, 51d

ולהבין ענין הלבושין ולמה צריכה הנשמה ללבושין שלא תהיה
ערומה וגם למה נכתב ענין זה בתורה להודיענו זאת?

*Let us better understand the matter of garments: Why
must the soul be clothed in garments so that it is not
naked? And why is this written in the Torah, to inform
us of this?*

Costume Change

TEXT 14

Rabbi Shneur Zalman of Liadi, Tanya, ch. 14

והנה מדת הבינוני היא מדת כל אדם ואחריה כל אדם ימשוך שכל
אדם יכול להיות בינוני בכל עת ובכל שעה כי הבינוני אינו מואס
ברע שזהו דבר המסור ללב ולא כל העתים שוות אלא סור מרע
ועשה טוב דהיינו בפועל ממש במעשה דבור ומחשבה שבהם
הבחירה והיכולת והרשות נתונה לכל אדם לעשות ולדבר ולחשוב
גם מה שהוא נגד תאות לבו והפכה ממש.
כי גם בשעה שהלב חומד ומתאוה איזו תאוה גשמיית בהיתר או
באיסור חס ושלום יכול להתגבר ולהסיח דעתו ממנה לגמרי באמרו
ללבו אינני רוצה להיות רשע אפילו שעה אחת כי אינני רוצה להיות
מובדל ונפרד חס ושלום מה' אחד בשום אופן... רק אני רוצה

לדבקה בו נפשי רוחי ונשמתי בהתלבשן בשלשה לבושיו יתברך
שהם מעשה דבור ומחשבה בה' ותורתו ומצותיו...
מה שאין כן בדבר המסור ללב דהיינו שיהא הרע מאוס ממש בלב
ושנאוי בתכלית שנאה או אפילו שלא בתכלית שנאה הנה זה אי
אפשר שיהיה באמת לאמיתו אלא על ידי גודל ותוקף האהבה לה'
בבחינת אהבה בתענוגים להתענג על ה' מעין עולם הבא... ואין כל
אדם זוכה לזה...

The rank of beinoni *is one that is attainable by every man, and each person should strive after it. Every person can at any time or hour be an "intermediate," because the "intermediate" man does not revile evil— for that is a feeling entrusted to the heart, and not all times are alike. [His task is] only to "turn away from evil and do good," in actual practice—in deed, speech, or thought, wherein the choice, ability, and freedom are given to every man that he may act, speak, and think even what is contrary to the desire of his heart and diametrically opposed to it.*

Even when the heart craves and desires a material pleasure, whether permitted or, G-d forbid, prohibited, he can steel himself and divert his attention from it altogether, declaring to himself, "I will not be wicked even for a moment, because I will not be parted and separated, Heaven forfend, from the One G-d under any circumstances. . . ."

It is different, however, with something that is entrust- ed to the heart, namely, that the evil should actually be despised in the heart and abhorred with absolute hatred, or even not quite so absolutely. This cannot be attained, truly and sincerely, except through great and intense love of G-d, the kind of ecstatic love and divine bliss that is akin to the World to Come . . . and not every person can attain this state.

TEXT 15A

The Rebbe, Rabbi Menachem Mendel Schneerson,
Maamar s.v. Vayishlach Yehoshua, 5736

Rabbi Menachem Mendel Schneerson
1902–1994

The towering Jewish leader of the 20th century, known as "the Lubavitcher Rebbe," or simply as "the Rebbe." Born in southern Ukraine, the Rebbe escaped Nazi-occupied Europe, arriving in the U.S. in June 1941. The Rebbe inspired and guided the revival of traditional Judaism after the European devastation, impacting virtually every Jewish community the world over. The Rebbe often emphasized that the performance of just one additional good deed could usher in the era of Mashiach. The Rebbe's scholarly talks and writings have been printed in more than 200 volumes.

המבואר בתניא בענין צדיקים ובינונים, שעבודת הבינונים היא (בעיקר) בלבושי הנפש, מחשבה דיבור ומעשה, ולכן מדת הבינוני היא מדת כל אדם, שגם כשהלב חומד ומתאוה איזו תאוה ביכלתו להתאפק ולמשול ברוח תאותו שבלבו שלא למלאותה במעשה דיבור ומחשבה (שלא לחשוב על דרך זה ברצונו), ועד שביכלתו להסיח דעתו ממנה לגמרי. מה שאין כן עבודת הצדיקים היא בעיקר במדות שבלב (אהבה ויראה), ואין כל אדם זוכה לזה. כי בדבר המסור ללב אין לאדם משפט הבחירה כל כך.

We can understand this by introducing a concept discussed in Tanya, *regarding* tzadikim *and* beinonim. *The divine service of the* beinonim *involves (primarily) the garments of the soul—thought, speech, and deed. Thus, the rank of* beinoni *is the rank attainable by every person. For when a person's heart craves and desires some material pleasure, he is capable of restraining himself and controlling the drive of his heart's lust by not allowing it to find expression in deed, speech, or thought (i.e., not to willingly think about his desire), to the extent of being able to divert his mind from it entirely.*

The service of tzadikim, *on the other hand, primarily involves the emotions of the heart (love and fear of G-d), and not every person merits this level of service. For man does not have that much jurisdiction over matters governed by the heart.*

TEXT 15B

Ibid.

הטעם לזה (שמחשבה דבור ומעשה הם ברשותו של אדם, מה
שאין כן המדות שבלב) הוא, כי מחשבה דיבור ומעשה הם לבושי
הנפש. ולכן, כמו שלבושי הגוף, עם היות שהאדם צריך ללבושים
[מצד ענין הצניעות כיון דיתבוששו, וגם בכדי להגן עליו מקור וחום],
מכל מקום ביכלתו לפושטם, ומכל שכן שאינו מוכרח בלבושים
אלו (שלובש עכשיו) וביכלתו להחליפם בלבושים אחרים, על דרך
זה הוא בלבושי הנפש, דהלבושים דיבור ומעשה אפשר לפושטם,
וגם המחשבה שהיא בתמידות, נחלפת במחשבה אחרת. מה שאין
כן השכל והמדות הרי הוא מהות הנפש, ולכן, בכדי לשנותם, צריך
ליגיעה, ועד לנתינת כח מיוחד מלמעלה.

*The reason that thought, speech, and deed are within
man's control, unlike the emotions of the heart, is
because thought, speech, and deed are the garments
of the soul. Therefore, just as regarding the garments
of the body—although man needs clothing [for the
purpose of modesty, since "they, Adam and Eve, were
ashamed" (of being naked after their sin), and also for
the purpose of protection from the cold and heat], nevertheless, he can remove them, and certainly he does
not need these particular clothes (that he is wearing
now) and can exchange them for others.*

*Similarly, with regard to the garments of the soul:
The garments of speech and deed can be "shed," and
even thought, which is constantly active and cannot be*

"shed" per se, can be replaced with a different thought. By contrast, the person's intellect and emotions are the very stuff of the soul itself, and, hence, much effort— even a special assistance from Above—is necessary to change them.

7

KI TISA

Forget Me Not!

Connection Is the Key to Memory

*Dedicated in loving memory of **Dror Shamir** on the occasion of his yahrtzeit, 12 Adar.
May the merit of the Torah study worldwide accompany his soul in the world of everlasting life and
be a source of blessings to his family with much health, happiness, nachat, and success.*

PARSHA OVERVIEW
Ki Tisa

The people of Israel are told to each contribute exactly half a shekel of silver to the Sanctuary. Instructions are also given regarding the making of the Sanctuary's water basin, anointing oil, and incense. "Wisehearted" artisans Betzalel and Aholiav are placed in charge of the Sanctuary's construction, and the people are once again commanded to keep the Shabbat.

When Moses does not return when expected from Mount Sinai, the people make a golden calf and worship it. G-d proposes to destroy the errant nation, but Moses intercedes on their behalf. Moses descends from the mountain carrying the tablets of the testimony engraved with the Ten Commandments; seeing the people dancing about their idol, he breaks the tablets, destroys the golden calf, and has the primary culprits put to death. He then returns to G-d to say: "If You do not forgive them, blot me out from the book that You have written."

G-d forgives, but says that the effects of their sin will be felt for many generations. At first, G-d proposes to send His angel along with them. But Moses insists that G-d Himself accompany His people to the Promised Land.

Moses prepares a new set of tablets and once more ascends the mountain, where G-d reinscribes the covenant on these second tablets. On the mountain, Moses is also granted a vision of the divine thirteen attributes of mercy. So radiant is Moses's face upon his return that he must cover it with a veil, which he removes only to speak with G-d and to teach His laws to the people.

Atonement for the Golden Calf

The Sin of the Calf

TEXT 1A

Shemot (Exodus) 32:1

וַיַּרְא הָעָם כִּי בֹשֵׁשׁ מֹשֶׁה לָרֶדֶת מִן הָהָר וַיִּקָּהֵל הָעָם עַל אַהֲרֹן וַיֹּאמְרוּ
אֵלָיו קוּם עֲשֵׂה לָנוּ אֱלֹהִים אֲשֶׁר יֵלְכוּ לְפָנֵינוּ כִּי זֶה מֹשֶׁה הָאִישׁ אֲשֶׁר
הֶעֱלָנוּ מֵאֶרֶץ מִצְרַיִם לֹא יָדַעְנוּ מֶה הָיָה לוֹ.

When the people saw that Moses was late in coming down from the mountain, the people gathered against Aaron, and they said to him, "Come on! Make us gods that will go before us, because this man Moses, who brought us up from the land of Egypt, we do not know what has become of him."

TEXT 1B

Ibid. 32:2–6

וַיֹּאמֶר אֲלֵהֶם אַהֲרֹן פָּרְקוּ נִזְמֵי הַזָּהָב אֲשֶׁר בְּאָזְנֵי נְשֵׁיכֶם בְּנֵיכֶם
וּבְנֹתֵיכֶם וְהָבִיאוּ אֵלָי. וַיִּתְפָּרְקוּ כָּל הָעָם אֶת נִזְמֵי הַזָּהָב אֲשֶׁר
בְּאָזְנֵיהֶם וַיָּבִיאוּ אֶל אַהֲרֹן:
וַיִּקַּח מִיָּדָם וַיָּצַר אֹתוֹ בַּחֶרֶט וַיַּעֲשֵׂהוּ עֵגֶל מַסֵּכָה וַיֹּאמְרוּ אֵלֶּה אֱלֹהֶיךָ
יִשְׂרָאֵל אֲשֶׁר הֶעֱלוּךָ מֵאֶרֶץ מִצְרָיִם:
וַיַּרְא אַהֲרֹן וַיִּבֶן מִזְבֵּחַ לְפָנָיו וַיִּקְרָא אַהֲרֹן וַיֹּאמַר חַג לַה' מָחָר.
וַיַּשְׁכִּימוּ מִמָּחֳרָת וַיַּעֲלוּ עֹלֹת וַיַּגִּשׁוּ שְׁלָמִים וַיֵּשֶׁב הָעָם לֶאֱכֹל וְשָׁתוֹ
וַיָּקֻמוּ לְצַחֵק:

Aaron said to them, "Remove the golden earrings that are on the ears of your wives, your sons, and your daughters and bring them [those earrings] to me." And all the people stripped themselves of the golden earrings that were on their ears and brought them to Aaron.

He took [them] from their hand[s], fashioned them with an engraving tool, and made it into a molten calf, upon which they said, "These are your gods, O Israel, who have brought you up from the land of Egypt!"

When Aaron saw [this], he built an altar in front of it, and Aaron proclaimed and said, "Tomorrow shall be a festival to the lord." On the next day they arose early, offered up burnt offerings, and brought peace offerings, and the people sat down to eat and to drink, and they got up to make merry.

TEXT 1C

Ibid. 32:11–13

וַיְחַל מֹשֶׁה אֶת פְּנֵי ה' אֱלֹקָיו וַיֹּאמֶר לָמָה ה' יֶחֱרֶה אַפְּךָ בְּעַמֶּךָ אֲשֶׁר הוֹצֵאתָ מֵאֶרֶץ מִצְרַיִם בְּכֹחַ גָּדוֹל וּבְיָד חֲזָקָה:
לָמָה יֹאמְרוּ מִצְרַיִם לֵאמֹר בְּרָעָה הוֹצִיאָם לַהֲרֹג אֹתָם בֶּהָרִים וּלְכַלֹּתָם מֵעַל פְּנֵי הָאֲדָמָה שׁוּב מֵחֲרוֹן אַפֶּךָ וְהִנָּחֵם עַל הָרָעָה לְעַמֶּךָ:
זְכֹר לְאַבְרָהָם לְיִצְחָק וּלְיִשְׂרָאֵל עֲבָדֶיךָ אֲשֶׁר נִשְׁבַּעְתָּ לָהֶם בָּךְ וַתְּדַבֵּר אֲלֵהֶם אַרְבֶּה אֶת זַרְעֲכֶם כְּכוֹכְבֵי הַשָּׁמָיִם וְכָל הָאָרֶץ הַזֹּאת אֲשֶׁר אָמַרְתִּי אֶתֵּן לְזַרְעֲכֶם וְנָחֲלוּ לְעֹלָם:

Moses pleaded before the L-rd, his G-d, and said, "Why, O G-d, should Your anger be kindled against Your people whom You have brought up from the land of Egypt with great power and with a strong hand?

"Why should the Egyptians say, 'He brought them out with evil [intent] to kill them in the mountains and to annihilate them from upon the face of the earth'? Retreat from the heat of Your anger and reconsider the evil [intended] for Your people.

"Remember Abraham, Isaac, and Israel, Your servants, to whom You swore by Your very Self, and to whom You said, 'I will multiply your seed like the stars of the heavens, and all this land which I said that I would give to your seed, they shall keep it as their possession forever.'"

Mercy and Atonement

TEXT 1D

Ibid. 33:18–23

וַיֹּאמַר הַרְאֵנִי נָא אֶת כְּבֹדֶךָ:
וַיֹּאמֶר אֲנִי אַעֲבִיר כָּל טוּבִי עַל פָּנֶיךָ וְקָרָאתִי בְשֵׁם ה' לְפָנֶיךָ וְחַנֹּתִי
אֶת אֲשֶׁר אָחֹן וְרִחַמְתִּי אֶת אֲשֶׁר אֲרַחֵם:
וַיֹּאמֶר לֹא תוּכַל לִרְאֹת אֶת פָּנָי כִּי לֹא יִרְאַנִי הָאָדָם וָחָי:
וַיֹּאמֶר ה' הִנֵּה מָקוֹם אִתִּי וְנִצַּבְתָּ עַל הַצּוּר:
וְהָיָה בַּעֲבֹר כְּבֹדִי וְשַׂמְתִּיךָ בְּנִקְרַת הַצּוּר וְשַׂכֹּתִי כַפִּי עָלֶיךָ עַד עָבְרִי:
וַהֲסִרֹתִי אֶת כַּפִּי וְרָאִיתָ אֶת אֲחֹרָי וּפָנַי לֹא יֵרָאוּ:

And Moses said, "Show me, now, Your glory!"

He said, "I will let all My goodness pass before you; I will proclaim the name of G-d before you, and I will favor when I wish to favor, and I will have compassion when I wish to have compassion."

And He said, "You will not be able to see My face, for man shall not see Me and live."

And G-d said, "Behold, there is a place with Me, and you shall stand on the rock.

"And it shall be that when My glory passes by, I will place you into the cleft of the rock, and I will cover you with My hand until I have passed by.

"Then I will remove My hand, and you will see My back, but My face shall not be seen."

TEXT 1E

Ibid. 34:5–8

וַיֵּרֶד ה' בֶּעָנָן וַיִּתְיַצֵּב עִמּוֹ שָׁם וַיִּקְרָא בְשֵׁם ה':
וַיַּעֲבֹר ה' עַל פָּנָיו וַיִּקְרָא ה' ה' אֵ-ל רַחוּם וְחַנּוּן אֶרֶךְ אַפַּיִם וְרַב
חֶסֶד וֶאֱמֶת:
נֹצֵר חֶסֶד לָאֲלָפִים נֹשֵׂא עָוֹן וָפֶשַׁע וְחַטָּאָה וְנַקֵּה לֹא יְנַקֶּה פֹּקֵד עֲוֹן
אָבוֹת עַל בָּנִים וְעַל בְּנֵי בָנִים עַל שִׁלֵּשִׁים וְעַל רִבֵּעִים. וַיְמַהֵר מֹשֶׁה
וַיִּקֹּד אַרְצָה וַיִּשְׁתָּחוּ:

And G-d descended in the cloud and stood with him there, and He called out in the name of G-d. And G-d passed before him and proclaimed:

"L-rd, L-rd, benevolent G-d, who is compassionate and gracious, slow to anger, and abundant in loving-kindness and truth.

"Preserving loving-kindness for thousands, forgiving iniquity and rebellion and sin, yet He does not completely clear [of sin]: He visits the iniquity of parents on children and children's children, to the third and fourth generations." And Moses hastened, bowed his head to the ground, and prostrated himself.

Instruction in Prayer

TEXT 2

Rashi to Shemot (Exodus) 33:19

"וקראתי בשם ה' לפניך". ללמדך סדר בקשת רחמים אף אם תכלה זכות אבות וכסדר זה שאתה רואה אותי מעוטף וקורא י"ג מדות הוי מלמד את ישראל לעשות כן ועל ידי שיזכירו לפני רחום וחנון יהיו נענין כי רחמי לא כלים.

"I will proclaim the name of G-d before you." To teach you the procedure for begging for compassion [i.e., praying] even if the merit of the patriarchs is depleted. According to this procedure, [during] which you [will] see Me enwrapped [in a talit] and proclaiming the Thirteen Attributes, teach the Israelites to do likewise. Through their mentioning before Me [the words] "compassionate and gracious," they will be answered, for My compassion never ends.

Rabbi Shlomo Yitzchaki (Rashi)
1040–1105
Most noted biblical and Talmudic commentator. Born in Troyes, France, Rashi studied in the famed *yeshivot* of Mainz and Worms. His commentaries on the Pentateuch and the Talmud, which focus on the straightforward meaning of the text, appear in virtually every edition of the Talmud and Bible.

TEXT 3

Rabbeinu Bechaye to Shemot (Exodus) 34:6

Rabbeinu Bechaye ben Asher

c. 1265–1340

Biblical commentator. Rabbeinu Bechaye lived in Spain and was a disciple of Rabbi Shlomo ben Aderet, known as Rashba. He is best known for his multifaceted commentary on the Torah, which interprets the text on literal, Midrashic, philosophical, and kabbalistic levels. Rabbeinu Bechaye also wrote *Kad Hakemach*, a work on philosophy and ethics.

כל המבין שלוש עשרה מידות... ומתפלל בהן בכוונה, אין תפילתו חוזרת ריקם...

בזמן הזה שאנחנו שרויים בגלות ואין לנו כהן גדול לכפר על חטאותינו ולא מזבח להקריב עליו קרבנות ולא בית המקדש להתפלל בתוכו – לא נשאר לנו לפני ה', בלתי אם תפלתנו ושלוש עשרה מידותיו.

Whoever understands these Thirteen Attributes . . . and invokes them with the correct intention in prayer will never find his prayer unanswered. . . .

In these times, when we find ourselves in exile without a High Priest to atone for us, nor an altar upon which to offer sacrifices nor a Temple in which to pray, nothing remains with which to appear before G-d, save our prayer and His Thirteen Attributes.

Seeing G-d's Presence

TEXT 4

Rashi to Shemot (Exodus) 33:18

"ויאמר הראני נא וגו'". ראה משה שהיה עת רצון ודבריו מקובלים
והוסיף לשאול להראותו מראית כבודו.

And he said, "Show me, now, Your glory!" Moses perceived that it was a time of [G-d's] goodwill, and his words were accepted, so he continued to ask that He show him the appearance of His glory.

TEXT 5

Midrash Pirkei DeRabbi Eliezer §46

Pirkei DeRabbi Eliezer

A Midrash bearing the name of Rabbi Eliezer ben Hyrcanus, a prominent rabbinic sage living during the 1st and 2nd centuries. *Pirkei Rabbi Eliezer* commences with the story of the early days of Rabbi Eliezer's life and then chronologically narrates and expounds upon events from the Creation until the middle of the journeys of the Children of Israel in the wilderness.

אמר לפני הקדוש ברוך הוא: רבונו של עולם "הראני נא את כבֹדך"?
אמר לו הקדוש ברוך הוא: משה, אין אתה יכול לראות את כבודי
שלא תמות שנאמר "כי לא יראני האדם וחי", אלא למען השבועה
שנשבעתי לך והשם שהודעתי לך אני אעשה רצונך. עמוד בפתח
מערה ואני אעביר לפניך את המלאכים המשרתים לפני שנאמר:
"ויאמר אני אעביר כל טובי על פניך", וכשאתה שומע את השם
שהודעתי לך שם אני עומד לפניך ועמוד בכחך ואל תפחד, שנאמר
"וחנֹתי את אשר אחֹן ורחמתי את אשר ארחם".
אמרו מלאכי השרת לפני הקדוש ברוך הוא: הרי אנו משרתים
לפניך ביום ובלילה ואין אנו יכולין לראות את כבודך, וזה ילוד אשה
רוצה לראות את כבודך!
ועמדו בזעף ובבהלה להמיתו והגיעה נפשו עד מות, מה עשה
הקדוש ברוך הוא נגלה עליו בענן שנאמר "וירד ה' בענן", וזו היא
ירידה שביעית, וסכך עליו הקדוש ברוך הוא בכף ידו שלא ימות,
שנאמר "והיה בעבור כבודי ושמתיך בנקרת הצור ושכתי כפי",
וכשעבר הסיר הקדוש ברוך הוא את כף ידו מעליו וראה אחורי
השכינה, שנאמר "והסירותי את כפי [וראית את אחורי]".

Moses spoke before the Holy One, blessed be He, "Sovereign of all the universe! Show me, now, Your glory!" The Holy One, blessed be He, said to him, "Moshe! You are not able to see My glory lest you should die, as it is said, 'For men shall not see me and live'; but for the sake of the oath which I have sworn to you, I will do as you ask. Stand at the entrance of the cave, and I will make all the angels who move before Me pass before your face. Stand mighty, and do not fear, as it is said, 'And He said, I will let all My goodness pass before you.' When you hear the Name which I have spoken to you, you'll know I am before you, as it is said, 'And he said, I will let all My goodness pass before you.'"

The ministering angels said, "Now, we serve before Him by day and by night, and we are unable to see His glory, and this one born of woman desires to see His glory?!" And they arose in wrath and excitement to slay him, and his soul came close to death. What did the Holy One, blessed be He, do? He revealed Himself unto him in a cloud, as it is said, "And G-d descended in the cloud." This was the seventh descent.

The Holy One, blessed be He, protected him with the hollow of His hand that he should not die, as it is said, "And it shall be that when My glory passes by, I will place you into the cleft of the rock, and I will cover you with My hand." When the Holy One, blessed be He, had passed by, He removed the hollow of His hand from him, and he saw the traces of the Shechinah, *the Divine presence, as it is said, "Then I will remove My hand, and you will see My back."*

TEXT 6A

Talmud Tractate Berachot, 7a

Babylonian Talmud
A literary work of monumental proportions that draws upon the legal, spiritual, intellectual, ethical, and historical traditions of Judaism. The 37 tractates of the Babylonian Talmud contain the teachings of the Jewish sages from the period after the destruction of the Second Temple through the 5th century CE. It has served as the primary vehicle for the transmission of the Oral Law and the education of Jews over the centuries; it is the entry point for all subsequent legal, ethical, and theological Jewish scholarship.

"והסירתי את כפי וראית את אחרי", אמר רב חנא בר ביזנא אמר רב שמעון חסידא מלמד שהראה הקדוש ברוך הוא למשה קשר של תפילין.

"I will remove My hand and you will see My back." Rabbi Chana bar Bizna said in the name of Rabbi Shimon Chasida, "G-d showed Moshe the knot of His tefilin."

TEXT 6B

Rashi to Tractate Berachot, 7a

"קשר של תפילין". מאחוריו הוא, ואמרינן לעיל דהקדוש ברוך הוא מניח תפילין.

"The knot of His tefilin." The knot is behind Him [as the knot of the head tefilin normally is]. And we already said earlier [in the Talmud] that G-d wears tefilin.

Jewish Ties

Tefilin *and* Tzitzit

TEXT 7A

Shemot (Exodus) 13:9–10

וְהָיָה לְךָ לְאוֹת עַל יָדְךָ וּלְזִכָּרוֹן בֵּין עֵינֶיךָ לְמַעַן תִּהְיֶה תּוֹרַת ה' בְּפִיךָ
כִּי בְּיָד חֲזָקָה הוֹצִאֲךָ ה' מִמִּצְרָיִם:
וְשָׁמַרְתָּ אֶת הַחֻקָּה הַזֹּאת לְמוֹעֲדָהּ מִיָּמִים יָמִימָה:

And it shall be to you as a sign upon your hand and as a remembrance between your eyes, in order that the law of G-d shall be in your mouth, for with a mighty hand G-d took you out of Egypt.

And you shall keep this statute at its appointed time, from year to year.

TEXT 7B

Bamidbar (Numbers) 15:37–40

וַיֹּאמֶר ה' אֶל מֹשֶׁה לֵּאמֹר:

דַּבֵּר אֶל בְּנֵי יִשְׂרָאֵל וְאָמַרְתָּ אֲלֵהֶם וְעָשׂוּ לָהֶם צִיצִת עַל כַּנְפֵי בִגְדֵיהֶם

לְדֹרֹתָם וְנָתְנוּ עַל צִיצִת הַכָּנָף פְּתִיל תְּכֵלֶת:

וְהָיָה לָכֶם לְצִיצִת וּרְאִיתֶם אֹתוֹ וּזְכַרְתֶּם אֶת כָּל מִצְוֹת ה' וַעֲשִׂיתֶם

אֹתָם וְלֹא תָתוּרוּ אַחֲרֵי לְבַבְכֶם וְאַחֲרֵי עֵינֵיכֶם אֲשֶׁר אַתֶּם זֹנִים אַחֲרֵיהֶם:

לְמַעַן תִּזְכְּרוּ וַעֲשִׂיתֶם אֶת כָּל מִצְוֹתָי וִהְיִיתֶם קְדֹשִׁים לֵאלֹקֵיכֶם:

G-d spoke to Moses, saying, "Speak to the Children of Israel, and you shall say to them that they shall make for themselves fringes on the corners of their garments, throughout their generations, and they shall affix a thread of sky blue [wool] on the fringe of each corner.

"This shall be fringes for you, and when you see it, you will remember all the commandments of G-d to perform them, and you shall not wander after your hearts and after your eyes after which you are going astray.

"So that you shall remember and perform all My commandments and you shall be holy to your G-d."

A Memory Aid

TEXT 8

Zohar, vol. 2, Ki Tisa 190a

אָמַר רִבִּי יוֹסֵי, זַכָּאָה אָרְחָא דָא, דְּזָכֵינָא לְהַאי מִלָּה. אָמַר לֵיהּ מִמָּאן
שְׁמַעַת לָהּ. אָמַר לֵיהּ, יוֹמָא חֲדָא הֲוֵינָא אָזִיל בְּאָרְחָא, וּשְׁמַעְנָא
וַחֲמֵינָא לֵיהּ לְרַב הַמְנוּנָא סָבָא, דַּהֲוָה דָּרִישׁ לְהַאי קְרָא לְרִבִּי אָחָא,
וְכֵיוָן דְּשָׁמַעְנָא חַדֵּינָא בֵּיהּ, וּנְטִירְנָא לֵיהּ צָרִיר בְּכַנְפָא דִּלְבוּשָׁאי, דְּלָא
יִתְעֲדֵי מִנַּאי לְעָלְמִין.

Rabbi Yossi said, "Praised be this way, that it merited to this teaching." They said to him, "From whom did you hear it?"

He said to them, "One day I was walking on the way, and I heard and saw Rabbi Hamnuna Sabba expounding upon this verse to Rabbi Acha, and when I heard it I was overjoyed. So, I tied a knot on the edge of my garment, so the teaching would never depart from me."

TEXT 9

Bereishit (Genesis) 40:23

וְלֹא זָכַר שַׂר הַמַּשְׁקִים אֶת יוֹסֵף וַיִּשְׁכָּחֵהוּ:

And the butler did not remember Joseph, and forgot him.

TEXT 10

Midrash Bereishit Rabah, 88:7

Bereishit Rabah

An early rabbinic commentary on the Book of Genesis. This Midrash bears the name of Rabbi Oshiya Rabah (Rabbi Oshiya "the Great"), whose teaching opens this work. This Midrash provides textual exegeses and stories, expounds upon the biblical narrative, and develops and illustrates moral principles. Produced by the sages of the Talmud in the Land of Israel, its use of Aramaic closely resembles that of the Jerusalem Talmud. It was first printed in Constantinople in 1512 together with 4 other Midrashic works on the other 4 books of the Pentateuch.

"וְלֹא זָכַר שַׂר הַמַּשְׁקִים וְגוֹ'". כל היום היה מתנה תנאים ומלאך בא
והופכן, וקושר קשרים ומלאך בא ומתירן.

"The butler did not remember." All day he would set reminders, and an angel would overturn them. He would tie knots, and an angel would loosen them.

TEXT 11

*Rabbi Shneur Zalman of Liadi, Shulchan
Aruch HaRav, Orach Chayim, 24:1*

**Rabbi Shneur
Zalman of Liadi**
(Alter Rebbe)
1745–1812

Chasidic rebbe, halachic
authority, and founder of
the Chabad movement. The
Alter Rebbe was born in
Liozna, Belarus, and was
among the principal students
of the Magid of Mezeritch.
His numerous works include
the *Tanya*, an early classic
containing the fundamentals
of Chabad Chasidism, and
Shulchan Aruch HaRav,
an expanded and reworked
code of Jewish law.

אַף עַל פִּי שֶׁאֵין אָדָם חַיָּיב לִקְנוֹת טַלִּית בַּת ד' כְּנָפוֹת כְּדֵי שֶׁיִּתְחַיֵּיב
בְּצִיצִית אֶלָּא דַּוְקָא אִם רוֹצֶה לְהִתְלַבֵּשׁ בְּטַלִּית בַּת ד' כְּנָפוֹת חַיָּיב
לְהָטִיל בָּהּ צִיצִית מִכָּל מָקוֹם טוֹב וְנָכוֹן לִהְיוֹת כָּל אָדָם זָהִיר וְזָרִיז
לִלְבּוֹשׁ טַלִּית מְצוּיֶּיצֶת כָּל הַיּוֹם כְּדֵי שֶׁיִּזְכּוֹר הַמִּצְוֹת בְּכָל רֶגַע.
דֻּגְמָא לְדָבָר כְּאָדָם הַמַּזְהִיר לַחֲבֵירוֹ עַל עִנְיָן אֶחָד שֶׁקּוֹשֵׁר קֶשֶׁר
בַּאֲזוֹרוֹ כְּדֵי שֶׁיִּזְכְּרֶנּוּ. וְעַל כֵּן יֵשׁ בְּצִיצִית ה' קְשָׁרִים כְּנֶגֶד ה' חוּמְשֵׁי
תּוֹרָה וְד' כְּנָפוֹת כְּדֵי שֶׁלְּכָל צַד שֶׁיִּפְנֶה יִזְכּוֹר הַמִּצְוֹת.

*One is not obligated to buy a garment with four corners
so that he will be required [to attach] tzitzit to it; rather,
only if he desires to wear a four-cornered garment is he
required to attach tzitzit. Nevertheless, it is preferable
and appropriate for everyone to be careful and eager
to wear a* talit *with* tzitzit *throughout the day, so that
he will remember the* mitzvot *at every moment.*

*To explain by example: If someone cautions his friend
to remember something, the friend will tie a knot in
his belt as a reminder. Accordingly, the* tzitzit *[at each
corner] have five knots which recall the Five Books of
the Torah, and there are four corners so that whichever
direction a person turns, he will remember the* mitzvot.

Holy Memory

What Is Forgetfulness?

TEXT 12

Rabbi Shneur Zalman of Liadi, Shulchan Aruch HaRav, Laws of Torah Study, 2:10

הנה זאת התורה היא העולה למעלה עד כסא הכבוד ועד בכלל
אך לא למעלה מהכסא "כי אין שכחה לפני כסא כבודך" שהוא
למעלה מהכסא עולם הזכרון והזכר המשפיע (כי השכחה באה
מצד הקליפה ואינה מגעת לינק אלא עד הכסא כמו שכתוב שאין
הכסא שלם כו').

The Torah one has studied but forgotten ascends above to the throne of glory, but not beyond the throne, as it is written that there is no forgetfulness before the throne of Your glory, since the world of memory is above the throne. (Forgetfulness comes from the concealment and is only able to derive life up until the throne.)

The Root of Evil

TEXT 13A

The Rebbe, Rabbi Menachem Mendel Schneerson,
Likutei Sichot, vol. 21, p. 235–6

The notion of sin in general . . . derives from forgetfulness. Forgetfulness itself derives from the concealment of G-dliness, whereas in the realm of holiness there is no forgetfulness before the throne of Your glory.

Jews are "believers, the sons of believers." Every Jew believes that, in the beginning, G-d created the heavens and the earth and everything within them, and that He is constantly creating the world every day and every moment from absolute nothingness.

The question arises: When a Jew profoundly feels that in this very moment he or she has been created by G-d, and that in the next moment he or she must depend on the word of G-d anew to continue creating them ex nihilo, how can a Jew fail to carry out G-d's will to not fulfill his desire? The Jew's desire, as part of his very existence, depends on G-d's will to create the Jew at this very moment!

(And even if the Jew reasons that there are many things which prevent him from serving G-d, he knows, in his soul, as a believer, with absolute clarity, that even these things which appear to prevent him have

Rabbi Menachem Mendel Schneerson
1902–1994
The towering Jewish leader of the 20th century, known as "the Lubavitcher Rebbe," or simply as "the Rebbe." Born in southern Ukraine, the Rebbe escaped Nazi-occupied Europe, arriving in the U.S. in June 1941. The Rebbe inspired and guided the revival of traditional Judaism after the European devastation, impacting virtually every Jewish community the world over. The Rebbe often emphasized that the performance of just one additional good deed could usher in the era of Mashiach. The Rebbe's scholarly talks and writings have been printed in more than 200 volumes.

also been created in this moment by G-d from absolute nothingness—and thus, they cannot possibly be against the will of the Creator! How can they truly prevent his proper fulfillment of Judaism, which is what G-d truly wants, if G-d Himself first created them at this very moment?)

How, then, does a Jew end up doing other than what his soul's clear understanding necessitates? The answer is: of course he or she knows; but at that moment, they forget.

Tie Yourself to Him

TEXT 13B

The Rebbe, Rabbi Menachem Mendel Schneerson,
Likutei Sichot, ibid., p. 236

When a Jew remembers as a Jew should, all forms of the opposing forces are automatically nullified, and one fulfills the Torah and mitzvot to perfection, to the point of "all your actions are for the sake of Heaven" and "know Him in all your ways." At this point, the Jew feels no extraneous, non-G-dly thoughts at all.

TEXT 14

Rabbi Shneur Zalman of Liadi, Tanya, Igeret Hateshuva, ch. 9

וזהו שכתוב בתנא דבי אליהו אדם עבר עבירה ונתחייב מיתה
למקום מה יעשה ויחיה אם היה רגיל לקרות דף אחד יקרא ב'
דפים לשנות פרק א' ישנה ב' פרקים וכו'.
והיינו כמשל חבל הנפסק וחוזר וקושרו שבמקום הקשר הוא כפול
ומכופל. וככה הוא בחבל נחלתו וכו'.

In Midrash Tanna Devei Eliahu *it is stated, "A man
commits a sin and is liable to death before the Almighty:
what shall he do and live? If he was accustomed to
studying one page, he shall study two, to studying
one chapter, he shall study two chapters. . . ." This
parallels the illustration of the cord severed and then
re-knotted—the place of the knot is so much thicker
than the unaffected portion. So it is with the "cord of
His possession" [namely, the Jewish people].*

Knot Below, Knot Above

TEXT 15A

The Rebbe, Rabbi Menachem Mendel Schneerson,
Likutei Sichot, ibid., p. 237

*From the spiritual source of matters—that a spiritual
"knot" negates any connection to negativity, the concealment of G-d—comes about in the physical reality
as well, that making a physical knot helps nullify one's
literal physical forgetfulness.*

Knots of Repentance

TEXT 15B

Ibid., p. 237

This is also the connection between "You will see My back" and "You will be shown the knot of the tefilin," with G-d teaching Moses the words for requesting mercy:

When G-d taught Moses how to request mercy (which repairs the damage of the transgression), He showed him what fixing a transgression truly means. He did so by revealing the knot of His tefilin—connoting a powerful connection, a knot, and the memory of the holy tefilin, and, more specifically, that everything is created at every moment by G-d.

TEXT 16

The Rebbe, Rabbi Menachem Mendel Schneerson,
Hayom Yom, entry for 4 Cheshvan

לימוד התורה בכל יום ויום נוגע בנפשות ממש, לא לבד בנפש הלומד, כי אם גם בנפשות בני ביתו, שאז אויר הבית הוא אויר תורה ויראת שמים.

Torah study every day is crucial to life itself. This applies not only to the soul of the one studying but also to the souls of his family. For then (through Torah study) the atmosphere of the home becomes an atmosphere of Torah and piety.

Hayom Yom

In 1942, Rabbi Yosef Y. Schneersohn, the 6th rebbe of Chabad, gave his son-in-law, the future Rebbe, the task of compiling an anthology of Chasidic aphorisms and customs arranged according to the days of the year. In describing the completed product, Rabbi Yosef Yitzchak wrote that it is "a book that is small in format but bursting with pearls and diamonds of the choicest quality."

VAYAKHEL

Flip the Script

Writing the Narrative of Your Own Life

ליבא חנה בת ר' דוד צבי הכהן ע"ה ~ *Dedicated in loving memory of* **Mrs. Leba Chana Lubin**
Marking her passing on 21 Cheshvan, 5779. May the merit of the Torah study worldwide accompany her soul in the world of everlasting life and be a source of blessings to her family with much health, happiness, nachas, and success.

PARSHA OVERVIEW
Vayakhel

Moses assembles the people of Israel and reiterates to them the commandment to observe the Shabbat. He then conveys G-d's instructions regarding the making of the Mishkan (Tabernacle). The people donate the required materials in abundance, bringing gold, silver and copper; blue-, purple-, and red-dyed wool; goat hair, spun linen, animal skins, wood, olive oil, herbs, and precious stones. Moses has to tell them to stop giving.

A team of wisehearted artisans make the Mishkan and its furnishings (as detailed in the previous Torah readings of Terumah, Tetzaveh, and Ki Tisa): three layers of roof coverings; 48 gold-plated wall panels and 100 silver foundation sockets; the parochet (veil) that separates between the Sanctuary's two chambers and the masach (screen) that fronts it; the ark and its cover with the cherubim; the table and its show-bread; the seven-branched menorah with its specially prepared oil; the golden altar and the incense burned on it; the anointing oil; the outdoor altar for burnt offerings and all its implements; the hangings, posts, and foundation sockets for the courtyard; and the basin and its pedestal, made out of copper mirrors.

Behind the Scenes of Building the Tabernacle

The National Construction Project

TEXT 1A

Shemot (Exodus) 35:21–29

וַיָּבֹאוּ כָּל אִישׁ אֲשֶׁר נְשָׂאוֹ לִבּוֹ וְכֹל אֲשֶׁר נָדְבָה רוּחוֹ אֹתוֹ הֵבִיאוּ אֶת תְּרוּמַת ה' לִמְלֶאכֶת אֹהֶל מוֹעֵד וּלְכָל עֲבֹדָתוֹ וּלְבִגְדֵי הַקֹּדֶשׁ:
וַיָּבֹאוּ הָאֲנָשִׁים עַל הַנָּשִׁים כֹּל נְדִיב לֵב הֵבִיאוּ חָח וָנֶזֶם וְטַבַּעַת וְכוּמָז כָּל כְּלִי זָהָב וְכָל אִישׁ אֲשֶׁר הֵנִיף תְּנוּפַת זָהָב לַיהֹוָה:
וְכָל אִישׁ אֲשֶׁר נִמְצָא אִתּוֹ תְּכֵלֶת וְאַרְגָּמָן וְתוֹלַעַת שָׁנִי וְשֵׁשׁ וְעִזִּים וְעֹרֹת אֵילִם מְאָדָּמִים וְעֹרֹת תְּחָשִׁים הֵבִיאוּ:
כָּל מֵרִים תְּרוּמַת כֶּסֶף וּנְחֹשֶׁת הֵבִיאוּ אֵת תְּרוּמַת ה' וְכֹל אֲשֶׁר נִמְצָא אִתּוֹ עֲצֵי שִׁטִּים לְכָל מְלֶאכֶת הָעֲבֹדָה הֵבִיאוּ:
וְכָל אִשָּׁה חַכְמַת לֵב בְּיָדֶיהָ טָווּ וַיָּבִיאוּ מַטְוֶה אֶת הַתְּכֵלֶת וְאֶת הָאַרְגָּמָן אֶת תּוֹלַעַת הַשָּׁנִי וְאֶת הַשֵּׁשׁ:
וְכָל הַנָּשִׁים אֲשֶׁר נָשָׂא לִבָּן אֹתָנָה בְּחָכְמָה טָווּ אֶת הָעִזִּים:
וְהַנְּשִׂאִם הֵבִיאוּ אֵת אַבְנֵי הַשֹּׁהַם וְאֵת אַבְנֵי הַמִּלֻּאִים לָאֵפוֹד וְלַחֹשֶׁן:
וְאֶת הַבֹּשֶׂם וְאֶת הַשָּׁמֶן לְמָאוֹר וּלְשֶׁמֶן הַמִּשְׁחָה וְלִקְטֹרֶת הַסַּמִּים:
כָּל אִישׁ וְאִשָּׁה אֲשֶׁר נָדַב לִבָּם אֹתָם לְהָבִיא לְכָל הַמְּלָאכָה אֲשֶׁר צִוָּה ה' לַעֲשׂוֹת בְּיַד מֹשֶׁה הֵבִיאוּ בְנֵי יִשְׂרָאֵל נְדָבָה לַה':

Every man whose heart uplifted him came, and every-
one whose spirit inspired him to generosity brought the

offering of G-d for the work of the Tent of Meeting, for all its service, and for the holy garments.

The men came with the women; every generous-hearted person brought bracelets and earrings and rings and buckles, all kinds of golden objects, and every man who waved a waving of gold to G-d.

And every man with whom was found blue, purple, or crimson wool, linen, goat hair, ram skins dyed red or tachash *skins, brought them.*

Everyone who set aside an offering of silver or copper brought the offering for G-d, and everyone with whom acacia wood was found for any work of the service brought it.

And every wisehearted woman spun with her hands, and they brought spun material: blue, purple, and crimson wool, and linen.

And all the women whose hearts uplifted them with wisdom spun the goat hair.

And the princes brought the shoham *stones and filling stones for the* ephod *and for the* choshen.

And the spice and the oil for lighting and for the anointing oil and for the incense.

Every man and woman whose heart inspired them to generosity to bring for all the work that G-d had commanded to make, through Moses, the Children of Israel brought a gift for G-d.

Donating Too Much

TEXT 1B

Ibid. 36:1–7

וְעָשָׂה בְצַלְאֵל וְאָהֳלִיאָב וְכֹל אִישׁ חֲכַם לֵב אֲשֶׁר נָתַן ה' חָכְמָה וּתְבוּנָה בָּהֵמָה לָדַעַת לַעֲשֹׂת אֶת כָּל מְלֶאכֶת עֲבֹדַת הַקֹּדֶשׁ לְכֹל אֲשֶׁר צִוָּה ה':

וַיִּקְרָא מֹשֶׁה אֶל בְּצַלְאֵל וְאֶל אָהֳלִיאָב וְאֶל כָּל אִישׁ חֲכַם לֵב אֲשֶׁר נָתַן ה' חָכְמָה בְּלִבּוֹ כֹּל אֲשֶׁר נְשָׂאוֹ לִבּוֹ לְקָרְבָה אֶל הַמְּלָאכָה לַעֲשֹׂת אֹתָהּ:

וַיִּקְחוּ מִלִּפְנֵי מֹשֶׁה אֵת כָּל הַתְּרוּמָה אֲשֶׁר הֵבִיאוּ בְּנֵי יִשְׂרָאֵל לִמְלֶאכֶת עֲבֹדַת הַקֹּדֶשׁ לַעֲשֹׂת אֹתָהּ וְהֵם הֵבִיאוּ אֵלָיו עוֹד נְדָבָה בַּבֹּקֶר בַּבֹּקֶר:

וַיָּבֹאוּ כָּל הַחֲכָמִים הָעֹשִׂים אֵת כָּל מְלֶאכֶת הַקֹּדֶשׁ אִישׁ אִישׁ מִמְּלַאכְתּוֹ אֲשֶׁר הֵמָּה עֹשִׂים:

וַיֹּאמְרוּ אֶל מֹשֶׁה לֵּאמֹר מַרְבִּים הָעָם לְהָבִיא מִדֵּי הָעֲבֹדָה לַמְּלָאכָה אֲשֶׁר צִוָּה ה' לַעֲשֹׂת אֹתָהּ:

וַיְצַו מֹשֶׁה וַיַּעֲבִירוּ קוֹל בַּמַּחֲנֶה לֵאמֹר אִישׁ וְאִשָּׁה אַל יַעֲשׂוּ עוֹד מְלָאכָה לִתְרוּמַת הַקֹּדֶשׁ וַיִּכָּלֵא הָעָם מֵהָבִיא:

וְהַמְּלָאכָה הָיְתָה דַיָּם לְכָל הַמְּלָאכָה לַעֲשׂוֹת אֹתָהּ וְהוֹתֵר:

Bezalel and Oholiab and every wisehearted man into whom G-d has imbued wisdom and insight to know how to do shall do all the work of the service of the Holy, according to all that G-d has commanded.

And Moses called Bezalel and Oholiab and every wisehearted man into whose heart G-d had given wisdom, everyone whose heart lifted him up to approach the work to do it.

So they took from before Moses all the offering[s] that the Children of Israel had brought for the work of the service of the Holy, and they brought him more gifts every morning.

Then all the wise men who were doing the work of the Holy came, each one from his work, which they had been doing.

And they spoke to Moses, saying, "The people are bringing very much, more than is enough for the labor of the articles which the L-rd has commanded to do."

So Moses commanded, and they announced in the camp, saying, "Let no man or woman do any more work for the offering for the Holy." So the people stopped bringing.

And the work was sufficient for them for all the work, to do it and to leave over.

Conspiracy Theories

TEXT 2A

Midrash Shemot Rabah, 51:6

Shemot Rabah

An early rabbinic commentary on the Book of Exodus. Midrash is the designation of a particular genre of rabbinic literature usually forming a running commentary on specific books of the Bible. *Shemot Rabah*, written mostly in Hebrew, provides textual exegeses, expounds upon the biblical narrative, and develops and illustrates moral principles. It was first printed in Constantinople in 1512 together with 4 other Midrashic works on the other 4 books of the Pentateuch.

רַבִּי חָמָא אָמַר הָיוּ אוֹמְרִים חָמֵי קְדָל דִּבְרֵיהּ דְּעַמְרָם, וַחֲבֵרוֹ אוֹמֵר לוֹ אָדָם שֶׁשָּׁלַט עַל מְלֶאכֶת הַמִּשְׁכָּן אֵין אַתָּה מְבַקֵּשׁ שֶׁיְּהֵא עָשִׁיר.

Rabbi Chama said: One would say, "[Look] how thick is the neck of the son of Amram!" His friend would reply, "Are you surprised that the one in charge of building the Mishkan would be wealthy?"

TEXT 2B

Ibid.

כְּשֶׁשָּׁמַע מֹשֶׁה כָּךְ אָמַר לָהֶם מֹשֶׁה, חַיֵּיכֶם, נִגְמַר הַמִּשְׁכָּן אֶתֵּן לָכֶם חֶשְׁבּוֹן. אָמַר לָהֶם בּוֹאוּ וְנַעֲשֶׂה חֶשְׁבּוֹן, הֱוֵי: וְאֵלֶּה פְקוּדֵי הַמִּשְׁכָּן.

When Moses heard this, he said, "By your lives, when the Mishkan is complete I will give you an account [of all the Mishkan's funds. When it was completed,] he said, "Come, let's make an accounting. Hence, the verse states, "These are the numbers of the Mishkan."

Missing Silver

TEXT 2C

Ibid.

אָמַר לָהֶם מֹשֶׁה: אֵלֶּה פְקוּדֵי הַמִּשְׁכָּן, כָּךְ וְכָךְ יָצָא עַל הַמִּשְׁכָּן, עַד
שֶׁהוּא יוֹשֵׁב וּמְחַשֵּׁב שָׁכַח בְּאֶלֶף וּשְׁבַע מֵאוֹת וַחֲמִשָּׁה וְשִׁבְעִים
שֶׁקֶל מַה שֶּׁעָשָׂה וָוִים לָעַמּוּדִים, הִתְחִיל יוֹשֵׁב וּמַתְמִיהַּ, אָמַר עַכְשָׁו
יִשְׂרָאֵל מוֹצְאִין יְדֵיהֶם לֵאמֹר מֹשֶׁה נְטָלָן.
מֶה עָשָׂה הֵאִיר הַקָּדוֹשׁ בָּרוּךְ הוּא עֵינָיו וְרָאָה אוֹתָם עֲשׂוּיִם וָוִים
לָעַמּוּדִים, אוֹתָהּ שָׁעָה נִתְפַּיְּסוּ כָּל יִשְׂרָאֵל עַל מְלֶאכֶת הַמִּשְׁכָּן.

Moses said to them, "These are the numbers of the Mishkan; such and such was spent on the Mishkan." While he was sitting and calculating, he forgot what was done with the sum of 1,775 shekels (which were used as hooks for the pillars of the Mishkan). He was sitting, wondering what to do. He said, "Now the Jewish people will have a pretext to say Moses took it."

What did he do? G-d illuminated his eyes, and he saw the silver used as hooks for the pillars of the Mishkan. At that moment, all of Israel were appeased regarding the work of the Mishkan.

Difficulty Making the Menorah

TEXT 3

Midrash Tanchuma, Behaalotecha 3

Midrash Tanchuma
A Midrashic work bearing the
name of Rabbi Tanchuma, a
4th-century Talmudic sage
quoted often in this work.
Midrash is the designation of
a particular genre of rabbinic
literature usually forming
a running commentary on
specific books of the Bible.
Midrash Tanchuma provides
textual exegeses, expounds
upon the biblical narrative,
and develops and illustrates
moral principles. *Tanchuma*
is unique in that many of its
sections commence with a
halachic discussion, which
subsequently leads into
non-halachic teachings.

שֶׁכֵּן הוּא אוֹמֵר, מִקְשָׁה תֵּעָשֶׂה הַמְּנוֹרָה. כֵּיוָן שֶׁנִּתְקַשָּׁה, אָמַר
הַקָּדוֹשׁ בָּרוּךְ הוּא לְמֹשֶׁה, טוֹל כִּכַּר זָהָב וְהַשְׁלִיכֵהוּ לָאֵשׁ וְהוֹצִיאֵהוּ,
וְהִיא נַעֲשֵׂית מֵעַצְמָהּ, וְכַפְתּוֹרֶיהָ וּפְרָחֶיהָ גְּבִיעֶיהָ וְקָנֶיהָ מִמֶּנָּה. אַתָּה
הֱיֵה מַכֶּה בַּפַּטִּישׁ, וּמֵעַצְמָהּ נַעֲשֵׂית. לְכָךְ הוּא אוֹמֵר, מִקְשָׁה תֵּעָשֶׂה
הַמְּנוֹרָה, יוּ"ד מָלֵא, וְלֹא כְּתִיב תַּעֲשֶׂה. כְּלוֹמַר, מֵעַצְמָהּ תֵּעָשֶׂה. מָה
עָשָׂה מֹשֶׁה. נָטַל אֶת הַכִּכָּר וְהִשְׁלִיכוּ לָאוּר, וְאָמַר מֹשֶׁה, רִבּוֹנוֹ שֶׁל
עוֹלָם, הֲרֵי הַכִּכָּר נִשְׁלַךְ בְּתוֹךְ הָאֵשׁ, כְּשֵׁם שֶׁאַתָּה רוֹצֶה, תֵּעָשֶׂה
לְפָנֶיךָ. מִיָּד יָצְאַת הַמְּנוֹרָה עֲשׂוּיָה כְּתִקּוּנָהּ.

*The verse states, "The Menorah shall be made of
hammered work." When Moses had difficulty with
the Menorah, G-d said to him, "Take a kikar of gold,
throw it into the fire, and remove it. It will be made
on its own, with its knobs, flowers, goblets, and arms
protruding from it. You bang with the hammer, and it
will take shape on its own."*

*Therefore the verse states, "The menorah shall be
made of hammered work." It does not say, "you shall
make," meaning, it shall be made on its own.*

*What did Moses do? He took the kikar and threw it
into the fire. He said, "Master of the Universe, here,
the kikar has been thrown into the fire. As You wish,
let it be made before you." Immediately, the Menorah
emerged complete.*

Sitting Idly

TEXT 4

Midrash Shemot Rabah, 52:2

דָּבָר אַחֵר, תֵּאָלַמְנָה שִׂפְתֵי שָׁקֶר, מְדַבֵּר בְּמֹשֶׁה, בְּשָׁעָה שֶׁאָמַר הַקָּדוֹשׁ בָּרוּךְ הוּא לַעֲשׂוֹת לוֹ מִשְׁכָּן, מִיָּד אָמַר מֹשֶׁה לְיִשְׂרָאֵל: "וְיִקְחוּ לִי תְרוּמָה", הָיָה מֹשֶׁה עוֹשֶׂה בַּמִּשְׁכָּן וְהָיוּ לֵיצָנֵי יִשְׂרָאֵל אוֹמְרִים אֶפְשָׁר שֶׁהַשְּׁכִינָה שׁוֹרָה עַל יְדֵי בֶּן עַמְרָם.

אָמַר רַבִּי יוֹחָנָן שִׁשָּׁה חֳדָשִׁים הָיָה עוֹסֵק בַּמִּשְׁכָּן, שְׁלֹשָׁה חֳדָשִׁים עֲשָׂאוּהוּ וּשְׁלֹשָׁה חֳדָשִׁים קִפְּלוּהוּ, אַף עַל פִּי כֵן הָיוּ מְלִיצִין אַחֲרָיו וְאוֹמְרִים הֲרֵי נַעֲשָׂה, לֹא הָיָה מֹשֶׁה אוֹמֵר שֶׁיַּשְׁרֶה שְׁכִינָתוֹ אֶצְלֵנוּ. וְהַקָּדוֹשׁ בָּרוּךְ הוּא נִתְכַּוֵּן לְהַעֲמִיד הַמִּשְׁכָּן בַּחֹדֶשׁ שֶׁנּוֹלַד בּוֹ יִצְחָק אָבִינוּ, לֹא עָשָׂה אֶלָּא כְּשֶׁהִגִּיעַ אוֹתוֹ הַחֹדֶשׁ אָמַר הַקָּדוֹשׁ בָּרוּךְ הוּא לְמֹשֶׁה: "בְּיוֹם הַחֹדֶשׁ הָרִאשׁוֹן תָּקִים אֶת הַמִּשְׁכָּן", אוֹתָהּ שָׁעָה אָמְרָה רוּחַ הַקֹּדֶשׁ: "תֵּאָלַמְנָה שִׂפְתֵי שָׁקֶר", אוֹתָם שֶׁמְּלִיצִים אַחַר מֹשֶׁה, לֹא עָשָׂה, אֶלָּא כֵּיוָן שֶׁאָמַר הָאֱלֹקִים לְמֹשֶׁה שֶׁיָּקִים אֶת הַמִּשְׁכָּן הִתְחִילוּ טוֹעֲנִין אוֹתוֹ וּבָאִין כָּל אֶחָד וְאֶחָד מִמְּלַאכְתּוֹ, שֶׁנֶּאֱמַר: "וַיָּבִיאוּ אֶת הַמִּשְׁכָּן אֶל מֹשֶׁה".

When G-d told Moses to build Him a Mishkan, Moses immediately told the Jewish people [of G-d's command, "Speak to the Children of Israel, and they shall] take for Me an offering [from every person whose heart inspires him to generosity, you shall take My offering]."

As Moses worked on the Mishkan, the scoffers of Israel would say, "Is it possible that the Divine Presence will rest through the work of the son of Amram?"

Rabbi Yochanan said: For six months he worked on the Mishkan. For three months he assembled it, and for three months it lay disassembled. Nevertheless, they would scoff and say, "Look, the Mishkan is complete! Didn't Moses say the Divine Presence would now rest among us?"

But G-d intended for the Mishkan to be erected in the month of Isaac's birth, so Moses did not erect it until that month arrived and G-d said to Moses, "On the day of the first month . . . you shall set up the Mishkan of the Tent of Meeting."

Then the Divine Spirit said, "Let lying lips become mute." To those who scoffed about Moses—once G-d told Moses to erect the Mishkan, they began to load it up, and each person came from his work, as the verse states, "They brought the Mishkan to Moses."

Six Days of Aggravation?

The Proper Balance

TEXT 5A

Bereishit (Genesis) 1:1

בְּרֵאשִׁית בָּרָא אֱלֹקִים אֵת הַשָּׁמַיִם וְאֵת הָאָרֶץ:

In the beginning of G-d's creation of the heavens and the earth.

TEXT 5B

Rashi, ad loc.

Rabbi Shlomo Yitzchaki
(Rashi)
1040–1105
Most noted biblical and
Talmudic commentator.
Born in Troyes, France,
Rashi studied in the famed
yeshivot of Mainz and
Worms. His commentaries
on the Pentateuch and
the Talmud, which focus
on the straightforward
meaning of the text, appear
in virtually every edition
of the Talmud and Bible.

"ברא אלקים." ולא אמר ברא ה', שבתחלה עלה במחשבה לבראתו
במדת הדין, ראה שאין העולם מתקיים, הקדים מדת רחמים ושתפה
למדת הדין, היינו דכתיב ביום עשות ה' א-להים ארץ ושמים.

"G-d's creation of the heavens and the earth.": But it
does not say "of G-d's creation of" [i.e., the verse does
not uses the name "Elokim" instead of G-d's four letter
name, which expresses kindness]. In the beginning,
G-d intended to create it with the Divine standard of
judgment, but he perceived that the world would not
endure. So He preceded it with the Divine standard of
mercy, allying it with the Divine standard of judgment.
And that is the reason it is written, "On the day the
L-rd, G-d [Hashem, Elokim] made earth and heaven."

Light Created, Light Stored Away

TEXT 6

Talmud Tractate Chagigah, 12a

דאמר רבי אלעזר אור שברא הקדוש ברוך הוא ביום ראשון אדם
צופה בו מסוף העולם ועד סופו כיון שנסתכל הקדוש ברוך הוא
בדור המבול ובדור הפלגה וראה שמעשיהם מקולקלים עמד וגנזו
מהן שנאמר "וימנע מרשעים אורם". ולמי גנזו? –לצדיקים לעתיד
לבא שנאמר "וירא אלקים את האור כי טוב", ואין טוב אלא צדיק,
שנאמר "אמרו צדיק כי טוב".

Babylonian Talmud

A literary work of monumental proportions that draws upon the legal, spiritual, intellectual, ethical, and historical traditions of Judaism. The 37 tractates of the Babylonian Talmud contain the teachings of the Jewish sages from the period after the destruction of the 2nd Temple through the 5th century CE. It has served as the primary vehicle for the transmission of the Oral Law and the education of Jews over the centuries; it is the entry point for all subsequent legal, ethical, and theological Jewish scholarship.

Rabbi Elazar said: By the light that the Holy One, blessed is He, created on the first day, man could observe from one end of the world to the other. But when the Holy One, blessed be He, looked upon the generation of the Flood and the generation of the Dispersion and saw that their ways were corrupt, He arose and concealed it from them, as it is stated, "And from the wicked their light is withheld."

And for whom did He conceal it? For the righteous people in the future, as it is stated, "And G-d saw the light, that it was good"; "good" refers to none other than the righteous, as it is stated, "Say of the righteous that it shall be good for them, for they shall eat the fruit of their actions."

The Trees Revolt

TEXT 7A

Bereishit (Genesis) 1:12

וַתּוֹצֵא הָאָרֶץ דֶּשֶׁא עֵשֶׂב מַזְרִיעַ זֶרַע לְמִינֵהוּ וְעֵץ עֹשֶׂה פְּרִי אֲשֶׁר
זַרְעוֹ בוֹ לְמִינֵהוּ וַיַּרְא אֱלֹהִים כִּי טוֹב:

And G-d said, "Let the earth sprout vegetation, seed yielding herbs, and fruit trees producing fruit according to its kind in which its seed is found, on the earth," and it was so.

TEXT 7B

Rashi, ad loc.

"עֵץ פְּרִי". שֶׁיְּהֵא טַעַם הָעֵץ כְּטַעַם הַפְּרִי, וְהִיא לֹא עָשְׂתָה כֵן, אֶלָּא
וַתּוֹצֵא הָאָרֶץ עֵץ עוֹשֶׂה פְּרִי, וְלֹא הָעֵץ פְּרִי, לְפִיכָךְ כְּשֶׁנִּתְקַלֵּל אָדָם
עַל עֲווֹנוֹ נִפְקְדָה גַּם הִיא עַל עֲווֹנָהּ וְנִתְקַלְּלָה.

"Fruit trees." That the taste of the tree should be like the taste of the fruit. The earth did not do so, however, as it is stated, "The earth gave forth . . . trees producing fruit," producing *fruit,* but the trees themselves were not *fruit.* Therefore, when man was cursed because of his iniquity, the earth too was punished for its iniquity and was cursed.

The Moon Protests

TEXT 8

Talmud Tractate Chulin, 60b

רבי שמעון בן פזי רמי כתיב "ויעש אלקים את שני המאורות
הגדולים" וכתיב "את המאור הגדול ואת המאור הקטן". אמרה
ירח לפני הקדוש ברוך הוא, "רבונו של עולם, אפשר לשני מלכים
שישתמשו בכתר אחד?" אמר לה, "לכי ומעטי את עצמך". אמרה
לפניו, "רבונו של עולם, הואיל ואמרתי לפניך דבר הגון אמעיט את
עצמי?" אמר לה "לכי ומשול ביום ובלילה". אמרה ליה "מאי רבותיה
דשרגא בטיהרא מאי אהני?" אמר לה "זיל לימנו בך ישראל ימים
ושנים". אמרה ליה "יומא נמי אי אפשר דלא מנו ביה תקופותא
דכתיב 'והיו לאותות ולמועדים ולימים ושנים' זיל ליקרו צדיקי
בשמיך יעקב הקטן שמואל הקטן דוד הקטן".
חזייה דלא קא מיתבא דעתה אמר הקדוש ברוך הוא "הביאו כפרה
עלי שמיעטתי את הירח".
והיינו דאמר רבי שמעון בן לקיש: מה נשתנה שעיר של ראש חדש
שנאמר בו "לה'"? אמר הקדוש ברוך הוא "שעיר זה יהא כפרה על
שמיעטתי את הירח".

*Rabbi Shimon ben Pazi raises a contradiction between
two verses. It is written, "And G-d made the two great
lights," and it is also written, "The greater light to rule
the day, and the lesser light to rule the night."*

*The moon said before the Holy One, blessed be He,
"Master of the Universe, is it possible for two kings to*

serve with one crown?" G-d therefore said to the moon, "You're right; go and diminish yourself."

She said before Him, "Master of the Universe, since I said a correct observation before You, must I diminish myself?" G-d said to her, "[As compensation,] go and rule both during the day along with the sun and during the night." She said to Him, "What use is a candle in the middle of the day?"

G-d said to her, "Go, let the Jewish people count the days and years with you, and this will be your greatness." She said to Him, "But the Jewish people will count with the sun as well, as it is impossible that they will not count seasons with it, as it is written, 'And let them be for signs and for seasons and for days and years.'" G-d said to her, "Go, let righteous men be named after you. [Just as you are called the lesser (hakatan) light,] there will be Ya'akov (Jacob) Hakatan, Shmuel (Samuel) Hakatan, and David Hakatan."

G-d saw that the moon was not appeased, so He said to the Jews, "Offer a sacrifice to atone for the fact that I diminished the moon."

Rabbi Shimon ben Lakish, said regarding this matter: Why is the goat offering of Rosh Chodesh unique among all sacrifices in that it is regarded in Scripture as being "for G-d"? The idea is that G-d said, "This goat offering shall be an atonement for the fact that I diminished the moon."

Demise of the Leviathan's Spouse

TEXT 9

Bereishit (Genesis) 1:21

> וַיִּבְרָא אֱלֹקִים אֶת הַתַּנִּינִם הַגְּדֹלִים וְאֵת כָּל נֶפֶשׁ הַחַיָּה הָרֹמֶשֶׂת אֲשֶׁר
> שָׁרְצוּ הַמַּיִם לְמִינֵהֶם וְאֵת כָּל עוֹף כָּנָף לְמִינֵהוּ וַיַּרְא אֱלֹקִים כִּי טוֹב:

And G-d created the great sea monsters and every living creature that crawls, with which the waters swarmed, according to their kind, and every winged fowl, according to its kind, and G-d saw that it was good.

TEXT 10A

Rashi, ad loc.

> "הַתַּנִּינִם." דגים גדולים שבים. ובדברי אגדה הוא לויתן ובן זוגו
> שבראם זכר ונקבה והרג את הנקבה ומלחה לצדיקים לעתיד לבא,
> שאם יפרו וירבו לא יתקיים העולם בפניהם.

"The great sea monsters": The great fish in the sea. In the Agadah, this refers to the Leviathan and its mate, for He created them male and female, and He slew the female and salted her away for the righteous in the future, for if they would propagate, the world could not exist because of them.

Heavenly Controversy

TEXT 10B

Midrash Bereishit Rabah, 8:5

Bereishit Rabah

An early rabbinic commentary on the Book of Genesis. This Midrash bears the name of Rabbi Oshiya Rabah (Rabbi Oshiya "the Great"), whose teaching opens this work. This Midrash provides textual exegeses and stories, expounds upon the biblical narrative, and develops and illustrates moral principles. Produced by the sages of the Talmud in the Land of Israel, its use of Aramaic closely resembles that of the Jerusalem Talmud. It was first printed in Constantinople in 1512 together with 4 other Midrashic works on the other 4 books of the Pentateuch.

אָמַר רַבִּי סִימוֹן, בְּשָׁעָה שֶׁבָּא הַקָּדוֹשׁ בָּרוּךְ הוּא לִבְרֹאת אֶת אָדָם הָרִאשׁוֹן, נַעֲשׂוּ מַלְאֲכֵי הַשָּׁרֵת כִּתִּים כִּתִּים, וַחֲבוּרוֹת חֲבוּרוֹת, מֵהֶם אוֹמְרִים אַל יִבָּרֵא, וּמֵהֶם אוֹמְרִים יִבָּרֵא... חֶסֶד אוֹמֵר יִבָּרֵא, שֶׁהוּא גוֹמֵל חֲסָדִים. וֶאֱמֶת אוֹמֵר אַל יִבָּרֵא, שֶׁכֻּלּוֹ שְׁקָרִים. צֶדֶק אוֹמֵר יִבָּרֵא, שֶׁהוּא עוֹשֶׂה צְדָקוֹת. שָׁלוֹם אוֹמֵר אַל יִבָּרֵא, דְּכוֹלֵיהּ קְטָטָה. מֶה עָשָׂה הַקָּדוֹשׁ בָּרוּךְ הוּא נָטַל אֱמֶת וְהִשְׁלִיכוֹ לָאָרֶץ, הֲדָא הוּא דִּכְתִיב: וְתַשְׁלֵךְ אֱמֶת אַרְצָה, אָמְרוּ מַלְאֲכֵי הַשָּׁרֵת לִפְנֵי הַקָּדוֹשׁ בָּרוּךְ הוּא, רִבּוֹן הָעוֹלָמִים מָה אַתָּה מְבַזֶּה תַּכְסִיס אַלְטִיכְסְיָה שֶׁלָּךְ, תַּעֲלֶה אֱמֶת מִן הָאָרֶץ, הֲדָא הוּא דִּכְתִיב: אֱמֶת מֵאֶרֶץ תִּצְמָח.

Rabbi Simon said: When the Holy One, blessed is He, was about to create Adam, the angels split into groups. Some said, "Let not man be created." Others said, "Let man be created."... The attribute of kindness said, "Let man be created, for he will perform acts of kindness."

The attribute of truth said, "Let not man be created, for he will be full of lies." The attribute of righteousness said, "Let man be created, for he will perform acts of righteousness." The attribute of peace said, "Let not man be created, for he will be full of quarrels."

What did G-d do? He took truth and threw it to the ground, as the verse states, "He threw truth to the ground." The serving angels said before G-d, "Master of

the Universe, why are you disgracing Your seal [truth]?
Lift truth from the earth!" This, then, is the meaning
of the verse, "Truth will sprout from the earth."

Very Good?

TEXT 11

Bereishit (Genesis) 1:31

וַיַּרְא אֱלֹקִים אֶת כָּל אֲשֶׁר עָשָׂה וְהִנֵּה טוֹב מְאֹד וַיְהִי עֶרֶב וַיְהִי בֹקֶר
יוֹם הַשִּׁשִּׁי:

*And G-d saw all that He had made, and, behold, it was
very good, and it was evening and it was morning, the
sixth day.*

TEXT 12

Talmud Tractate Sukkah, 53a

בשעה שכרה דוד שיתין קפא תהומא ובעא למשטפא עלמא אמר
דוד מי איכא דידע אי שרי למכתב שם אחספא ונשדיה בתהומא
ומנח? ליכא דקאמר ליה מידי. אמר דוד כל דידע למימר ואינו
אומר יחנק בגרונו? נשא אחיתופל קל וחומר בעצמו ומה לעשות
שלום בין איש לאשתו אמרה תורה שמי שנכתב בקדושה ימחה
על המים לעשות שלום לכל העולם כולו על אחת כמה וכמה! אמר
ליה שרי. כתב שם אחספא ושדי לתהומא ונחית תהומא שיתסר
אלפי גרמידי. כי חזי דנחית טובא אמר כמה דמידלי טפי מירטב
עלמא! אמר חמש עשרה מעלות ואסקיה חמיסר אלפי גרמידי
ואוקמיה באלפי גרמידי.

When David dug the drainpipes for the Temple, the waters of the depths rose and sought to inundate the world. David said, "Is there anyone who knows whether it is permitted to write the sacred name on an earthenware shard? If it is permitted, we will write it and throw it into the depths, and they will subside." No one replied.

David said, "Anyone who knows what to say and does not say anything: may he be strangled in his throat!"

Ahithophel [who was present] reasoned: If G-d says, "My name that was written in sanctity shall be erased on the water, in order to make peace between a man and his wife," certainly it must be permissible [to write the sacred name on an earthenware shard and throw it into the depths] to establish peace for the entire world!

So he said to David, "It is permitted."

David wrote the sacred name on an earthenware shard and cast it into the depths, and the waters in the depths subsided sixteen thousand cubits. When he saw that they subsided excessively, he said, "The higher the waters in the aquifers, the moister and more fertile the soil of the world!"

He recited the fifteen Songs of the Ascents and elevated them fifteen thousand cubits and established them at a depth of one thousand cubits.

When the Gates Were Glued Shut

TEXT 13

Talmud Tractate Shabbat, 30a

כשבנה שלמה את בית המקדש ביקש להכניס ארון לבית קדשי
הקדשים דבקו שערים זה בזה אמר שלמה עשרים וארבעה רננות
ולא נענה פתח ואמר שאו שערים ראשיכם והנשאו פתחי עולם
ויבא מלך הכבוד רהטו בתריה למיבלעיה אמרו מי הוא זה מלך
הכבוד אמר להו ה' עזוז וגבור חזר ואמר שאו שערים ראשיכם
ושאו פתחי עולם ויבא מלך הכבוד מי הוא זה מלך הכבוד ה' צבאות
הוא מלך הכבוד סלה ולא נענה כיון שאמר ה' אלהים אל תשב פני
משיחך זכרה לחסדי דוד עבדך מיד נענה באותה שעה נהפכו פני
כל שונאי דוד כשולי קדירה וידעו כל העם וכל ישראל שמחל לו
הקדוש ברוך הוא על אותו עון.

*When Solomon built the Temple and sought to bring
the ark into the Holy of Holies, the gates clung together
[and could not be opened]. Solomon uttered twenty-
four songs of praise, and his prayer was not answered.*

*He began and said, "Lift up your heads, O you gates,
and be you lifted up, you everlasting doors, that the
King of Glory may come in." Immediately, the gates
ran after him to swallow him. They said, "Who is the
King of Glory?" He said to them, "G-d, strong and
mighty, G-d mighty in battle." And he said again, "Lift
up your heads, O you gates, yea, lift them up, you
everlasting doors, that the King of Glory may come in.*

Who then is the King of Glory? The G-d of hosts; He is the King of Glory. Selah," and he was not answered. When he said, "O L-rd, G-d, turn not away the face of Your anointed; remember the good deeds of David Your servant," he was immediately answered, and a fire descended from heaven. At that moment, the faces of all of David's enemies turned dark like the charred bottom of a pot. And all of Israel knew that the Holy One, blessed be He, forgave him for that sin.

When King Solomon Slept In

TEXT 14

Midrash Bamidbar Rabah, 10:4

Bamidbar Rabah

An exegetical commentary on the first 7 chapters of the book of Numbers and a homiletic commentary on the rest of the book. The first part of *Bamidbar Rabah* is notable for its inclusion of esoteric material; the second half is essentially identical to *Midrash Tanchuma* on the book of Numbers. It was first printed in Constantinople in 1512, together with 4 other midrashic works on the other 4 books of the Pentateuch.

אָמַר רַבִּי יִשְׁמָעֵאל בְּאוֹתוֹ הַלַּיְלָה שֶׁהִשְׁלִים שְׁלֹמֹה מְלֶאכֶת בֵּית הַמִּקְדָּשׁ נָשָׂא בִּתְיָה בַּת פַּרְעֹה, וְהָיָה שָׁם צַהֲלַת שִׂמְחַת בֵּית הַמִּקְדָּשׁ, וְצַהֲלַת בַּת פַּרְעֹה, וְעָלְתָה צַהֲלַת שִׂמְחַת בַּת פַּרְעֹה יוֹתֵר מִצַּהֲלַת בֵּית הַמִּקְדָּשׁ... וּבְאוֹתָהּ שָׁעָה עָלְתָה בַּמַּחְשָׁבָה לִפְנֵי הַקָּדוֹשׁ בָּרוּךְ הוּא לְהַחֲרִיב אֶת יְרוּשָׁלַיִם...רַבָּנָן אָמְרִי אֶלֶף מִינֵי זֶמֶר הִכְנִיסָה לוֹ בַּת פַּרְעֹה...וְהָיְתָה אוֹמֶרֶת לוֹ, כָּךְ מְזַמְּרִין לִפְנֵי עֲבוֹדַת כּוֹכָבִים פְּלוֹנִית וְכָךְ מְזַמְּרִין לִפְנֵי עֲבוֹדַת כּוֹכָבִים פְּלוֹנִית...וְהָיָה יָשֵׁן לוֹ עַד אַרְבַּע שָׁעוֹת. אָמַר רַבִּי לֵוִי אוֹתוֹ הַיּוֹם נִתְקְרַב תָּמִיד בְּאַרְבַּע שָׁעוֹת, וְעַל אוֹתָהּ שָׁעָה שָׁנִינוּ, מַעֲשֶׂה הָיָה וְנִתְקְרַב תָּמִיד שֶׁל שַׁחַר בְּאַרְבַּע שָׁעוֹת וְהָיוּ יִשְׂרָאֵל עֲצֵבִים שֶׁהָיָה יוֹם חֲנֻכַּת בֵּית הַמִּקְדָּשׁ וְלֹא הָיוּ יְכוֹלִין לַעֲשׂוֹת מִפְּנֵי שֶׁהָיָה יָשֵׁן שְׁלֹמֹה וְהָיוּ מִתְיָרְאִים לַהֲקִיצוֹ מִפְּנֵי אֵימַת הַמַּלְכוּת, הָלְכוּ וְהוֹדִיעוּ לְבַת שֶׁבַע אִמּוֹ, וְהָלְכָה הִיא וֶהֱקִיצַתּוּ וְהוֹכִיחַתּוּ, הֲדָא הוּא דִכְתִיב: מַשָּׂא אֲשֶׁר יִסְּרַתּוּ אִמּוֹ.

Rabbi Ishmael said: On the night that Solomon completed the work of the Holy Temple, he wed Batya, the daughter of Pharaoh. There was rejoicing there for the Temple and rejoicing for daughter of Pharaoh, and the rejoicing for the daughter of Pharaoh exceeded the rejoicing of the Temple. . . . At that time, it occurred to G-d to destroy Jerusalem. . . .

The rabbis said: Pharaoh's daughter brought him one thousand types of instruments . . . and she would say,

"This is the music we play before this idol; this is the music we play before that idol. . . ." He slept the next morning until four hours after dawn.

Rabbi Levi said: That day, the daily offering was brought at the conclusion of the fourth hour. Regarding this incident, we learned: There was an incident where the daily morning offering was brought at the conclusion of the fourth hour. The Jewish people were troubled, for it was the day of the Temple's dedication, and they couldn't bring the offering because Solomon was sleeping, and due to their fear of the monarchy, they were afraid to wake him. They went and informed his mother, Bathsheba. She went and woke him and rebuked him. This is the meaning of the verse, "A prophecy that his mother chastised him."

The Art of Storytelling

Evil Inclination = Good?

TEXT 15

Midrash Kohelet Rabah, 3:15

Kohelet Rabah

A Midrashic text on the Book of Ecclesiastes. *Midrash* is the designation of a particular genre of rabbinic literature. The term Midrash is derived from the root *d-r-sh (dalet-raish-shin)*, which means "to search," "to examine," and "to investigate." This particular Midrash provides textual exegeses and develops and illustrates moral principles. It was first printed in Pesaro, Italy, in 1519, together with four other Midrashic works on the other four biblical *megilot*.

"והנה טוב" - זה יצר טוב. "מאד" - זה יצר הרע.

"It is good" refers to the human inclination to do good. "It is very good" refers to the human inclination to do evil.

It's All a Matter of Perspective

TEXT 16A

The Rebbe, Rabbi Menachem Mendel Schneerson,
Sichot Kodesh 5732, vol. 1, pp. 361–362

אז מ'הייבט זיך אן ארום קוקן בעיני בשר, מיט פליישיגע אויגן, זעהט מען דאן די "פלייש" און די גשמיות שבכל דבר, ווערט מען דערשראקן: וואס טוט זיך אין דער וועלט? וואס מדור לדור ומשנה לשנה איז "אכשור דרא בתמי'". אז מ'גיט א קוק, איז ניט דער חלק הטוב איז גובר, און ניט דער סדר ווערט אלץ שטארקער און ניט קדושה ורוחניות איז מושל ושולט, נאר לכאורה להיפך. ובפרט אין ענינים וואס זיינען פארבונדן מיט אידן. אידן זיינען דאך אלעמאל "אתם המעט מכל העמים", על אחת כמה וכמה איצטער. לויט דעם חשבון קאן איינפאלן על פי טבע, לויט דעם חשבון פון עיני בשר, אז דאס איז אן ענין פון א יער וואו עס געוועלטיגן חיות רעות, ניט א גארטן וואס גיט פירות מאכל אדם . . . מ'קאן דאך ווערן ביי זיך אראפגעפאלן, ווי קאן מען האבן א האפענונג אויפטאן מיט דער וועלט און איבערמאכן וועלט ווען מיר זעהען אז מדור לדור ומשנה לשנה איז הולך ופוחת, "אכשור דרא בתמי'"? אפילו אז ער וועט טאן מיט קבלת עול . . . ביי אים ווייזט זיך אויס אז ער וועט זיכער ניט מצליח זיין, ווארום די וועלט איז א יער וואו עס געוועלטיגן חיות רעות, איז טוט ער טאקע כל ענינ*י*ו, אבער ניט מיט דעם חיות, על אחת כמה וכמה ניט מיט שמחה ווי ס'דארף זיין בעבודת ה'.

Rabbi Menachem Mendel Schneerson
1902–1994

The towering Jewish leader of the 20th century, known as "the Lubavitcher Rebbe," or simply as "the Rebbe." Born in southern Ukraine, the Rebbe escaped Nazi-occupied Europe, arriving in the U.S. in June 1941. The Rebbe inspired and guided the revival of traditional Judaism after the European devastation, impacting virtually every Jewish community the world over. The Rebbe often emphasized that the performance of just one additional good deed could usher in the era of Mashiach. The Rebbe's scholarly talks and writings have been printed in more than 200 volumes.

When we look about with physical eyes, we only per-
ceive the physical aspects in all that we see, and we
naturally wonder: What is happening with the world?

The situation is steadily deteriorating, from one gen-
eration to the next and even from one year to the next.
Goodness does not prevail. Conditions are not improv-
ing. Holy and spiritual values do not dominate. This
is especially true with regard to Jewish concerns. Our
nation has always been a small minority among the
world's inhabitants, and this is certainly the case today.

Such thoughts easily lead to the conclusion that this
world is but a jungle dominated by vicious animals,
and that it certainly does not remotely resemble a gar-
den that yields edible fruit. . . . Such thoughts also lead
to dejection and despair. How can we hope to affect
and change the world for the better if the situation is
consistently degenerating?

If we reach this conclusion, even if we dutifully obey
[and continue to study Torah and do good deeds] . . .
we will lack the morale and happiness that is necessary
to fulfill our mission and properly serve G-d, inasmuch
as it appears that we will certainly fail, for the world
is no more than a wild jungle ruled by vicious beasts.

TEXT 16B

Ibid.

מיר זאלן וויסן זיין אז די וועלט . . . איז א "גן". דאס הייסט, ניט
סתם א שדה עושה תבואה, נאר דאס איז א גן עושה פירות. און
דאס איז ניט סתם א גן פון אבי וועמען, במילא איז דאס בערך
לבעל הפרדס והגן, איז פאר עם גענוג אז די פירות האבן די און
די חשיבות וואס זיי האבן. זאגט מען גלייך מלכתחילה אז דער
פסוק זאגט: "באתי לגני". דאס איז א זאך אין וועלט וואס דער
אויבערשטער זאגט אז דאס איז זיין פרדס.

*We must know that the world . . . is a garden. Not just
a field that yields grain [which is necessary in order
to subsist], but a garden that yields luxurious fruits
[that provide enjoyment and pleasure]. Moreover, the
pleasure provided by a given entity is subjective, its
extent determined by the needs and taste of its owner.
This world is not just anyone's garden; it is G-d's garden, as the verse states, "I have come to My garden."
[Its goodness is therefore measured according to His
infinite terms.]*

TEXT 16C

Ibid.

דעמאלט, קוקט ער אויף אויף וועלט אנדערש. און אז ער קוקט אנדארש,
דערזעהט ער אז דאס וואס בעיני בשר, בשטחיות, אויף דעם
ערשטן קוק, באמערקט מען ניט, איז אבער ווען ער דארף זוכן, און
ער זוכט, און ער זוכט אין דער ריכטונג - אויסצוגעפינען וואס ס'געפינט
זיך אונטער דער קליפה, אונטער דער אויסווייניגסטע שאלעכץ, די
פירות פון דעם גן, איז בשעת ער זוכט אין דער ריכטונג - איז צום
אלעם ערשטן איז ער זיכער אז ער וועט דאס זיכער געפינען, וּוארום
תורת אמת זאגט עם אז ס'איז דא, און וויסנדיק אז ער וועט זיכער
געפינען א אוצר יקר מכל יקר - פירות וואס דער אויבערשטער
איז אויף זיי מעיד אז דאס איז פירות פון זיין פרדס אין וועלכען
ער געפינט זיך, "עיקר שכינה בתחתונים היתה" - איז לפי ערך פון
יוקר הפירות וועט עס אים ניט אפשרעקן און ניט אפשטעלן פון
קיין השתדלות און קיין יגיעה און ער וועט זיך ניט לאזן אפציען,
אפרעדן און פארנעמען זיך מיט זייטיגע זאכן וויסנדיק אז אויף
אים ווארט א אוצר יקר מכל יקר ער זאל עס מגלה זיין אין וועלט
. . . מ'זאל וויסן אז מ'געפינט זיך אין א טייערע וועלט, נאר דער
יצר הרע איז זיך משתדל בכל האופנים אויף צודעקן די טייערקייט
וואס געפינט זין אין וועלט, כדי מיר זאלן זיך מייאש זיין חס ושלום,
אדער על כל פנים טאן מער ניט ווי אויף יוצא געווען וכו' . . . און
דורך דער התבוננות, גייט ער לבטח דרכו . . . וויסנדיק א זיכערע
זאך אז מ'וועט צוקומען און געפינען די פירות פון דעם גן.

*With this perspective, we view the world differently,
and when we do so, we begin to notice things that
we missed at first glance. When we realize that it is
our responsibility to constantly be on the search, we
endeavor to look around us and perceive that which*

is beneath the shell, the fruit that is under the peel. We are confident that we will successfully uncover the garden that is latent in creation because the Torah tells us that it is indeed there, waiting to be discovered. The knowledge that we will surely find precious fruit, fruit that G-d says is a part of the garden in which He dwells, infuses us with supreme confidence and enthusiasm. Knowing that a precious treasure awaits discovery, we remain focused on our task and do not allow ourselves to be sidetracked by other endeavors. . . .

We must know that we inhabit a wonderful world. The evil inclination endeavors in every way possible to obscure the world's preciousness, in the hope that we lose all hope, G-d forbid, or, at least, to lull us into doing the bare required minimum. . . . Through contemplating the above, however, we assuredly traverse through life . . . secure in the knowledge that we will find the fruits of G-d's garden.

Is the Glass Half-Full?

TEXT 17

The Rebbe, Rabbi Menachem Mendel Schneerson, Igrot Kodesh, 20:41

I acknowledge receipt of your letter. . . . Despite its tone and content . . . I have not, G-d forbid, lost hope that eventually you will appreciate the good in life, including *the good in your own life, and that this appreciation will impact your emotions and frame of mind. . . . In our world, everything is a mixture of good and bad. Human beings must choose which aspects they will emphasize, contemplate, and pursue. In everyone's life there are two paths—to see the good or [the opposite]. . . .*

How instructive is that which our sages tell us, that Adam was an ingrate. Even before he was banished from the Garden of Eden [while living in a literal paradise,] he complained about his circumstances. On the other hand, there were Jewish men and women who thanked and blessed the Creator and recited the morning blessings while living through most horrifying times in the German concentrations camps. Ultimately, everyone's circumstances will be somewhere between these two extremes. . . .

Needless to say, my intention is not to imply that anyone deserves suffering, G-d forbid. My point is simply to underscore the reality: the type of lives that we live, whether full of satisfaction and meaning or the opposite, depends, in large measure, on our willpower, which dictates whether we will focus on the positive or on the negative.

9

PEKUDEI

Did Plato Get It Right?

Jewish Realism vs. Greek Idealism

*Dedicated to **Reb Hershel Lazaroff**, on the occasion of his birthday on 25 Adar. May he go from strength to strength and enjoy good health, happiness, nachat from his loved ones, and success in all his endeavors.*

PARSHA OVERVIEW
Pekudei

An accounting is made of the gold, silver and copper donated by the people for the making of the Mishkan. Betzalel, Aholiav, and their assistants make the eight priestly garments—the apron, breastplate, cloak, crown, hat, tunic, sash and breeches—according to the specifications communicated to Moses in the parsha of Tetzaveh.

The Mishkan is completed and all its components are brought to Moses, who erects it and anoints it with the holy anointing oil, and initiates Aaron and his four sons into the priesthood. A cloud appears over the Mishkan, signifying the Divine Presence that has come to dwell within it.

Plato's Error

Plato's Theory of Forms

TEXT 1

The Rebbe, Rabbi Menachem Mendel Schneerson,
Sichot Kodesh 5724, p. 82

Rabbi Menachem Mendel Schneerson
1902–1994

The towering Jewish leader of the 20th century, known as "the Lubavitcher Rebbe," or simply as "the Rebbe." Born in southern Ukraine, the Rebbe escaped Nazi-occupied Europe, arriving in the U.S. in June 1941. The Rebbe inspired and guided the revival of traditional Judaism after the European devastation, impacting virtually every Jewish community the world over. The Rebbe often emphasized that the performance of just one additional good deed could usher in the era of Mashiach. The Rebbe's scholarly talks and writings have been printed in more than 200 volumes.

איז דא דער סיפור הידוע אז מ'האט עם אמאל געכאפט ביי ניט
קיין שיינער מעשה, האט מען עם געפרעגט ס'טייטש דו אריסטו
האסט דאך מייסד געווען און פאנאדערגעארבעט א שיטה אין
מוסר און הנהגת האדם וכו', ווי קומסטו צו דער מעשה? האט ער
געענטפערט אז איצטער איז ער ניט דער אריסטו וואס האט מייסד
געווען תורת המוסר.
מען קאן לערנען תורה און תורה זאל זיין א באזונדער ענין.

The story is told about Aristotle: He was once caught doing a very not nice act. His students asked him how he—Aristotle—could be involved with such a low thing? "You, Aristotle, the one who has founded and developed a philosophy on human morals: How could you come to do such an immoral act?" To which he answered, "When I am involved in logic, spirituality, and writing books, I am Aristotle. However, when I deal with materialism, I am not Aristotle."

Similarly, one can study Torah, and yet the Torah remains abstract. . . .

TEXT 2

Zohar, Vayikra, 15b

אמר רבי יודאי אמר רבי ייסא נשבע הקדוש ברוך הוא שלא יכנס בירושלם דלעילא עד שיכנסו ישראל בירושלם דלתתא.

G-d promised that He would not enter into the heavenly Jerusalem until Israel entered into the earthly Jerusalem.

Zohar

The seminal work of kabbalah, Jewish mysticism. The *Zohar* is a mystical commentary on the Torah, written in Aramaic and Hebrew. According to the Arizal, the *Zohar* contains the teachings of Rabbi Shimon bar Yochai, who lived in the Land of Israel during the 2nd century. The *Zohar* has become one of the indispensable texts of traditional Judaism, alongside and nearly equal in stature to the Mishnah and Talmud.

Preserving a Letter

TEXT 3

Talmud Tractate Menachot, 29b

Babylonian Talmud

A literary work of monumental proportions that draws upon the legal, spiritual, intellectual, ethical, and historical traditions of Judaism. The 37 tractates of the Babylonian Talmud contain the teachings of the Jewish sages from the period after the destruction of the 2nd Temple through the 5th century CE. It has served as the primary vehicle for the transmission of the Oral Law and the education of Jews over the centuries; it is the entry point for all subsequent legal, ethical, and theological Jewish scholarship.

בשעה שעלה משה למרום, מצאו להקדוש ברוך הוא שיושב וקושר כתרים לאותיות, אמר לפניו: רבונו של עולם, מי מעכב על ידך? אמר לו: אדם אחד יש שעתיד להיות בסוף כמה דורות ועקיבא בן יוסף שמו, שעתיד לדרוש על כל קוץ וקוץ תילין תילין של הלכות. אמר לפניו: רבונו של עולם, הראהו לי, אמר לו: חזור לאחורך. הלך וישב בסוף שמונה שורות, ולא היה יודע מה הן אומרים, תשש כחו; כיון שהגיע לדבר אחד, אמרו לו תלמידיו: רבי, מנין לך? אמר להן: הלכה למשה מסיני, נתיישבה דעתו.

חזר ובא לפני הקדוש ברוך הוא, אמר לפניו: רבונו של עולם, יש לך אדם כזה ואתה נותן תורה על ידי? אמר לו: שתוק, כך עלה במחשבה לפני.

Rav Yehudah said in the name of Rav: When Moses ascended to the heavenly heights, he found the Holy One, blessed is He, as He was sitting and attaching crowns to some of the letters. Moses said before Him, "Master of the Universe, who is holding you back from giving the Torah as it is?" G-d said to him, "There is one man who is destined to exist at the end of many generations: Akiva ben Yosef is his name, and it is he who will expound upon each and every point of the letters in the sefer Torah's mounds upon mounds of laws."

Moses said before G-d, "Master of the Universe, show him to me!" G-d said to him, "Turn around." Moses found himself in Rabbi Akiva's class. Moses went and sat at the end of eight rows of students, but he did not understand what they were saying. Disheartened, Moses's strength ebbed. However, once they reached a certain matter that required a source, Rabbi Akiva's students asked him, "Teacher, from where do you know this?" Rabbi Akiva replied to them, "It is a halachah transmitted orally to Moses at Sinai." Upon hearing this, Moses's mind was relieved.

He returned and came before the Holy One, blessed is He. Moses said before Him, "Master of the Universe, You have someone like this, and you give the Torah through me?!" G-d said to him, "Quiet! Thus has it arisen in the thoughts before Me."

TEXT 4

Rashi to Shemot (Exodus) 35:5

כבר פירשתי נדבת המשכן ומלאכתו במקום צואתן.

I have already explained the contribution to the Tabernacle and its construction in the verses where their commands were presented.

Rabbi Shlomo Yitzchaki (Rashi)
1040–1105
Most noted biblical and Talmudic commentator. Born in Troyes, France, Rashi studied in the famed *yeshivot* of Mainz and Worms. His commentaries on the Pentateuch and the Talmud, which focus on the straightforward meaning of the text, appear in virtually every edition of the Talmud and Bible.

Possible Solutions

No Other Deviation

TEXT 5

Rabbi Don Yitzchak Abarbanel, Commentary to Shemot (Exodus) 36:8

Rabbi Don Yitzchak Abarbanel
1437–1508

Biblical exegete and statesman. Abarbanel was born in Lisbon, Portugal, and served as a minister in the court of King Alfonso V of Portugal. After intrigues at court led to accusations against him, he fled to Spain, where he once again served as a counselor to royalty. It is claimed that Abarbanel offered King Ferdinand and Queen Isabella large sums of money for the revocation of their Edict of Expulsion of 1492, but to no avail. After the expulsion, he eventually settled in Italy where he wrote a commentary on Scripture, as well as other venerated works.

למה הגיד הכתוב כל המלאכה הזאת בפרטיות הזה כל כך מהפעמים, ולא הספיק לומר בכלל: ויעשו כל חכם לב כאשר צוה ה' את משה?...

הטעם בזה אצלי הוא, מפני שלא עשו האומנים המלאכה הזאת באותו סדר מהקדימה והאיחור שצוה ה' למשה בסדר "ויקחו לי תרומה". ולכך הוצרך הכתוב להגיד כאן איך עשו הכלים והדברים ההם, שהיה באופן מתחלף למה שנצטווה בהם משה, וכמו שביארתי בסדר הנזכר הסבה בחלוף הזה. ומפני שלא יחשוב אדם, שכמו ששנו בסדר המלאכה כך שנו בעצמותה ובמספרה, הוצרך לבאר כאן כל דבר ודבר שעשו, כדי להודיע שעשו כל הדברים שצוה ה', ולא שנו דבר אלא בקדימה והאיחור בסדר המעשה. ואין אם כן בזה מותר כלל.

Why does the Torah repeat the entire narrative again with such detail and not simply state, "And the craftsmen did what G-d instructed Moses?" . . .

The Tabernacle was actually constructed by the craftsmen in a different sequence to that which G-d transmitted to Moses in parshat *Terumah. When the reader sees that the order is different to that of* parshat

Terumah, *he may suspect that, in addition to chang-
ing the order of construction, perhaps further changes
were made. Therefore, the Torah repeated the construction process in intricate detail to show that only
the order was changed, and that all the measurements
and weights were preserved. Thus, it is not superfluous
at all.*

Cherished Topics Get Repeated

TEXT 6

Rashi to Bereishit (Genesis) 24:42

אמר רבי אחא יפה שיחתן של עבדי אבות לפני המקום מתורתן
של בנים, שהרי פרשה של אליעזר כפולה בתורה, והרבה גופי
תורה לא נתנו אלא ברמיזה.

*Rabbi Acha said: The ordinary conversation of the
servants of the patriarchs is more beloved before the
Omnipresent than the Torah of their sons, for the
section dealing with Eliezer is repeated in the Torah,
whereas many fundamentals of the Torah were given
only through allusions.*

TEXT 7

Rashi to Shemot (Exodus) 38:21

"משכן העדת". עדות לישראל שויתר להם הקדוש ברוך הוא על
מעשה העגל, שהרי השרה שכינתו ביניהם.

*"The Mishkan of the testimony": [The Mishkan] was
testimony for Israel that the Holy One, blessed is He,
forgave them for the incident of the calf, for He caused
His shechinah to rest among them [in the Mishkan].*

TEXT 8

The Rebbe, Rabbi Menachem Mendel Schneerson,
Likutei Sichot, vol. 16, p. 461

דער משכן וכליו איז פון די ענינים הכי עקריים וחביבים ביי אידן,
דורך דעם איז געווען השראת השכינה ביי אידן וכו';
ובפרט, אז דער משכן... עדות לישראל שויתר להם הקדוש ברוך
הוא על מעשה העגל.. וואס דערפון איז נאך מער מובן די חביבות
און ענין הכללי שבזה, ווארום חטא העגל איז געווען דער חטא הכי
גדול (וכללי) וואס האט גורם געווען צום גרעסטן הסתר פנים פון
דעם אויבערשטן, ביז צו דער גזירת כליה רחמנא ליצלן אויף אידן...
און דערפון איז מובן (לאידך גיסא), אז דער משכן, וואס דורך אים
איז "השרה שכינתו ביניהם" איז אן ענין כללי ונעלה מאד.
ובמילא איז פארשטאנדיק אז אט די גרויסע חביבות פון דעם
משכן ביים אויבערשטן (און ביי אידן), דאס איז דער טעם וואס
די תורה רעכנט אויס אלע פרטי המשכן און חזר'ט זיי איבער איין
מאל און נאכאמאל כו' מיט אלע פרטים

*The Tabernacle and its vestments were especially cher-
ished and beloved by the Jewish people, for through
them the Divine Presence dwelled among the people.*

*This is especially so considering the fact that the
Tabernacle was . . . testimony that G-d had forgiven
the Jewish people for the sin of the golden calf. The
sin of the golden calf was the greatest and broadest
sin committed by the Jewish people, a sin that caused
unprecedented damage to our relationship with G-d—
almost resulting in a death sentence for the nation. . . .*

A Tale of Two Sanctuaries

A Tabernacle Above vs. a Tabernacle Below

TEXT 9

Shemot (Exodus) 26:30

וַהֲקֵמֹתָ אֶת הַמִּשְׁכָּן כְּמִשְׁפָּטוֹ אֲשֶׁר הָרְאֵיתָ בָּהָר:

You shall erect the Tabernacle according to its laws, as you have been shown on the mountain.

TEXT 10

The Rebbe, Rabbi Menachem Mendel Schneerson,
Likutei Sichot, vol. 1, p. 196

דער משכן וואס דער אויבערשטער האט געזאגט צו משה'ן, ווי ער
ווערט באשריבן אין פרשיות תרומה ותצוה, און דער משכן וואס
די אידן האבן געמאכט לויט ווי עס ווערט דערציילט אין פרשיות
ויקהל ופקודי, זיינען מרמז אויף צוויי באזונדערע משכנות... און
דערפאר רעכנט ער אויס אלע פרטים נאך אמאל.

*The Tabernacle that G-d spoke of to Moses, as it is
transcribed in the parshiot of Terumah and Tetzaveh,
and the Tabernacle that the Jews actually erected, as
is described in the parshiot of Vayakhel and Pekudei,
allude to two different edifices. . . . For this reason, the
Torah reviews all the details again.*

G-d's Choice

TEXT 11

Shemot (Exodus) 40:34–38

וַיְכַס הֶעָנָן אֶת אֹהֶל מוֹעֵד וּכְבוֹד ה' מָלֵא אֶת הַמִּשְׁכָּן:
וְלֹא יָכֹל מֹשֶׁה לָבוֹא אֶל אֹהֶל מוֹעֵד כִּי שָׁכַן עָלָיו הֶעָנָן וּכְבוֹד ה' מָלֵא
אֶת הַמִּשְׁכָּן:
וּבְהֵעָלוֹת הֶעָנָן מֵעַל הַמִּשְׁכָּן יִסְעוּ בְּנֵי יִשְׂרָאֵל בְּכֹל מַסְעֵיהֶם:
וְאִם לֹא יֵעָלֶה הֶעָנָן וְלֹא יִסְעוּ עַד יוֹם הֵעָלֹתוֹ:
כִּי עֲנַן ה' עַל הַמִּשְׁכָּן יוֹמָם וְאֵשׁ תִּהְיֶה לַיְלָה בּוֹ לְעֵינֵי כָל בֵּית יִשְׂרָאֵל
בְּכָל מַסְעֵיהֶם:

The cloud covered the Tent of Meeting, and the glory of G-d filled the Mishkan.

Moses could not enter the Tent of Meeting because the cloud rested upon it and the glory of G-d filled the Mishkan.

When the cloud rose up from over the Mishkan, the Children of Israel set out in all their journeys.

But if the cloud did not rise up, they did not set out until the day that it rose.

For the cloud of G-d was upon the Mishkan by day, and there was fire within it at night, before the eyes of the entire house of Israel in all their journeys.

TEXT 12

Rabbi Shneur Zalman of Liadi, Tanya, Chapter 36

Rabbi Shneur Zalman of Liadi (Alter Rebbe) 1745–1812

Chasidic rebbe, halachic authority, and founder of the Chabad movement. The Alter Rebbe was born in Liozna, Belarus, and was among the principal students of the Magid of Mezeritch. His numerous works include the *Tanya*, an early classic containing the fundamentals of Chabad Chasidism, and *Shulchan Aruch HaRav*, an expanded and reworked code of Jewish law.

והנה מודעת זאת מאמר רבותינו זכרונם לברכה שתכלית בריאת
עולם הזה הוא שנתאוה הקדוש ברוך הוא להיות לו דירה
בתחתונים... שכך עלה ברצונו יתברך להיות נחת רוח לפניו יתברך
כד אתכפיא סטרא אחרא ואתהפך חשוכא לנהורא שיאיר אור ה'
אין סוף ברוך הוא במקום החשך והסטרא אחרא של כל עולם הזה
כולו ביתר שאת ויתר עז.

We already know from our sages that the purpose behind the creation of this world is G-d's desire to dwell in the lowest realms. . . . It must be that this goal does not arise out of any need or to profit any gain. It simply was His decision that He would have pleasure when the sense of otherness is suppressed and darkness transformed into light; when the light of Havayeh, *the Infinite, shines in the place of darkness and otherness throughout all of this world, shining with great intensity and great power.*

TEXT 13

Ethics of the Fathers, 3:10

Ethics of the Fathers
(Pirkei Avot)
A 6-chapter work on Jewish
ethics that is studied widely
by Jewish communities,
especially during the summer.
The first 5 chapters are from
the Mishnah, tractate Avot.
Avot differs from the rest of
the Mishnah in that it does
not focus on legal subjects;
it is a collection of the sages'
wisdom on topics related
to character development,
ethics, healthy living, piety,
and the study of Torah.

רבי חנינא בן דוסא אומר... כל שמעשיו מרובין מחכמתו חכמתו
מתקיימת וכל שחכמתו מרובה ממעשיו אין חכמתו מתקיימת.

Rabbi Hanina ben Dosa used to say, . . . "Anyone whose [good] deeds exceed his wisdom, his wisdom will endure; but anyone whose wisdom exceeds his [good] deeds, his wisdom will not endure."

TEXT 14

The Rebbe, Rabbi Menachem Mendel Schneerson, Likutei Sichot, ad loc.

ניט געקוקט אויף דעם גרויסן אונטערשייד פון דעם "בכח" און
דעם "בפועל", איז ווען האט זיך אויסגעפירט דער תכלית הרצון
פון דעם אויבערשטן און ווען איז מקוים געווארן זיין הבטחה פון
ושכנתי בתוכם? –דוקא אין גשמיות'דיקן משכן פון ויקהל פקודי
און ניט אין רוחניות'דיקן משכן פון דעם "הראת בהר", ווי ער זאגט
אין מדרש דארט.

ווארום נתאוה הקדוש ברוך הוא להיות לו יתברך דירה בתחתונים
דוקא, און ווי ער זאגט אין תניא גייט דאס אויפן עולם הזה שאין
תחתון למטה ממנו. כאטש ער איז א גשמי און א חומרי און דערצו
נאך איז דארט א חושך כפול ומכופל... פונדעסטוועגן, און מצד
דעם גופא, פירט זיך אויס דער תכלית הכוונה אין עולם הזה דוקא.

Considering the great difference between "abstract" and "reality," when do you think G-d's true desire was fulfilled? When was His presence truly expressed in this world? Counterintuitively, it was specifically through the material Tabernacle of Vayakhel/Pekudei, not through the spiritual, abstract Tabernacle that was spoken of "on the mountain" [transcribed in Terumah/Tetzaveh].

Why? Because G-d wishes to be expressed in the earthly arena, which—as explained in Tanya—is the world we know of today, after which there is nothing lower. Yes, it is mundane and crass, and dark to boot. Nevertheless—actually, precisely because of all that—it is where G-d's true desire is realized.

Conclusion: Two Types of Beauty

TEXT 15

Midrash Shir Hashirim Rabah, 8:11

Shir Hashirim Rabah
A Midrashic text and exegetical commentary on the book of Song of Songs. This Midrash explicates this biblical book based on the principle that its verses convey an allegory of the relationship between G-d and the people of Israel. It was compiled and edited in the Land of Israel during the 6th century.

"הַיּוֹשֶׁבֶת בַּגַּנִּים חֲבֵרִים מַקְשִׁיבִים לְקוֹלֵךְ הַשְׁמִיעִנִי". רַבִּי נָתָן בְּשֵׁם רַבִּי אַחָא אָמַר לְמֶלֶךְ שֶׁכָּעַס עַל עֲבָדָיו וַחֲבָשָׁן בְּבֵית קוֹלִין, מֶה עָשָׂה הַמֶּלֶךְ נָטַל כָּל קַצְרְקְטִין שֶׁלּוֹ וַעֲבָדָיו וְהָלַךְ לִשְׁמוֹעַ מֶה הָיוּ, מִן הֵן אוֹמְרִים, שָׁמַע שֶׁהָיוּ אוֹמְרִים אֲדוֹנֵינוּ הַמֶּלֶךְ הוּא שִׁבְחֵנוּ הוּא חַיֵּינוּ אַל נֶחְסַר לַאֲדוֹנֵינוּ הַמֶּלֶךְ לְעוֹלָם, אָמַר לָהֶם בְּנֵי הַגְבִּיהוּ קוֹלְכֶם כְּדֵי שֶׁיִּשְׁמְעוּ חֲבֵרִים שֶׁעַל גַּבְּכֶם.

כָּךְ אַף עַל פִּי שֶׁיִּשְׂרָאֵל עֲסוּקִין בִּמְלַאכְתָּן כָּל שֵׁשֶׁת יָמִים, וּבַיוֹם הַשַׁבָּת מַשְׁכִּימִים וּבָאִים לְבֵית הַכְּנֶסֶת, וְקוֹרִין קְרִיאַת שְׁמַע, וְעוֹבְרִין לִפְנֵי הַתֵּבָה, וְקוֹרִין בַּתּוֹרָה, וּמַפְטִירִין בַּנָּבִיא, וְהַקָּדוֹשׁ בָּרוּךְ הוּא אוֹמֵר לָהֶם בְּנֵי הַגְבִּיהוּ קוֹלְכֶם כְּדֵי שֶׁיִּשְׁמְעוּ חֲבֵרִים שֶׁעַל גַּבְּכֶם, וְאֵין חֲבֵרִים אֶלָּא מַלְאֲכֵי הַשָּׁרֵת.

"You who dwell in the gardens, friends listen to your voice; let me hear it."

Rabbi Nathan said in the name of Rabbi Acha: This can be compared to a king who becomes angry with his servants and imprisons them. The king then gathers his entire entourage and goes to listen to what the prisoners are discussing. He hears them saying, "Our master, the king, he is our praise, he is our life, may he lack nothing, forever." The king then says to the prisoners, "Raise your voices, so your friends out here will hear you too."

Similarly, Jews are busily working for six days. Then, on Shabbat, they rise early and come to shul; *they read the Shema and the prayers, the Torah, and the* haftarah. *G-d then says to them, "My children, raise your voices so that your friends above can hear you too." The "friends" in the verse is a reference to the* ministering angels.

10

VAYIKRA

Today Is the First Day of the Rest of Your Life

Make the Most of It

dicated in loving memory of **Rabbi Daniel Moscowitz,** *Regional Director of Chabad of Illinois, marking his* yahrtzeit *on 2 Adar*

לעילוי נשמת השליח הרה"ח ר' דניאל יצחק ע"ה בן יבלחט"א ר' אפרים שליט"א

PARSHA OVERVIEW
Vayikra

G-d calls to Moses from the Tent of Meeting, and communicates to him the laws of the korbanot, *the animal and meal offerings brought in the Sanctuary. These include:*

1. The "ascending offering" (olah) *that is wholly raised to G-d by the fire atop the altar;*

2. Five varieties of "meal offering" (minchah) *prepared with fine flour, olive oil, and frankincense;*

3. The "peace offering" (shelamim), *whose meat was eaten by the one bringing the offering, after parts are burned on the altar and parts are given to the* kohanim *(priests);*

4. The different types of "sin offering" (chatat) brought to atone for transgressions committed erroneously by the High Priest, the entire community, the king or the ordinary Jew; and

5. *The "guilt offering" (asham) brought by one who has misappropriated property of the Sanctuary, who is in doubt as to whether he transgressed a divine prohibition, or who has committed a "betrayal against G-d" by swearing falsely to defraud a fellow man.*

Sacrifices Spelled Out

Book of Sacrifices

TEXT 1

Nachmanides, Pirush Haramban, introduction to Vayikra

Rabbi Moshe ben Nachman
(Nachmanides, Ramban)
1194–1270

Scholar, philosopher, author, and physician. Nachmanides was born in Spain and served as leader of Iberian Jewry. In 1263, he was summoned by King James of Aragon to a public disputation with Pablo Cristiani, a Jewish apostate. Though Nachmanides was the clear victor of the debate, he had to flee Spain because of the resulting persecution. He moved to Israel and helped reestablish communal life in Jerusalem. He authored a classic commentary on the Pentateuch and a commentary on the Talmud.

הספר הזה הוא תורת כהנים והלוים, יבאר בו עניני הקרבנות כולן ומשמרת המשכן, כי כאשר היה ספר אחד בענין הגלות והגאולה ממנו, והשלימו בענין אהל מועד וכבוד השם אשר מלא את המשכן, צוהו בקרבנות ובשמירת המשכן, שיהו הקרבנות כפרה להן ולא יגרמו העונות לסלק השכינה.

וצוה בכהנים הנגשים אל ה' שיתקדשו, שהזהיר על טומאת מקדש וקדשיו, וגם שלא יהרסו לעלות אל ה', כמו שאמר: דבר אל אהרן אחיך ואל יבא בכל עת אל הקדש מבית לפרוכת אל פני הכפרת אשר על הארון ולא ימות כי בענן אראה על הכפרת. כאזהרת: פן יהרסו אל ה' לראות ונפל ממנו רב. ואחר כך יגביל המשכן כהגבלת הר סיני בעת היות שם כבוד אלהי ישראל.

והנה רוב הספר הזה בקרבנות בתורת הקרבן והמקריבים, ובמקום שיתקרב בו. ויבואו בו קצת מצות נגררות עם אלה . . ורוב פרשיות הספר הזה ידבר בהן עם הכהנים: דבר אל אהרן ואל בניו, צו את אהרן ואת בניו. ובפרשת קדושים תהיו קצת מצות לבני ישראל, רובן נגררות עם עניני הקרבנות בדומים להם, ובמקומם אפרש בעזרתו של הקדוש ברוך הוא.

This book contains the laws of the priests and the Levites; all matters pertaining to the sacrifices and to the Tabernacle's upkeep are explained in it. Just as there is a book pertaining to the enslavement of Israel and the subsequent Exodus, culminating with the topic of the Tabernacle and G-d's glory which filled it, [the following book] contains commandments of the sacrifices and the Tabernacle's upkeep, so that the sacrifices will atone for the Jewish people, and their sins will not cause the Divine Presence to depart.

G-d commands the priests, who approach G-d, to sanctify themselves. He warns us against allowing any impurity of the Sanctuary and its holy artifacts, and forbids us from unrestrictedly approaching the Sanctuary, as the verse states, "[And G-d said to Moses: Speak to your brother Aaron, that] he should not come at all times into the Holy within the dividing curtain, in front of the cover that is upon the ark, so that he should not die, for I appear over the ark cover in a cloud." This is analogous to the warning [at Sinai, "G-d said to Moses, 'Go down, warn the people] lest they break [their formation to go nearer] to G-d, to see, and many of them will fall.'" The Sanctuary should then be cordoned off, just as Mount Sinai was cordoned off when the glory of the G-d of Israel was there.

Most of this book deals with the laws of the sacrifices, of those who may offer them, and of where they may be offered. A few other related mitzvot *are recorded in it . . . and most chapters of this book are addressed to the priests, for example, "Speak to Aaron and his sons," and, "Command Aaron and his sons." The portion of "kedoshim tiheyu" contains a few commandments to the Children of Israel, mostly relating to the sacrifices. I will explain them in their proper place with G-d's help.*

Intro to Sacrifices

TEXT 2

Vayikra (Leviticus) 1:1–3

וַיִּקְרָא אֶל מֹשֶׁה וַיְדַבֵּר ה' אֵלָיו מֵאֹהֶל מוֹעֵד לֵאמֹר:
דַּבֵּר אֶל בְּנֵי יִשְׂרָאֵל וְאָמַרְתָּ אֲלֵהֶם אָדָם כִּי יַקְרִיב מִכֶּם קָרְבָּן לַה' מִן
הַבְּהֵמָה מִן הַבָּקָר וּמִן הַצֹּאן תַּקְרִיבוּ אֶת קָרְבַּנְכֶם:
אִם עֹלָה קָרְבָּנוֹ מִן הַבָּקָר זָכָר תָּמִים יַקְרִיבֶנּוּ אֶל פֶּתַח אֹהֶל מוֹעֵד
יַקְרִיב אֹתוֹ לִרְצֹנוֹ לִפְנֵי ה':

And He called to Moses, and G-d spoke to him from the Tent of Meeting, saying:

"Speak to the Children of Israel, and say to them: When a man from [among] you brings a sacrifice to G-d, from animals, from cattle, or from the flock you shall bring your sacrifice.

"If his sacrifice is a burnt offering from cattle, an unblemished male he shall bring it. He shall bring it willingly to the entrance of the Tent of Meeting, before G-d."

The Voluntary Peace Offering

TEXT 3A

Ibid. 3:1–5

וְאִם זֶבַח שְׁלָמִים קָרְבָּנוֹ אִם מִן הַבָּקָר הוּא מַקְרִיב אִם זָכָר אִם נְקֵבָה תָּמִים יַקְרִיבֶנּוּ לִפְנֵי ה':

וְסָמַךְ יָדוֹ עַל רֹאשׁ קָרְבָּנוֹ וּשְׁחָטוֹ פֶּתַח אֹהֶל מוֹעֵד וְזָרְקוּ בְּנֵי אַהֲרֹן הַכֹּהֲנִים אֶת הַדָּם עַל הַמִּזְבֵּחַ סָבִיב:

וְהִקְרִיב מִזֶּבַח הַשְּׁלָמִים אִשֶּׁה לַה' אֶת הַחֵלֶב הַמְכַסֶּה אֶת הַקֶּרֶב וְאֵת כָּל הַחֵלֶב אֲשֶׁר עַל הַקֶּרֶב:

וְאֵת שְׁתֵּי הַכְּלָיֹת וְאֶת הַחֵלֶב אֲשֶׁר עֲלֵהֶן אֲשֶׁר עַל הַכְּסָלִים וְאֶת הַיֹּתֶרֶת עַל הַכָּבֵד עַל הַכְּלָיוֹת יְסִירֶנָּה:

וְהִקְטִירוּ אֹתוֹ בְנֵי אַהֲרֹן הַמִּזְבֵּחָה עַל הָעֹלָה אֲשֶׁר עַל הָעֵצִים אֲשֶׁר עַל הָאֵשׁ אִשֶּׁה רֵיחַ נִיחֹחַ לַה':

If his sacrifice is a peace offering, if he brings it from cattle, whether male or female, unblemished he shall bring it before G-d.

And he shall lean his hand [forcefully] upon the head of his sacrifice and slaughter it at the entrance of the Tent of Meeting. And Aaron's descendants, the koha-nim, shall dash the blood upon the altar, around.

And from the peace offering he shall bring a fire offer-ing to G-d [comprised of] the fat covering the innards and all the fat that is on the innards.

And he shall bring the two kidneys [along] with the fat that is upon them which is over the flanks. And he shall remove the diaphragm with the liver, along with the kidneys.

And Aaron's descendants shall cause it to [go up in] smoke on the altar, apart from the burnt offering, which is on top of the wood that is on the fire; [it is] a fire offering [with] a pleasing fragrance to G-d.

The Daily Burnt Offering

TEXT 3B

Rashi to Vayikra 3:5

"על העולה". מלבד העולה, למדנו שתקדים עולת תמיד לכל קרבן על המערכה.

"*Apart from the burnt offering*": [From here] we learn that the daily burnt offering precedes any other sacrifice upon the woodpile [of the altar].

Rabbi Shlomo Yitzchaki (Rashi)
1040–1105

Most noted biblical and Talmudic commentator. Born in Troyes, France, Rashi studied in the famed *yeshivot* of Mainz and Worms. His commentaries on the Pentateuch and the Talmud, which focus on the straightforward meaning of the text, appear in virtually every edition of the Talmud and Bible.

TEXT 4

Bamidbar (Numbers) 28:1–4

וַיְדַבֵּר ה' אֶל מֹשֶׁה לֵּאמֹר:

צַו אֶת בְּנֵי יִשְׂרָאֵל וְאָמַרְתָּ אֲלֵהֶם אֶת קָרְבָּנִי לַחְמִי לְאִשַּׁי רֵיחַ נִיחֹחִי תִּשְׁמְרוּ לְהַקְרִיב לִי בְּמוֹעֲדֹו:

וְאָמַרְתָּ לָהֶם זֶה הָאִשֶּׁה אֲשֶׁר תַּקְרִיבוּ לַה' כְּבָשִׂים בְּנֵי שָׁנָה תְמִימִם שְׁנַיִם לַיּוֹם עֹלָה תָמִיד:

אֶת הַכֶּבֶשׂ אֶחָד תַּעֲשֶׂה בַבֹּקֶר וְאֵת הַכֶּבֶשׂ הַשֵּׁנִי תַּעֲשֶׂה בֵּין הָעַרְבָּיִם:

G-d spoke to Moses, saying:

Command the Children of Israel and say to them: My offering, My food for My fire offerings, a spirit of satisfaction for Me, you shall take care to offer to Me at its appointed time.

And you shall say to them: This is the fire offering that you shall offer to G-d: two unblemished lambs in their first year each day as a continual burnt offering.

The one lamb you shall offer up in the morning, and the other lamb you shall offer up in the afternoon.

Institution of Prayer

TEXT 5

Talmud Tractate Berachot, 26b

רבי יהושע בן לוי אמר תפלות כנגד תמידין תקנום . . ותניא כוותיה
דרבי יהושע בן לוי מפני מה אמרו תפלת השחר עד חצות שהרי
תמיד של שחר קרב והולך עד חצות ורבי יהודה אומר עד ארבע
שעות שהרי תמיד של שחר קרב והולך עד ארבע שעות ומפני
מה אמרו תפלת המנחה עד הערב שהרי תמיד של בין הערבים
קרב והולך עד הערב רבי יהודה אומר עד פלג המנחה שהרי תמיד
של בין הערבים קרב והולך עד פלג המנחה ומפני מה אמרו תפלת
הערב אין לה קבע שהרי אברים ופדרים שלא נתעכלו מבערב
קרבים והולכים כל הלילה.

Babylonian Talmud

A literary work of monumental proportions that draws upon the legal, spiritual, intellectual, ethical, and historical traditions of Judaism. The 37 tractates of the Babylonian Talmud contain the teachings of the Jewish sages from the period after the destruction of the 2nd Temple through the 5th century CE. It has served as the primary vehicle for the transmission of the Oral Law and the education of Jews over the centuries; it is the entry point for all subsequent legal, ethical, and theological Jewish scholarship.

Rabbi Joshua ben Levi said: The prayers were insti-tuted based on the daily offerings sacrificed in the Holy Temple. . . . It was taught in a Baraita in accordance with the opinion of Rabbi Joshua ben Levi: Why did the rabbis say that the morning prayer may be recited until noon? Because the daily morning offering may be sacrificed until noon. Rabbi Judah says: [The morning prayer may be recited only] until four hours into the day, because the daily morning offering is sacrificed until four hours.

And why did the rabbis say that the afternoon prayer may be recited until the evening? Because the daily afternoon offering is sacrificed until the evening. Rabbi

Judah said: [The afternoon prayer may be recited only] until the midpoint of the afternoon because the daily afternoon offering is sacrificed until the midpoint of the afternoon.

And why did they say that the evening prayer is not fixed? Because the burning of the limbs and fats of the offerings that were not consumed by the fire on the altar until the evening remained on the altar and were offered continuously throughout the entire night.

Origins of the Musaf

TEXT 6A

Bamidbar (Numbers) 28:9–10

וּבְיוֹם הַשַּׁבָּת שְׁנֵי כְבָשִׂים בְּנֵי שָׁנָה תְּמִימִם וּשְׁנֵי עֶשְׂרֹנִים סֹלֶת מִנְחָה
בְּלוּלָה בַשֶּׁמֶן וְנִסְכּוֹ:
עֹלַת שַׁבַּת בְּשַׁבַּתּוֹ עַל עֹלַת הַתָּמִיד וְנִסְכָּהּ:

And on the Sabbath day, two unblemished lambs in the first year, and two tenths of an ephah of fine flour as a meal offering, mixed with oil, and its libation.

[This is] the burnt offering of each Sabbath on its Sabbath, in addition to the daily burnt offering and its libation.

TEXT 6B

Maimonides, Mishneh Torah, Hilchot Tefilah 1:58

Rabbi Moshe ben Maimon
(Maimonides, Rambam)
1135–1204

Halachist, philosopher, author, and physician. Maimonides was born in Córdoba, Spain. After the conquest of Córdoba by the Almohads, he fled Spain and eventually settled in Cairo, Egypt. There, he became the leader of the Jewish community and served as court physician to the vizier of Egypt. He is most noted for authoring the *Mishneh Torah*, an encyclopedic arrangement of Jewish law, and for his philosophical work, *Guide for the Perplexed*. His rulings on Jewish law are integral to the formation of halachic consensus.

וכן תקנו שיהא מנין התפלות כמנין הקרבנות שתי תפלות בכל יום כנגד שני תמידין וכל יום שיש קרבן מוסף תקנו בו תפלה שלישית כנגד קרבן מוסף ותפלה שהיא כנגד תמיד של בקר היא הנקראת תפלת השחר ותפלה שכנגד תמיד של בין הערבים היא הנקראת תפלת מנחה ותפלה שכנגד המוספין היא נקראת תפלת המוספין. וכן התקינו שיהא אדם מתפלל תפלה אחת בלילה שהרי איברי תמיד של בין הערבים מתעכלין והולכין כל הלילה שנאמר היא העולה... נמצאו התפלות בכל יום שלש ערבית ושחרית ומנחה ובשבתות ובמועדים ובראשי חדשים ארבע שלש של כל יום ותפלת המוספין.

[The rabbis] also decreed that the number of prayers correspond to the number of sacrifices—i.e., two prayers every day, corresponding to the two daily sacrifices. On any day that an additional sacrifice [was offered], they instituted a third prayer, corresponding to the additional offering.

The prayer that corresponds to the daily morning sacrifice is called the shacharit *prayer. The prayer that corresponds to the daily sacrifice offered in the afternoon is called the* minchah *prayer, and the prayer corresponding to the additional offerings is called the* musaf *prayer. . . . They also instituted a prayer to be recited at night, since the limbs of the daily afternoon offering could be burnt the whole night, as the verse* states, "The burnt offering [shall remain on the altar hearth all night until morning]." . . . Thus, three prayers are recited daily: the evening prayer, the morning prayer, and the minchah prayer. There are four on Sabbaths, festivals, and Rosh Chodesh: the three that are recited daily and the musaf prayer.

Two Kinds of Mitzvot

Every Day, Every Moment

TEXT 7

Sefer Hachinuch, Author's Foreward

החיוב של אלו [=המצוות] לעשותן אינו בכל עת, רק בזמנים ידועים
מן השנה או מן היום, חוץ משש מהן, שחיובן תמידי, לא יפסק
מעל האדם אפילו רגע בכל ימיו, ואלו הן:

א. להאמין בשם.

ב. שלא להאמין זולתו.

ג. ליחדו.

ד. לאהבה אותו.

ה. ליראה אותו.

ו. שלא לתור אחר מחשבת הלב וראית העינים.

Sefer Hachinuch

A work on the biblical commandments. Four aspects of every mitzvah are discussed in this work: the definition of the mitzvah; ethical lessons that can be deduced from the mitzvah; basic laws pertaining to the observance of the mitzvah; and who is obligated to perform the mitzvah, and when. The work was composed in the 13th century by an anonymous author who refers to himself as "the Levite of Barcelona." It has been widely thought that this referred to Rabbi Aharon Halevi of Barcelona (Re'ah); however, this view has been contested.

Almost every mitzvah is not constant; rather, it is observed at certain times of the year or of the day. There are six exceptions, six mitzvot *whose obligations are constant and do not cease for a person for even a moment all his days. They are:*

1. *To believe in G-d.*
2. *Not to believe in anything besides for G-d.*
3. *To unify Him.*
4. *To fear Him.*
5. *To love Him.*
6. *Not to go astray after the thoughts of the heart and the sight of the eyes.*

TEXT 8

Maimonides, Mishneh Torah, Laws of Reciting the Shema 1:1

פעמים בכל יום קוראין קריאת שמע בערב ובבקר שנאמר "ובשכבך ובקומך" בשעה שדרך בני אדם שוכבין וזה הוא לילה ובשעה שדרך בני אדם עומדין וזה הוא יום.

We [are obligated to] recite the Shema twice daily—in the evening and in the morning, as the verse states, ". . . When you lie down and when you rise," i.e., when people are accustomed to sleep—namely, at night—and when people are accustomed to rise, namely during the day.

Two Modes of Connection

A Sacrifice from Whom?

TEXT 9

Vayikra (Leviticus) 1:2

דַּבֵּר אֶל בְּנֵי יִשְׂרָאֵל וְאָמַרְתָּ אֲלֵהֶם אָדָם כִּי יַקְרִיב מִכֶּם קָרְבָּן לַה' מִן הַבְּהֵמָה מִן הַבָּקָר וּמִן הַצֹּאן תַּקְרִיבוּ אֶת קָרְבַּנְכֶם:

Speak to the Children of Israel, and say to them: When a man from [among] you brings [literally: when a man brings from you] a sacrifice to G-d, from animals, from cattle, or from the flock you shall bring your sacrifice.

TEXT 10A

Rabbi Shneur Zalman of Liadi, Likutei Torah, Vayikra 2b

להבין . . . דהוה ליה למימר מלת "מכם" קודם "כי יקריב" היינו אדם מכם כי יקריב כו'?

It is puzzling. . . . One would think that the verse should state the word mikem *[from you] before the words* ki yakriv *[who will bring]; the verse should have stated, "A person from you who will bring, etc."*

Rabbi Shneur Zalman of Liadi (Alter Rebbe) 1745–1812
Chasidic rebbe, halachic authority, and founder of the Chabad movement. The Alter Rebbe was born in Liozna, Belarus, and was among the principal students of the Magid of Mezeritch. His numerous works include the *Tanya*, an early classic containing the fundamentals of Chabad Chasidism, and *Shulchan Aruch HaRav*, an expanded and reworked code of Jewish law.

A Sacrifice from You

TEXT 10B

Ibid.

אך הנה נודע שיש בכל אחד ב' נפשות. נפש האלקית ונפש
הבהמית... ותכלית ירידת הנשמה לעולם הזה הוא כדי לברר נפש
הבהמית להיות בבחינת אתכפייא ואתהפכא והיינו על ידי נפש
האלקית המתלבשת בה ומתבוננת בה' אחד בקראית שמע שמע
ישראל כו' ועל ידי זה ואהבת בכל לבבך בשני יצריך כו'...
וזהו כי יקריב מכם מכם ממש שיקריב את נפש האדם שלמטה
לה'. ולכן אמר תיבת מכם אחר אומרו כי יקריב. ולא אמר אדם מכם
כי יקריב שאם כן היה הפירוש רק כפשוטו לבד שאדם הגשמי
שלמטה יקריב. אבל באומרו כי יקריב מכם בא לרמז אל ענין הנ"ל...
ופירוש מן הבקר ומן הצאן היינו שני מדרגות חלוקות שיש בנפשות
הבהמיות. יש מי שהוא מבחינת בקר... הוא בחינת גבורות קשות
והיינו מי שהוא כעסן בטבעו שמדה רעה זו היא בו בתגבורת יותר
ויכונה בשם בקר על שם הרתחנות כו'. ויש מי שאינו רתחן בטבעו
וחלק הרע שבו הוא היותו בעל תאוה והוא שנפשו הבהמית היא
מבחינת צאן שאינן נגחנית אדרבה קולם ברחמנות. אלא שהם
בעלי תאות כו', הנה כל אלה צריך לאכפיא.
וזהו שכתוב מן הבקר ומן הצאן תקריבו את קרבנכם כל אחד לפי
מה דידע בנפשו מהותו וטבעו כך יראה לאכפיא מדה זו ואז יהיה
דבר המתקיים.

*It is a popular notion that every person possesses two
souls, a G-dly soul and an animal soul. . . . The purpose of the soul's descent to this world is to elevate the
animal soul by subduing and transforming it. This is
accomplished by the G-dly soul, which is vested within*

[the animal soul] and contemplates the one G-d while reciting, "Shema Yisrael, etc.," which leads one to love G-d with both inclinations [with the animal soul and the G-dly soul], etc. . . .

This is the meaning of, "[When a person] brings from you," meaning, literally from you—when a person brings his soul to G-d. Therefore, the word mikem [from you] is stated after the words ki yakriv [will bring]. The verse did not state, "When a person from you will bring," for that would only have expressed the simple meaning that a physical person should bring his sacrifice. But in stating, "A person who will bring from you," the verse alludes to this [internal sacrifice of one's animal soul]. . . .

Now, the words, "from cattle or from the flock," refer to two distinct types of animal souls. Some people are like cattle . . . exhibiting strong character, i.e., a person who by nature possesses a strong measure of the evil trait of anger. He is referred to by the moniker "cattle," due to his boiling nature, etc. Others are not heated by nature; their evil lies in the fact that they have physical desires. Such a person's animal soul can be likened to herd animals, who do not gore. To the contrary, they speak with a merciful voice, but they are full of desires. All of this needs to be subdued.

This is the meaning of, "From cattle or from the flock you shall bring your sacrifice." Each person should, according to his awareness of his own personality and nature, seek to subdue the necessary trait, and then it will have a lasting effect.

TEXT 11

The Rebbe, Rabbi Menachem Mendel Schneerson,
Hayom Yom, entry for 12 Adar II

Rabbi Menachem Mendel Schneerson
1902–1994
The towering Jewish leader of the 20th century, known as "the Lubavitcher Rebbe," or simply as "the Rebbe." Born in southern Ukraine, the Rebbe escaped Nazi-occupied Europe, arriving in the U.S. in June 1941. The Rebbe inspired and guided the revival of traditional Judaism after the European devastation, impacting virtually every Jewish community the world over. The Rebbe often emphasized that the performance of just one additional good deed could usher in the era of Mashiach. The Rebbe's scholarly talks and writings have been printed in more than 200 volumes.

דער אנהויב פון פרשות הקרבנות איז: אדם כי יקריב מכם קרבן לה'. עס האט דאך געדארפט שטיין אדם מכם כי יקריב גו', זאגט דער אלטער רבי: אדם כי יקריב, בכדי א מענש זאל ווערען נעהנטער צו השם יתברך איז מכם קרבן לה', פון אייך אליין דארף זיין דער קרבן, מקריב זיין זיין אייגענע בהמה, דעם יצר הרע וואס ווערט אנגערופען נפש הבהמית.

The Torah portion dealing with altar offerings begins, "A man who offers (yakriv) of you an offering to G-d." The logical order of the words should be, "A man from [among] you who offers, etc." The Alter Rebbe answers, "A man who offers"—for a person to become closer to G-d—"of you an offering to G-d"—he or she must bring the offering of him or herself. They must sacrifice their personal "animal," the desire for evil that is called the animal soul.

Mitzvah = Connection

TEXT 12

Rabbi Shneur Zalman of Liadi, Likutei Torah, Bechukotai 45c

כי המצוה היא כלי לאורו יתברך הנמשך מסתימא דכל סתימין
למטה להשגת האדם... והוא לשון צוותא לשון חיבור.

*A mitzvah is a receptacle for Divine light which flows
down from the most hidden of the hidden spiritual
realms into the grasp of a lowly person . . . as expressed
in the word "mitzvah," which is etymologically related
to the word tzavta [bond].*

Consistency vs. Creativity

TEXT 13

The Rebbe, Rabbi Menachem Mendel Schneerson,
Igrot Melech, vol. 2, pp. 254–255

כאשר נתבונן, נראה כי קיים הבדל בין האופנים שבהם מאירים השמש והלבנה את הארץ: השמש זורח ומאיר יום יום באותו אופן, ללא כל שינוי. לעומתו הלבנה מתחדשת מדי חודש בהופעתה או בהיוולדה. בראשית החודש [היא מופיעה] תחילה כרצועה צרה חצי-עגולה והיא הולכת ומתמלאת ומגביהה אורה מיום ליום עד שהיא מגיע לשלימותה ושיא אורה, ביום ארבעה עשר-חמשה עשר לחודש.

במלים אחרות: השמש והירח מסמלים שני כחות. השמש מייצגת אחידות ויציבות, והלבנה– תמורה והתחדשות. שני גורמים אלה קיימים גם בעבודת ה', ולמרות שהם, לכאורה, ענינים הפכיים ומנוגדים, הרי דווקא שניהם יחד הכרחיים ודרושים להשגת שלימות בעבודת השם.

ביאור הדבר: ישנם ענינים בעבודת השם החוזרים ונשנים מדי יום ביומו ללא הבדל. כך לדוגמא פותח כל יהודי את יומו מיד עם הקיצו משנתו באמירת "מודה אני לפניך". הוא מכיר ומודה לה' על שהעניק לו חיים וכוחות רעננים לעבדו. כך גם מצות קריאת שמע וקבלת עול מלכות שמים, והתפילות הנאמרות בכל יום, כך גם מצות לימוד תורה, אהבת ישראל וכו', שיהודי חייב לקיימן בכל יום ומדי יום.

אך יחד עם זה חייבת להתווסף מדי יום התלהבות מחודשת בכל עניני היהדות, ובפרט בעניינים החוזרים ונשנים מדי יום, בדיוק כאילו באו היום מפי הגבורה.

התלהבות חדשה ושמחה באה בימים של שבת ויום טוב וכו', כאשר מתווספות תפילות מיוחדות ומצוות מיוחדות הקשורות רק עם ימים מיוחדים אלה, כגון: הדלקת נרות וקידוש בשבת, ובחגים – אכילת מצה בזמן חרותנו וכו', באופן עד שקדושת השבת מורגשת גם בימי החול, ותוכן כל חג חודר לחיי כל ימי השנה.

There are readily discernable differences between how the sun and moon illuminate the earth. The sun is unchanging, shining, giving off light each day in the same way. By contrast, the moon reinvents itself every month: in the beginning of the month the moon first appears as a thin sliver and then expands, radiating more light each day until it reaches its zenith on the fourteenth/fifteenth day of the month.

In other words: The sun represents uniformity and stability, whereas the moon represents change and regeneration. These two modes exist in Divine service; though they seem opposite and contrary to one another, they are in fact both necessary to achieve complete service of the Divine.

To explain: Some aspects of Divine service repeat themselves constantly every day without fail. For example, immediately upon awakening from sleep, every Jew begins his or her day saying the Modeh Ani. He is cognizant of and thankful to G-d Who grants him life and renewed energy with which to serve Him. [He continues the daily routine] with reciting the Shema, accepting the yoke of Heaven, and daily *prayers. Similarly, [every day he fulfills] the mitzvah of Torah study and loving your fellow Jew, etc. A Jew is required to keep all these obligations on a daily basis.*

However, together with this [consistency], there is a need to add and inject new excitement in all aspects of Judaism, and specifically in those things that repeat themselves on a constant basis so that fulfilling them will feel like following a command issued today. This new energy and excitement come from special days such as Shabbat, Yom Tov, and the like when we add special prayers and perform special mitzvot such as lighting Shabbat candles, making Kiddush, eating matzah, etc., in such a way that the holiness of Shabbat is felt throughout the week, and the message of each holiday permeates one's life all the days of the year.

Making Each Day Count

TEXT 14

Midrash Tanchuma, Ki Teitzei

אמר רב אדא: מאתים וארבעים ושמונה מצוות עשה יש בתורה,
כמניין איברין שבאדם, ובכל יום ויום צועקים על האדם: עשה
אותנו שתחיה בזכותינו ותאריך ימים.
ושלש מאות וששים וחמש מצוות לא תעשה, כמניין ימות החמה,
ובכל יום ויום שהחמה זורחת עד שהיא שוקעת, צווחת ואומרת
לאדם: 'גוזרני עליך במי שהגיע ימיך ליום הזה, אל תעבור בי את
העבירה הזאת, ואל תכריע אותך ואת העולם כלו לכף חובה.

Rabbi Abba said, "There are 248 positive commandments in the Torah, corresponding to the organs that are in a human being; each day they cry out at the person, 'Perform us [i.e., do a mitzvah] so that you may live through our merit and you may lengthen your life.'"

There are also 365 negative commandments, like the number of solar days. So on each and every day, from when the sun rises until it sets, it speaks and cries out at a person, "Heed the warning of the One who has brought your days up to this day. Do not commit this transgression against me, and do not tilt yourself and the whole world toward the scale of guilt."

Midrash Tanchuma

A Midrashic work bearing the name of Rabbi Tanchuma, a 4th-century Talmudic sage quoted often in this work. Midrash is the designation of a particular genre of rabbinic literature usually forming a running commentary on specific books of the Bible. *Midrash Tanchuma* provides textual exegeses, expounds upon the biblical narrative, and develops and illustrates moral principles. *Tanchuma* is unique in that many of its sections commence with a halachic discussion, which subsequently leads into non-halachic teachings.

Square Tablets

TEXT 15

Rabbeinu Bechaye ben Asher, Shemot (Exodus) 31:18

Rabbeinu Bechaye ben Asher
c. 1265–1340
Biblical commentator. Rabbeinu Bechaye lived in Spain and was a disciple of Rabbi Shlomo ben Aderet, known as Rashba. He is best known for his multifaceted commentary on the Torah, which interprets the text on literal, midrashic, philosophical, and kabbalistic levels. Rabbeinu Bechaye also wrote *Kad Hakemach*, a work on philosophy and ethics.

ודע כי הלוחות היו מרובעות ששה טפחים באורך וששה טפחים ברוחב, וכן דרשו רבותינו זכרונם לברכה בבבא בתרא פרק השותפין הלוחות ארכם ששה ורחבם ששה ועבים שלשה.

Know that the tablets were box shaped, six hand-breadths long by six handbreadths wide. As the rabbis taught in Tractate Bava Batra, *chapter* "Hashutafin": *The tablets were six [handbreadths] long, six [hand-breadths] wide, and three [handbreadths] deep.*

TEXT 16

The Rebbe, Rabbi Menachem Mendel Schneerson,
Torat Menachem 5742, vol. 1, p. 275

והנה ידוע הכלל שלא ברא הקדוש ברוך הוא בעולמו דבר אחד
לבטלה, ובפרט כאשר מדובר אודות ענייני קדושה. ועל פי זה מובן
שהלוחות היו ממלאים את כל חלל הארון, באופן שלא נשאר
מקום פנוי ומקום ריק, כי אם היה נשאר מקום ריק, הרי מקום זה
הוא לבטלה חס ושלום...וכמפורש בגמרא... זאת אומרת, שעל פי
חשבון הגמרא היה הארון מלא באופן שלא היה בו מקום פנוי.
ועל פי זה הרי בהכרח לומר שכל א' מהלוחות היה ריבוע של ששה
טפחים על ששה טפחים, ואי אפשר לומר שקצהו העליון של
הלוחות הי' בצורת חצי עיגול, כי אז יוצא שמלמטה היה אמנם
הארון מלא לגמרי, אבל מלמעלה נשאר מקום פנוי, בגלל הצורה
דחצי עיגול — וזה היפך משמעות הגמרא.

It is axiomatic that "G-d did not create anything in
His world for naught," which certainly applies with
regard to holy matters. It is thus understood that the
tablets filled the entire space of the ark, leaving no
empty space, for if there were empty space, it would
emerge that some space would have been for naught,
G-d forbid. . . .

The Talmud goes to great lengths to explain how
every inch of the ark was utilized to the maximum:
the ark was full, with no empty space. It emerges that
each of the tablets must have been a box of six hand-
breadths by six handbreadths; the top of the tablets
cannot have been in the shape of a semicircle, because

then only the bottom of the ark would have been full, while in the top, in the place of the semicircle, there would have been empty space, which contradicts the Talmud's implication.

11

PURIM

Do It Because You Care

Personal Touch Is All the Difference

*Dedicated in loving memory of **Dr. Yitzchok** and **Laya Block** who together reconnected countless Jews to their heritage. May their memory be a blessing to their children, grandchildren, and great-grandchildren, and all those whose lives they impacted.*

PARSHA OVERVIEW
Purim

The jolly festival of Purim is celebrated every year on the fourteenth day of the Hebrew month of Adar (late winter/early spring). It commemorates the salvation of the Jewish people in ancient Persia from Haman's plot "to destroy, kill, and annihilate all the Jews, young and old, infants and women, in a single day," as recorded in the Megilah (book of Esther).

The Persian Empire of the fourth century BCE extended over 127 lands, and all the Jews were its subjects. When King Ahasuerus had his wife, Queen Vashti, executed for failing to follow his orders, he arranged a beauty pageant to find a new queen. A Jewish girl, Esther, found favor in his eyes and became the new queen, though she refused to divulge her nationality.

Meanwhile, the Jew-hating Haman was appointed prime minister of the empire. Mordechai, the leader of the Jews (and Esther's cousin), defied the king's orders and refused to bow to Haman. Haman was incensed, and he convinced the king to issue a decree ordering the extermination of all the Jews on the thirteenth day of Adar, a date chosen by a lottery Haman made.

Mordechai galvanized all the Jews, convincing them to repent, fast, and pray to G-d. Meanwhile, Esther asked the king and Haman to join her for a feast. At a subsequent feast, Esther revealed to the king her Jewish identity. Haman was hanged, Mordechai was appointed prime minister in his stead, and a new decree was issued, granting the Jews the right to defend themselves against their enemies.

On the thirteenth of Adar, the Jews mobilized and killed many of their enemies. On the fourteenth of Adar, they rested and celebrated. In the capital city of Shushan, they took one more day to finish the job.

Not Just a Hebrew Halloween

What Makes Purim, Purim?

TEXT 1

Megilat Esther 9:19–23, 28

עַל כֵּן הַיְּהוּדִים הַפְּרָזִים הַיּשְׁבִים בְּעָרֵי הַפְּרָזוֹת עֹשִׂים אֵת יוֹם
אַרְבָּעָה עָשָׂר לְחֹדֶשׁ אֲדָר שִׂמְחָה וּמִשְׁתֶּה וְיוֹם טוֹב וּמִשְׁלוֹחַ מָנוֹת
אִישׁ לְרֵעֵהוּ:
וַיִּכְתֹּב מָרְדֳּכַי אֶת הַדְּבָרִים הָאֵלֶּה וַיִּשְׁלַח סְפָרִים אֶל כָּל הַיְּהוּדִים
אֲשֶׁר בְּכָל מְדִינוֹת הַמֶּלֶךְ אֲחַשְׁוֵרוֹשׁ הַקְּרוֹבִים וְהָרְחוֹקִים:
לְקַיֵּם עֲלֵיהֶם לִהְיוֹת עֹשִׂים אֵת יוֹם אַרְבָּעָה עָשָׂר לְחֹדֶשׁ אֲדָר וְאֵת
יוֹם חֲמִשָּׁה עָשָׂר בּוֹ בְּכָל שָׁנָה וְשָׁנָה:
כַּיָּמִים אֲשֶׁר נָחוּ בָהֶם הַיְּהוּדִים מֵאוֹיְבֵיהֶם וְהַחֹדֶשׁ אֲשֶׁר נֶהְפַּךְ לָהֶם
מִיָּגוֹן לְשִׂמְחָה וּמֵאֵבֶל לְיוֹם טוֹב לַעֲשׂוֹת אוֹתָם יְמֵי מִשְׁתֶּה וְשִׂמְחָה
וּמִשְׁלוֹחַ מָנוֹת אִישׁ לְרֵעֵהוּ וּמַתָּנוֹת לָאֶבְיוֹנִים:
וְקִבֵּל הַיְּהוּדִים אֵת אֲשֶׁר הֵחֵלּוּ לַעֲשׂוֹת וְאֵת אֲשֶׁר כָּתַב
מָרְדֳּכַי אֲלֵיהֶם:...
וְהַיָּמִים הָאֵלֶּה נִזְכָּרִים וְנַעֲשִׂים בְּכָל דּוֹר וָדוֹר מִשְׁפָּחָה וּמִשְׁפָּחָה
מְדִינָה וּמְדִינָה וְעִיר וָעִיר וִימֵי הַפּוּרִים הָאֵלֶּה לֹא יַעַבְרוּ מִתּוֹךְ
הַיְּהוּדִים וְזִכְרָם לֹא יָסוּף מִזַּרְעָם:

*Therefore, the Jewish villagers who live in open towns
make the fourteenth day of the month of Adar [a day
of] joy and feasting and a festive day, and of sending
portions to one another.*

And Mordechai inscribed these things and sent letters to all the Jews who were in all the provinces of King Ahasuerus, both near and far: to enjoin them to make the fourteenth day of the month of Adar and the fifteenth day thereof, every year.

As the days when the Jews rested from their enemies, and the month that was reversed for them from grief to joy and from mourning to a festive day, to make them days of feasting and joy, and sending portions one to another and gifts to the poor.

And the Jews took upon themselves what they had commenced to do and what Mordechai had written to them. . . .

Consequently, these days are recalled and observed in every generation: by every family, every province, and every city. And these days of Purim shall never cease among the Jews, and the memory of them shall never perish among their descendants.

TEXT 2A

Shulchan Aruch, Orach Chayim 687:1

Rabbi Yosef Caro
(Maran, Beit Yosef)
1488–1575
Halachic authority and author.
Rabbi Caro was born in Spain
but was forced to flee during
the expulsion in 1492 and
eventually settled in Safed,
Israel. He authored many
works including the *Beit Yosef*,
Kesef Mishneh, and a mystical
work, *Magid Meisharim*.
Rabbi Caro's magnum opus,
the Shulchan Aruch (Code
of Jewish Law), has been
universally accepted as the
basis for modern Jewish law.

חייב אדם לקרות המגילה בלילה ולחזור ולשנותה ביום. ושל לילה,
זמנה כל הלילה; ושל יום, זמנה כל היום מהנץ החמה עד סוף היום.

One is obligated to read the Megillah at night and return and repeat it during the day. It can be read all night, while the day reading is all day, from sunrise until the end of the day. If one read it from daybreak, he has fulfilled his obligation.

TEXT 2B

Ibid. 694:1–3

חייב כל אדם ליתן לפחות שתי מתנות לשני עניים...
אין משנין מעות פורים לצדקה אחרת...
אין מדקדקים במעות פורים אלא כל מי שפושט ידו ליטול
נותנים לו.

One must give at least two gifts to two poor people. . . .

[Those entrusted with] monies donated in honor of Purim may not transfer toward a different charitable cause.

One ought not to be discerning with Purim money; rather, whoever stretches out his hand to ask should be given.

TEXT 2C

Ibid. 695:1–2

הגה: מצוה להרבות בסעודת פורים ובסעודה אחת יוצאים. סעודת פורים שעשאה בלילה לא יצא ידי חובתו. הגה: ומכל מקום גם בלילה ישמח וירבה קצת בסעודה.

One should add a festive meal on Purim; this obligation is met with one meal. Making a Purim meal at night does not fulfill this obligation. Nevertheless, one should be happy and add more during his meal even at night.

TEXT 2D

Ibid. 695:4

חייב לשלוח לחבירו שתי מנות בשר או של מיני אוכלים, שנאמר: "ומשלוח מנות איש לרעהו", שתי מנות לאיש אחד. וכל המרבה לשלוח לריעים משובח.

One must send to his fellow two portions of meat or foodstuffs, as the verse states, "And of sending portions to one another." Two portions to one man [is the obligation]. And anyone who sends more to his fellows is praiseworthy.

Mikra Megillah—*Reading the* Megillah

TEXT 3

Maimonides, Mishneh Torah, Laws of Megilah *and Chanukah, 3:6*

Rabbi Moshe ben Maimon (Maimonides, Rambam) 1135–1204

Halachist, philosopher, author, and physician. Maimonides was born in Córdoba, Spain. After the conquest of Córdoba by the Almohads, he fled Spain and eventually settled in Cairo, Egypt. There, he became the leader of the Jewish community and served as court physician to the vizier of Egypt. He is most noted for authoring the *Mishneh Torah*, an encyclopedic arrangement of Jewish law, and for his philosophical work, *Guide for the Perplexed*. His rulings on Jewish law are integral to the formation of halachic consensus.

ולא הלל של חנוכה בלבד הוא שמדברי סופרים אלא קריאת ההלל לעולם מדברי סופרים בכל הימים שגומרין בהן את ההלל, ושמונה עשר יום בשנה מצוה לגמור בהן את ההלל, ואלו הן: שמונת ימי החג, ושמונת ימי חנוכה, וראשון של פסח ויום עצרת, אבל ראש השנה ויום הכפורים אין בהן הלל לפי שהן ימי תשובה ויראה ופחד לא ימי שמחה יתירה, ולא תקנו הלל בפורים שקריאת המגילה היא ההלל.

It is not the recitation of Hallel on Chanukah alone that is a Rabbinic ordinance, but rather, at all times—i.e., on all the days that the complete Hallel is recited, [the obligation to do so] is a Rabbinic ordinance.

There are eighteen days during the year when it is a mitzvah to recite the entire Hallel. They are: the eight days of Sukkot, the eight days of Chanukah, the first day of Pesach, and the holiday of Shavuot. Hallel is not recited on Rosh Hashanah and Yom Kippur, since they are days of repentance, awe, and fear, and are not days of extra celebration. The [sages] did not ordain the recitation of Hallel on Purim, because the reading of the Megillah [serves the purpose of Hallel].

Mishloach Manot—*Food Gifts*

TEXT 4

Rabbi Shlomo Alkabetz, Manot Halevi to Megilat Esther 9:16, 20

עוד הוסיפו הפרזים על בני שושן ומשלוח מנות וגו' כי זה רומז
כי הם באגודה אחת ובאהבה ואחוה היפך מה שאמר הצורר
מפוזר ומפורד...
כי הנוסף להם היה היה משלוח מנות ומתנות כי זה מורה שהם בלב
אחד ואחוה... ובענין המנות הסכים עמם כי על ידי מרעות ואחוה
נקהלו וניצולו לא בפירוד לבבות.

Rabbi Shlomo Alkabetz
ca. 1500–1580
Born in Salonica, Greece.
Kabbalist and poet; best
known for his composition of
the Shabbat hymn, *Lechah
Dodi*. He eventually moved
to Safed, Israel, where he
was accepted into the circle
of Rabbi Moshe Alshich,
Rabbi Yosef Caro, and
Rabbi Moshe Cordovero.

The village dwellers went further than the inhabitants of Shushan in [initiating the practice of] mishloach manot, *symbolizing that they had joined together, in love and fraternity—the opposite of their oppressor [Haman's] statement that they were "scattered and divided."* . . .

The added practices of mishloach manot *and* matanot le'evyonim *show that they were of one heart and in a state of brotherhood.* . . . *[Mordechai] assented [to the practice of* mishloach manot*] for it was through friendship and brotherhood that they were saved, and not through division.*

TEXT 5

Talmud Yerushalmi Tractate Nedarim, 9:4

Jerusalem Talmud
A commentary to the Mishnah, compiled during the fourth and fifth centuries. The Jerusalem Talmud predates its Babylonian counterpart by 100 years and is written in both Hebrew and Aramaic. While the Babylonian Talmud is the most authoritative source for Jewish law, the Jerusalem Talmud remains an invaluable source for the spiritual, intellectual, ethical, historical, and legal traditions of Judaism.

"ואהבת לרעך כמוך", אמר רבי עקיבא זה כלל גדול בתורה.

The verse states, "You should love your fellow as yourself." Rabbi Akiva said, "This is a basic principle of the Torah."

More of the Same

The Real Celebration

TEXT 6

Halachot Gedolot, End of Hilchot Megilah

ועדיף יומא דפוריא כיום שניתנה בו תורה.

The day of Purim is as great as the day on which the Torah was given.

An Offer They Couldn't Refuse

TEXT 7

Talmud Tractate Shabbat, 88a

Babylonian Talmud
A literary work of monumental proportions that draws upon the legal, spiritual, intellectual, ethical, and historical traditions of Judaism. The 37 tractates of the Babylonian Talmud contain the teachings of the Jewish sages from the period after the destruction of the 2nd Temple through the 5th century CE. It has served as the primary vehicle for the transmission of the Oral Law and the education of Jews over the centuries; it is the entry point for all subsequent legal, ethical, and theological Jewish scholarship.

ויתיצבו בתחתית ההר, אמר רב אבדימי בר חמא בר חסא: מלמד שכפה הקדוש ברוך הוא עליהם את ההר כגיגית, ואמר להם: אם אתם מקבלים התורה - מוטב, ואם לאו - שם תהא קבורתכם. אמר רב אחא בר יעקב: מכאן מודעא רבה לאורייתא. אמר רבא: אף על פי כן, הדור קבלוה בימי אחשורוש. דכתיב "קימו וקבלו היהודים"; קיימו מה שקיבלו כבה.

The verse states, "And they stood under the mount." Rabbi Abdimi ben Hama ben Hasa said: This teaches that the Holy One, blessed be He, overturned the mountain upon them like an [inverted] cask and said to them, "If you accept the Torah, all is well; if not, there shall be your burial."

Rabbi Acha ben Jacob observed: This furnishes a strong protest against the Torah.

Said Raba: Yet, even so, they reaccepted it in the days of Ahasuerus, for it is written, "[The Jews] confirmed and took upon them [etc.]"; [i.e.,] they confirmed what they had accepted long before.

TEXT 8

Tosafot, loc. cit.

כפה עליהן הר כגיגית: ואף על פי שכבר הקדימו נעשה לנשמע.

"He overturned the mountain upon them like an [inverted] cask." Why would this be necessary if the Jews already [accepted the Torah] by saying, "We will do and we will obey"?

Tosefot

A collection of French and German Talmudic commentaries written during the 12th and 13th centuries. Among the most famous authors of *Tosafot* are Rabbi Yaakov Tam, Rabbi Shimshon ben Avraham of Sens, and Rabbi Yitschak ("the Ri"). Printed in almost all editions of the Talmud, these commentaries are fundamental to basic Talmudic study.

Everlasting Love

TEXT 9

Rabbi Shneur Zalman of Liadi, Torah Or, Megilat Esther, 98d

לזה היה ענין שכפה עליהם הר כגיגית שהוא בחינת ימינו תחבקני דהיינו התגלות אהבה העליונה מלמעלה על ישראל... שאהבה זו תחבקני לכנסת ישראל ומקפת אותו מכל צד אפילו לבחינת אחוריים עד שאינו מניחו לפנות ממנו ומוכרח להיות עומד עמו פנים בפנים. דהיינו שעל ידי אהבה עליונה זו נתעורר גם כן האהבה בנשמות ישראל עד שבאו למעלה ומדרגה שהקדימו נעשה כו'... שעל ידי התגלות אור האהבה מלמעלה בחינת אהבתי אתכם על ידי זה מתעורר גם כן האהבה מלמטה למעלה והוא העלאת כנסת ישראל בכלות הנפש אליו יתברך...

וזהו ענין שכפה עליהם הר הוא בחינת אהבה עליונה שנקרא הר. כגיגית שהוא בחינת דבר המקיף סחור כל עלמין שעל ידי זה נתעורר בהם האהבה.

Rabbi Shneur Zalman of Liadi
(Alter Rebbe)
1745–1812

Chasidic rebbe, halachic authority, and founder of the Chabad movement. The Alter Rebbe was born in Liozna, Belarus, and was among the principal students of the Magid of Mezeritch. His numerous works include the *Tanya*, an early classic containing the fundamentals of Chabad Chasidism, and *Shulchan Aruch HaRav*, an expanded and reworked code of Jewish law.

This is why "[G-d] overturned the mountain upon them like a cask"; as in the verse, "His right hand embraces me," it implies a degree of expression of G-d's supernal love for the Jewish people. . . . This love "embraces" the collective Jewish people, [as when one hugs another person,] surrounding him from all sides, even the back, so that he cannot move away and is compelled to stand there, facing him.

In other words, because of G-d's supernal love, a love awakened within the souls of the Jewish people, uplifting them to the point where they would declare, "We will do [and we will obey]!" . . . Revealing this light of love from above—such as it says, "I loved you [said G-d]"—awakens a corresponding love from below to above; this is the elevation of the Jewish collective, the expiration of their souls toward Him. . . .

This is the meaning of "overturning of the mountain"; it suggests the supernal love, which is referred to as a "mountain." It is likened to a "cask," which suggests something that surrounds and overwhelms all worlds, a light so intense that it awakens a love within them.

TEXT 10

Talmud Tractate Shabbat, 88b

אמר רבי יהושע בן לוי: כל דיבור ודיבור שיצא מפי הקדוש ברוך
הוא יצתה נשמתן של ישראל, שנאמר נפשי יצאה בדברו. ומאחר
שמדיבור ראשון יצתה נשמתן, דיבור שני היאך קיבלו? - הוריד טל
שעתיד להחיות בו מתים, והחיה אותם.

*Rabbi Joshua ben Levi also said: At every word that
went forth from the mouth of the Holy One, blessed
be He, the souls of Israel departed, for it is said, "My
soul went forth when he spoke." If their souls departed
at the first word, how could they receive the second
word? G-d brought down the dew with which He will
resurrect the dead and revived them. . . .*

TEXT 11A

Rabbi Shneur Zalman of Liadi, Torah Or, Megilat Esther, 98d.

זהו ענין על כל דבור פרחה נשמתן. שעל ידי הדבור והגילוי מלמעלה
פרחה נשמתן בבחינת בטול לאור אין סוף ברוך הוא.

*This, then, is the meaning of the notion that, "At every
word . . . the souls of Israel departed": on account of
each commandment [spoken by G-d], and the atten-
dant revelation from above, their souls flew up in a
state of surrender [bitul] to the Ein Sof.*

TEXT 11B

Rabbi Shneur Zalman of Liadi, Torah Or, ibid.

וזהו פירוש מה שאמר רבותינו זכרונם לברכה מכאן מודעא רבא
לאורייתא. דהיינו שהתעוררות זו בלבם לקבלת התורה בבחינת
מסירת נפש ובטול עד שהקדימו נעשה לנשמע לא היה זה מצדם
בבחירה ורצון אשר מעצמם לבד אלא שעל ידי הגילוי מלמעלה
דבחינת אהבתי אתכם על ידי זה דוקא נתעורר בהם הרצון
והאהבה כו'.

*This, then, is the meaning of our sages' statement,
"This furnishes a strong protest against the Torah." In
other words, the feeling that stirred in their hearts to
accept the Torah with such sacrifice and surrender that
they declared, "We will do and we will obey," was not
entirely a result of their own choice and desire. Rather,
it was on account of the revelation of G-d's love from
on high that inspired their reciprocal love to Him.*

Going Crazy with the Divine

The Love Below

TEXT 11C

Rabbi Shneur Zalman of Liadi, Torah Or, 99b

ואם היו כופרים חס ושלום לא היו עושים להם כלום שהרי לא גזר
רק על היהודים. אך כולם כאחד לא עלה על דעתם מחשבת חוץ
חס ושלום ומסרו נפשם על אחדותו יתברך.

*Had they apostatized, G-d forbid, nothing would have
happened to them, for the decree only applied to Jews.
Nevertheless, not one of them even entertained an outside thought, G-d forbid, and instead sacrificed their
lives for G-d.*

TEXT 11D

Torah Or, ibid., 99a–b

ואף על פי כן הדר וקבלוה ברצון גמור בימי אחשורוש. שהיה
מסירת נפש בכל ישראל מעצמם שלא על ידי התעוררות מלמעלה
בתחלה על דרך גלוי בחינת וימינו תחבקני. דהא אז היה בחינת
הסתר פנים... ואם כן היה בחינת אתערותא דלתתא מצד עצמם
וזהו הדר וקבלוה ברצון גמור...
שבמתן תורה שהקדימו נעשה לנשמע ועל כל דבור פרחה נשמתם
שהוא בחינת בטול ומסירת נפש שלכך זכו למתן תורה התגלות
אלקות. וכך היה בימי אחשורוש הבטול הזה ביתר שאת כי במתן
תורה היה בטול זה מחמת כח האתערותא דלעילא שכפה עליהם
הר כו׳. וכמים הפנים כו׳. אבל בימי אחשורוש היה הבטול מצד
עצמם בחינת אתערותא דלתתא תחלה. ולכן גם ההמשכה שנמשך
על ידי זה הוא ממקום עליון יותר עד שהגילוי שבמתן תורה נקרא
רק החלו התחלה לגבי אור ההמשכה שנמשך להם בפורים שנקרא
וקבל שזהו הגמר וזהו וקבל היהודים כו׳.

*Notwithstanding all the challenges, the Jews accepted
[the Torah] completely willingly in the days of Ahasuerus; they performed a collective act of self-sacrifice,
on their own, totally unprompted by any supernal
initiation in the form of a "Divine embrace." After all,
it was a time of spiritual concealment . . . Therefore,
it was an organic, collective spiritual awakening from
below. This is the meaning of the [Talmudic state-
ment] that they then accepted [the Torah] completely
willingly. . . .*

At Matan Torah *[the Giving of the Torah on Mount
Sinai] they declared, "We will do and then we will*

obey," and their souls expired every time G-d spoke. *This indicates the state of self-nullification [bitul] and sacrifice they achieved, which made them worthy of the G-dly revelation that* Matan Torah *was.*

This same spiritual state of bitul *was achieved in the days of Ahasuerus, only to a greater degree: At* Matan Torah, *this state of* bitul *was initiated from above and then reciprocated by the Jewish people, while in the days of Ahasuerus this state of* bitul *came from* them, *on their own initiative. Therefore, the spiritual flow that resulted came from an even higher place, so much so that the revelation of* Matan Torah *was only the "beginning," relative to the spiritual light that came down on Purim, which is referred to as the [subsequent] and final "acceptance." This is the meaning of the verse, "And the Jews accepted. . . ."*

Service with a Smile

TEXT 12A

The Rebbe, Rabbi Menachem Mendel Schneerson,
Likutei Sichot, vol. 15, p. 365

Rabbi Menachem Mendel Schneerson
1902–1994

The towering Jewish leader of the 20th century, known as "the Lubavitcher Rebbe," or simply as "the Rebbe." Born in southern Ukraine, the Rebbe escaped Nazi-occupied Europe, arriving in the U.S. in June 1941. The Rebbe inspired and guided the revival of traditional Judaism after the European devastation, impacting virtually every Jewish community the world over. The Rebbe often emphasized that the performance of just one additional good deed could usher in the era of Mashiach. The Rebbe's scholarly talks and writings have been printed in more than 200 volumes.

דעם חילוק צווישן א מעשה וואס א מענטש טוט דורך כפיה ואונס,
און א מעשה וואס ער טוט ברצון ודעת: ווען דאס איז בעל כרחו
ובכפיה טוט ער דאס נאר אויף וויפל ער מוז און עס פאדערט זיך
(צו יוצא זיין ידי חובתו); מה שאין כן ווען ער טוט עס מיט אן
אייגענעם חפץ ורצון, באנוגנט ער זיך ניט מיט בלויז יוצא זיין ידי
חובתו, נאר ער איז זיך משתדל און זוכט צו מוסיף זיין ומהדר זיין
אין דער פעולה, מער ווי עס פאדערט זיך מצד דער פליכט וואס
ליגט אויף אים.

The difference between doing something under duress and doing something willingly and consciously is this:

When someone is being forced, he or she will only do as much as they have to do (to fulfill their obligation). However, when a person acts of their own volition and desire, they do not suffice with simply meeting their obligation; rather, they strive and search for ways to add and enhance the act, more than is demanded of them out of duty.

The Purim Difference

TEXT 12B

The Rebbe, Rabbi Menachem Mendel Schneerson, ibid., p. 366

און דאס דריקט זיך אויס אין דעם... דורך די מצוות קריאת המגילה,
משלוח מנות און מתנות לאביונים.

והביאור: פון איין זייט זיינען די דריי ענינים ניט קיין דברים חדשים
ממש, און לאידך, האבן זיי אין זיך א הוספה לגבי דעם ווי זיי זיינען
פאראן פון פריער: דער ענין המגילה איז ניט קיין חידוש... אף
על פי כן קומט דא צו די קריאה בלילה פון א מגילה מתוך הקלף
פרסומי ניסא וכו'.

משלוח מנות:... מצד מצות אהבת ישראל איז ניטא קיין חיוב אז
מ'דארף זוכן א אידן צו מקיים זין די מצוה פון "ואהבת לרעך כמוך".
דער חידוש אין דער מצוה פון "משלוח מנות איש לרעהו": משתדל
זיין זיך געפינען "רעהו" און דורך משלוח מנות צו ארויסברענגען
בפועל... דעם ואהבת לרעך כמוך.

מתנות לאביונים: דער ענין הצדקה איז א מצוה בכל השנה כולה;
אין פורים קומט צו דער יתרון, אז ס'איז ניט גענוג דאס וואס בשעת
ער טרעפט אן עני ער איז ער מקיים די מצוה... נאר ער דארף עס זוכן
און געפינען און—צוויי עניים און זיי געבן "מתנות".

This is expressed . . . through the mitzvot *of* mikra
Megilah, mishloach manot, *and* matanot le'evyonim.

*To explain: On the one hand, these three things aren't
entirely new, but on the other, they are each enhanced
in some way, relative to before:*

The concept of [reading the] Megillah isn't at all novel . . . nevertheless we have an additional public reading at nighttime, from a scroll of parchment, and so on.

Mishloach manot . . . [T]he mitzvah of ahavat Yisrael *does not mandate us to search for another to fulfill the commandment to "love your fellow as yourself." [However,] the mitzvah of "sending gifts from one person to his friend" is novel in that, in doing so, we work to find a "friend" and, by sending him a gift, we put "loving your fellow as yourself" into practice.*

Matanot le'evyonim: While the mitzvah of tzedakah *applies year-round, [the charity we perform] on Purim is superior in that it isn't enough to perform the mitzvah upon encountering a poor person. Rather, one must go seek out two poor people, and give them charity.*

TEXT 12C

Ibid.

און דאס איז מודגש אויך אין די ווערטער "קיימו מה שקבלו כבר":
דאס זיינען ענינים וואס "קבלו כבר"—וואס מ'איז אין זיי מחוייב
און מ'טוט זיי בלאו הכי; בפורים אבער קומט אין זיי צו דער ענין פון
"קיימו"—דער אויפטו פון קיום וחיזוק.

This is emphasized in the words [of the Talmud],
"They confirmed what they had accepted long before."
These are things that we "already accepted"—we are
already obligated in them and do them regardless. On
Purim, however, they receive added "confirmation":
they achieve a degree of validation and strength.

Going All Out

TEXT 13

Maimonides, Mishneh Torah, Laws of Megillah and Chanukah, 2:15

כיצד חובת סעודה זו שיאכל בשר ויתקן סעודה נאה כפי אשר
תמצא ידו, ושותה יין עד שישתכר וירדם בשכרות.

What is the nature of our obligation for this feast? A
person should eat meat and prepare as attractive a
feast as his means permit. He should drink wine until
he becomes intoxicated and falls asleep in a stupor.

TEXT 14

Maimonides, ibid., 2:17

מוטב לאדם להרבות במתנות אביונים מלהרבות בסעודתו ובשלוח
מנות לרעיו, שאין שם שמחה גדולה ומפוארה אלא לשמח לב
עניים ויתומים ואלמנות וגרים, שהמשמח לב האמללים האלו
דומה לשכינה שנאמר להחיות רוח שפלים ולהחיות לב נדכאים.

*It is preferable for a person to be more liberal with his
donations to the poor than to be lavish in his preparation of the Purim feast or in sending portions to his
friends. For there is no greater and more splendid
happiness than to gladden the hearts of the poor, the
orphans, the widows, and the converts.*

*One who brings happiness to the hearts of these un-
fortunate individuals resembles the Divine Presence,
which the verse describes as having the tendency "to
revive the spirit of the lowly and to revive those with
broken hearts."*

12

SHEMINI

The Day Aaron Argued with Moses

Sorry, You Were Never Meant to Be Perfect

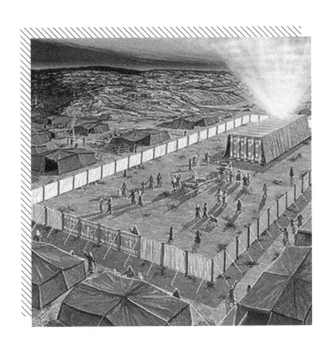

Dedicated to **Roberto** and **Margie Szerer** in appreciation of their friendship and partnership with JLI and their dedication to bringing the light of Torah to communities across the globe.

PARSHA OVERVIEW
Shemini

On the eighth day, following the seven days of their inauguration, Aaron and his sons begin to officiate as kohanim (priests); a fire issues forth from G-d to consume the offerings on the altar, and the Divine Presence comes to dwell in the Sanctuary.

Aaron's two elder sons, Nadav and Avihu, offer a "strange fire before G-d, which He commanded them not," and die before G-d. Aaron is silent in the face of his tragedy. Moses and Aaron subsequently disagree as to a point of law regarding the offerings, but Moses concedes to Aaron that Aaron is in the right.

G-d commands the kosher laws, identifying the animal species permissible and forbidden for consumption. Land animals may be eaten only if they have split hooves and also chew their cud; fish must have fins and scales; a list of nonkosher birds is given, and a list of kosher insects (four types of locusts).

Also in Shemini are some of the laws of ritual purity, including the purifying power of the mikveh (a pool of water meeting specified qualifications) and the wellspring. Thus the people of Israel are enjoined to "differentiate between the impure and the pure."

Between Moses and Aaron

The Story

TEXT 1A

Vayikra (Leviticus) 10:16–17

וְאֵת שְׂעִיר הַחַטָּאת דָּרֹשׁ דָּרַשׁ מֹשֶׁה וְהִנֵּה שֹׂרָף וַיִּקְצֹף עַל אֶלְעָזָר
וְעַל אִיתָמָר בְּנֵי אַהֲרֹן הַנּוֹתָרִם לֵאמֹר:
מַדּוּעַ לֹא אֲכַלְתֶּם אֶת הַחַטָּאת בִּמְקוֹם הַקֹּדֶשׁ כִּי קֹדֶשׁ קָדָשִׁים הוּא
וְאֹתָהּ נָתַן לָכֶם לָשֵׂאת אֶת עֲוֹן הָעֵדָה לְכַפֵּר עֲלֵיהֶם לִפְנֵי ה':

And Moses thoroughly investigated concerning the sin offering goat, and, behold, it had been burnt! So he was angry with Elazar and Itamar, Aaron's surviving sons, saying:

"Why did you not eat the sin offering in the holy place? For it is Holy of Holies, and He has given it to you to gain forgiveness for the sin of the community, to effect their atonement before G-d!"

TEXT 1B

Rashi, ad loc.

Rabbi Shlomo Yitzchaki
(Rashi)
1040–1105
Most noted biblical and
Talmudic commentator.
Born in Troyes, France,
Rashi studied in the famed
yeshivot of Mainz and
Worms. His commentaries
on the Pentateuch and
the Talmud, which focus
on the straightforward
meaning of the text, appear
in virtually every edition
of the Talmud and Bible.

"שעיר החטאת". שעיר מוספי ראש חודש. ושלשה שעירי חטאות
קרבו בו ביום שעיר עזים, ושעיר נחשון ושעיר ראש חודש, ומכולן
לא נשרף אלא זה. ונחלקו בדבר חכמי ישראל יש אומרים, מפני
הטומאה שנגעה בו נשרף. ויש אומרים, מפני אנינות נשרף, לפי
שהוא קדשי דורות, אבל בקדשי שעה סמכו על משה שאמר להם
במנחה "ואכלוה מצות".

*"The sin-offering goat": The goat of the additional
offerings of Rosh Chodesh. On that day of Rosh Chodesh Nisan, three sin-offering goats were sacrificed:
a) "[Take] a goat [as a sin-offering]"; b) the goat of
Nahshon [the son of Amminadab, leader of the tribe
of Judah]; and c) the goat [of the additional offering]
of Rosh Chodesh.*

*Now, of all of these, the only one burnt was this one
[the additional offering of Rosh Chodesh. And why
did they burn it?] The sages of Israel are divided on
the matter. Some said that it was burnt on account of
[the] uncleanness that had come into contact with it,
[while] others said that it was burnt because [Aaron's
sons were] onenim, because this [sacrifice came under
the category of] holy [sacrifices] that would also be
sacrificed in [future] generations. [Thus they deemed it
fit for burning, as the law would require for future generations.] However, when it came to holy [sacrifices]*

that were [brought] only at that time [like the other two goat offerings], they relied on Moses, who had said to them regarding the meal-offering, "Eat it as unleavened loaves" [even though they were onenim, assuming that since that meal-offering was exclusive to this day, so must Moses's command apply to all holy sacrifices exclusive to this day].

TEXT 2A

Vayikra (Leviticus) 10:19

וַיְדַבֵּר אַהֲרֹן אֶל מֹשֶׁה הֵן הַיּוֹם הִקְרִיבוּ אֶת חַטָּאתָם וְאֶת עֹלָתָם לִפְנֵי ה' וַתִּקְרֶאנָה אֹתִי כָּאֵלֶּה וְאָכַלְתִּי חַטָּאת הַיּוֹם הַיִּיטַב בְּעֵינֵי ה':

And Aaron spoke to Moses, "But today, did they offer up their sin offering and their burnt offering before the L-rd? But [if tragic events] like these had befallen me, and if I had eaten a sin offering today, would it have pleased G-d?"

TEXT 2B

Rashi, ad loc.

רש״י: הייטב בעיני ה': אם שמעת בקדשי שעה אין לך להקל
בקדשי דורות:

"Would it have pleased G-d?": If you heard this special law that an onen *may eat holy sacrifices brought exclusively for a special occasion, you have no right to be lenient regarding holy sacrifices offered for [future] generations [like the sacrifice on Rosh Chodesh].*

Truth vs. Peace

The Roles of Moses and Aaron

TEXT 3

Zohar, vol. 2, p. 49b

Zohar

The seminal work of kabbalah, Jewish mysticism. The *Zohar* is a mystical commentary on the Torah, written in Aramaic and Hebrew. According to the Arizal, the *Zohar* contains the teachings of Rabbi Shimon bar Yochai, who lived in the Land of Israel during the 2nd century. The *Zohar* has become one of the indispensable texts of traditional Judaism, alongside and nearly equal in stature to the Mishnah and Talmud.

כתיב, "ויקח אהרן את אלישבע בת עמינדב", ורזא הוא על כנסת ישראל, דאהרן הוא שושבינא דילה, לתקנא ביתה, ולשמשא לה, ולמיעל לה למלכא לאזדווגא כחדא, מכאן ולהלאה כל כהן דמשמש במקדשא כגוונא דאהרן.

The verse states, "And Aaron married Elisheva, the daughter of Amminadab." The secret meaning of this verse refers to the community of Israel: Aaron is her shushvina, *to put her house in order and to serve her, to escort her to the King to unify them as one. From here onward, any* kohen *that serves in the Temple is similar to Aaron.*

TEXT 4

Zohar, vol. 3, p. 20a

שבעין סנהדרי גדולה היו, ומשה עלייהו, ושבעים סנהדרי קטנה
הוו ואהרן עלייהו, ובגין דא אמרו מארי מתניתין, משה שושבינא
דמלכא הוה, ודא תפארת, מתמן סנהדרי גדולה, אהרן שושבינא
דמטרוניתא, ודא מלכות, הא, זעירא קרינן לה, כגון "אעבדך שבע
שנים ברחל בתך הקטנה", ועל שמה אתקרי סנהדרי קטנה.

There were seventy great Sanhendrins, and Moses pre-sides over them. There were seventy lesser Sanhedrins, and Aaron presides over them. Because of this, the rabbis of the Mishnah said: Moses is the shushvina of the King, which is Tiferet, called the great Sanhedrin. Aaron is the shushvina of the queen, which is Malchut: the letter hei, which is called small . . . and therefore it is called the lesser Sanhendrin.

TEXT 5

Rabbi Shneur Zalman of Liadi, Likutei Torah, Bamidbar 2d

Rabbi Shneur Zalman of Liadi
(Alter Rebbe)
1745–1812

Chasidic rebbe, halachic authority, and founder of the Chabad movement. The Alter Rebbe was born in Liozna, Belarus, and was among the principal students of the Magid of Mezeritch. His numerous works include the *Tanya*, an early classic containing the fundamentals of Chabad Chasidism, and *Shulchan Aruch HaRav*, an expanded and reworked code of Jewish law.

והנה ב' בחינות אלו שהם מדבר סיני ואוהל מועד הם נעשים ונמשכים על ידי בחינת משה ואהרן כי משה שושבינא דמלכא פירוש כמו על דרך משל שושבינו של החתן שמוליך את החתן למקום הכלה, כך משה רבינו עליו השלום הוא הממשיך בחי' יחוד אור אין סוף ברוך הוא למטה שיהא שורה ומתגלה בנפש האדם שיהיה בבחינת אוהל מועד כו'. ואתפשטותא דמשה בכל דרא שהוא משבעה רועים כו' הוא בחינת משה דעת ה' דהיינו לידע את ה' שהוא חיי החיים ואין עוד מלבדו כו'...

ובבחינת דעת אינה הידיעה לבדה אלא דעת מלשון הרגשה שהיא ההרגשה בלב שיכיר וירגיש כאלו רואה לעיני בשר בראיה חושיית ממש וכמו שכתוב "ראו עתה כי אני הוא ואין אלקים עמדי". והגם שמקרא זה נאמר על לעתיד שאז יאמרו ראו עתה כי אני כו' כנ"ל, מכל מקום כח זה יש בכל נפש ונשמה מישראל ביניקתה מנשמת משה רבינו עליו השלום לקשר מחשבתו בה' בקשר אמיץ וחזק כמו שהיא מקושרת בדבר גשמי שרואה בעיני בשר כו' אלא שצריכה ליגיעה רבה כו'...

ואהרן שושבינא דמטרוניתא, פירוש מטרוניתא היא בחינת כנסת ישראל מקור נשמות ישראל ולהעלות נשמות ישראל ולקשרם בה' ולדבקה בו ית' חיי החיים ברוך הוא הוא על ידי אהרן שהוא גם כן משבעה רועים כו' הממשיך לכללות נשמות ישראל להיות התפעלות הנפש בחינת מדבר וצמאון ורשפי אש כו' כי עבודת אהרן הוא בהעלותך את הנרות. פירוש הנרות הם הנשמות כי נר ה' נשמת אדם ועל ידי אהרן היתה הדלקתם והתלהבותם כרשפי שלהבת כו'.

The two elements of the Sinai Desert and the Sanctuary are influenced by "Moses" and "Aaron" since Moses is the shushvina *of the King. Just as the* shushvina *escorts the groom to the place of the bride, so does Moses draw down G-d's unity, so that it may rest upon and become manifest in the soul of man, which is the element of Sanctuary. And there is an extension of Moses in each generation, since Moses is one of the "seven shepherds," representing the function of knowing G-d, Who enlivens all life, and there is none else aside from Him. . . .*

Daat *is not merely knowing; it actually means feeling: a feeling in the heart, that one recognizes and feels as if he sees clearly with his eyes. As it is stated, "See now that I, I am Him, there is no god aside from Me." Although this verse speaks of the messianic era, nevertheless, this ability exists in each and every Jewish soul, on account of the sustenance it receives from the soul of Moses, namely, to firmly bind his thoughts to G-d in the same manner that one is bound to a visible scene that is witnessed. But to be bound to G-d requires great effort. . . .*

Aaron is the shushvina *of the queen, which refers to the souls of the Jewish people. Aaron is the one who raises these souls to become bound with G-d, the source of life, for Aaron is one of the "seven shepherds," drawing down the ability for our souls to become aroused, which is the level of thirst and flames of passionate fire.*

Aaron's role is to lift up the flames, which are the souls of the Jewish people, for the candle of G-d is the soul of man. Aaron caused the flames to be kindled and to become a raging flame.

TEXT 6

Ethics of the Fathers, 1:12

Ethics of the Fathers
(Pirkei Avot)
A six-chapter work on Jewish ethics that is studied widely by Jewish communities, especially during the summer. The first five chapters are from the Mishnah, tractate Avot. Avot differs from the rest of the Mishnah in that it does not focus on legal subjects; it is a collection of the sages' wisdom on topics related to character development, ethics, healthy living, piety, and the study of Torah.

הלל אומר הוי מתלמידיו של אהרון אוהב שלום ורודף שלום אוהב את הבריות ומקרבן לתורה.

Hillel said: Be among the disciples of Aaron, loving peace and pursuing peace, loving the creations and drawing them near to the Torah.

TEXT 7

Midrash Shemot Rabah, 5:10

Shemot Rabah

An early rabbinic commentary on the Book of Exodus. Midrash is the designation of a particular genre of rabbinic literature usually forming a running commentary on specific books of the Bible. *Shemot Rabah*, written mostly in Hebrew, provides textual exegeses, expounds upon the biblical narrative, and develops and illustrates moral principles. It was first printed in Constantinople in 1512 together with 4 other Midrashic works on the other 4 books of the Pentateuch.

"ויאמר ה' אל אהרן, לך לקראת משה המדברה וילך ויפגשהו בהר
האלקים וישק לו" - וילך ויפגשהו הדא הוא דכתיב "חסד ואמת
נפגשו צדק ושלום נשקו" חסד זה אהרן שנאמר "וללוי אמר תומיך
ואוריך לאיש חסידך" ואמת זה משה שנאמר "לא כן עבדי משה וגו'"
הוי חסד ואמת נפגשו כמה דתימא "וילך ויפגשהו בהר האלקים".
צדק זה משה שנאמר "צדקת ה' עשה ושלום זה אהרן שנאמר
"בשלום ובמישור הלך אתי נשקו".

"And G-d said to Aaron, 'Go greet Moses in the desert'; and he went and encountered him at the mountain of G-d (Mount Sinai), and he went and he kissed him."

"And he went and he kissed him": This is the meaning of the verse (in Tehilim [Psalms]), "Kindness and truth encounter one another, justice and peace kiss." Kindness refers to Aaron, as it is stated, "And to Levi he said, 'Your urim and tumim to a man of peace." Truth refers to Moses, as it states "Not so Moses my servant; he is faithful throughout My house." Thus, kindness and peace encounter each other, as it says, "and he went and encountered him at the mountain of G-d."

Justice is Moses, as it states, "The justice of G-d he has done." Peace is Aaron, as it states, "In peace and in equity he went with me." And the two kiss.

TEXT 8

The Rebbe, Rabbi Menachem Mendel Schneerson,
Likutei Sichot, vol. 17, pp. 113–114

**Rabbi Menachem
Mendel Schneerson**
1902–1994

The towering Jewish leader
of the 20th century, known
as "the Lubavitcher Rebbe,"
or simply as "the Rebbe."
Born in southern Ukraine,
the Rebbe escaped Nazi-
occupied Europe, arriving
in the U.S. in June 1941. The
Rebbe inspired and guided
the revival of traditional
Judaism after the European
devastation, impacting
virtually every Jewish
community the world over.
The Rebbe often emphasized
that the performance of
just one additional good
deed could usher in the era
of Mashiach. The Rebbe's
scholarly talks and writings
have been printed in more
than 200 volumes.

און דעריבער איז נטית סברת משה, מדת האמת, אז בכל ענין וואס
עס איז דא א ספק - פסק'נען אז עס איז ניטא קיין שינוי פון איין
זמן און מעמד ומצב ביז א צווייטן; דעריבער בנידון דידו—האט ער
געהאלטן אז ס'איז ניטא קיין חילוק פון קדשי דורות און קדשי
שעה: די זעלבע קדושה וואס איז דא "בשעה" (זו), אין דעם זעלבן
אופן דארף זיין די קדושה ל"דורות".

מצד בחינת חסד אבעה, מדריגת אהרן, וואס זיין ענין איז געווען
"אוהב שלום ורודף שלום אוהב את הבריות ומקרבן לתורה", ער
האט זיך איבערגעגעבן צו אידן ביז צו אזעלכע וואס זיינען אין סוג
פון "בריות" און זיי משפיע געווען יעדן לויט זיין דרגא ומצב—
דערפאר האט ער געזען אז ס'איז דא א חילוק צווישן "קדשי שעה"
און "קדשי דורות": מצד המקבלים, די וואס דארפן אנקומען צום
(חסד, צום) קרבן וקדשים קען מען ניט מאנען אז די קדושה זאל
זיין אין דעם זעלבן אופן ותוקף אין אלע שינויי דרגות און זמנים...
מצד משה שושבינא דמלכא, (התעסקות—במלכא) ו"גדריו", וואס
איז ממשיך אלקות אין אידן מלמעלה למטה, ווערט דער אור נמשך
למטה אזוי ווי ער איז למעלה (אין אצילות) אן חילוקים—און אזוי
איז געווען אופן עבודתו למטה אין דער המשכת אלקות וואס ער
האט ממשיך געווען צו אידן.

מצד בחינת אהרן שושבינא דמטרוניתא (התעסקות—במטרוניתא)
ו"גדריה", וואס איז מעלה כנסת ישראל מלמטה למעלה, איז די
העלאה תלויה אין דעם מצב או מדריגה פון אידן, און דעריבער איז
אין דער עבודה דא שינויים לפי ערך המצב פון דעם מטה.

From Moses's perspective, whenever there is uncer-
tainty we choose to make no differentiation between

276 *Torah Studies* Season Two 5779

one situation and another. In this specific instance, Moses chose not to make a differentiation between the sacrifices of the day and the sacrifices that would last for all generations. The holiness that is felt at this moment must remain for all generations.

Aaron was different. Aaron reflected the kind view; Aaron was one who "loved all creation and drew them close to Torah." He was dedicated to all Jews, even those who are on the level of "creatures," no matter their status in life. Thus, from Aaron's perspective, he could see the distinction between the holiness of the moment and the holiness that would remain for generations. It is too much to demand that these people maintain a constant aura of great holiness throughout the vicissitudes of time. . . .

For Moses, the shushvina of the King, whose role was to draw down G-dliness from above to below, he transmitted the G-dly light in a manner that preserved it whole, without any degradation. This was the path that Moses took when dealing with bestowing G-dly energy upon the Jewish nation.

But for Aaron, the shushvina of the queen, whose role was to elevate the Jewish people from below to above, this elevation was dependent upon the state of the Jewish people. Accordingly, he understood that the service would also be subject to differences congruent to the fluctuation that exists in the human experience.

The Verdict

Moses's Concession

TEXT 9A

Vayikra (Leviticus) 10:20

וַיִּשְׁמַע מֹשֶׁה וַיִּיטַב בְּעֵינָיו:

And Moses heard, and it was good in his eyes.

TEXT 9B

Rashi, ad loc.

"וַיִּיטַב בעיניו". הודה ולא בוש לומר לא שמעתי.

"And it was good in his eyes": He admitted and was not ashamed to say, "I did not hear."

TEXT 10

Rabbi Shneur Zalman of Liadi, Tanya, ch. 13

והנה מדת אהבה זו האמורה בבינונים בשעת התפלה על ידי
התגברות הנפש האלהית כו' הנה לגבי מדרגת הצדיקים עובדי ה'
באמת לאמיתו אין בחינת אהבה זו נקראת בשם עבודת אמת כלל
מאחר שחולפת ועוברת אחר התפלה וכתיב שפת אמת תכון לעד
ועד ארגיעה לשון שקר.

ואף על פי כן לגבי מדרגת הבינונים נקראת עבודה תמה באמת
לאמיתו שלהם איש איש כפי מדרגתו במדרגת הבינונים והריני
קורא באהבתם שבתפלתם גם כן שפת אמת תכון לעד הואיל ובכח
נפשם האלהית לחזור ולעורר בחינת אהבה זו לעולם בהתגברותה
בשעת התפלה מדי יום ביום על ידי הכנה הראויה לכל נפש כפי
ערכה ומדרגתה כי הנה מדת אמת היא מדתו של יעקב הנקרא
בריח התיכון המבריח מן הקצה אל הקצה מרום המעלות ומדרגות
עד סוף כל דרגין ובכל מעלה ומדרגה מבריח תוך נקודה האמצעית
שהיא נקודת ובחינת מדת אמת שלה.

By virtue of the preponderance of the divine soul, the beinoni *is able to reach a state of love during prayer. However, in comparison with the degree of love reached by* tzadikim *who serve G-d in perfect truth, the* beinoni's *love is not called "true service" at all, since it passes and disappears after prayer. Something really true will live up to the words of the verse, "The lip of truth shall be established forever, but a lying tongue is but for a moment."*

Nevertheless, in relation to the rank of the "interme-diate" people, his love is regarded as a truly perfect service in terms of their [level of] truth, every beinoni according to their level. And yes, in this case, too, the beinoni's love during prayer may be termed as "the lip of truth shall be established forever" since their divine soul has the power to reawaken this kind of love constantly, during its preponderance in time of prayer day after day, by means of an appropriate [mental] preparation, each soul according to its intrinsic quality and rank. Truth is the attribute of Jacob, who is called the "middle bolt that secures [everything] from end to end," from the highest gradations and degrees to the end of all grades. And in each gradation and plane it fixes its bolt through the most central point, which is the point and quality of its attribute of truth.

TEXT 11

Rabbi Shalom Dovber Schneersohn, Sefer Hamaamarim 5672, ch. 129

Rabbi Shalom Dovber Schneersohn
(Rashab)
1860–1920

Chasidic rebbe. Rabbi Shalom Dovber became the 5th leader of the Chabad movement upon the passing of his father, Rabbi Shmuel of Lubavitch. He established the Lubavitch network of *yeshivot* called Tomchei Temimim. He authored many volumes of Chasidic discourses and is renowned for his lucid and thorough explanations of kabbalistic concepts.

אמצעית האצילות הוא בב' דברים, הא' שיהיה על ידי זה התהוות
העולמות בריאה יצירה עשיה בבחינת המציאות שלהם שזהו העיקר
על ידי הכלים וכמו שכתוב באגרת הקדש איהו וגרמוהי חד לברוא
כו', והב' שעל ידי האצילות דוקא יכול להיות גילוי אלקות בעולם,
והוא ענין ידיעות והשגות אלקות והרגישות אלקות שבעולם.

The spiritual world of atzilut *serves a dual purpose. First, it enables the creation of lower worlds such as* beriah, yetzirah, *and* asiyah. *These worlds are able to emanate forth from the vehicles that contain the energy of* atzilut, *as is discussed in* Igeret Hakodesh, *epistle 20. Atzilut's second role is to bring about a revelation of G-dliness in the world, namely, the ability to understand and to feel G-d in this world.*

TEXT 12

The Rebbe, Rabbi Menachem Mendel Schneerson,
Likutei Sichot, Vol. 16, p. 116

איז דער ביאור אין דעם: ס'איז ידוע אז דער תכלית ופנימיות
הכוונה פון עולם האצילות איז צוליב דער עבודה וגילוי אלקות
אין נבראים למטה. דאס הייסט אין אצילות איז דא צווי ענינים:
אצילות מצד עצמה, וואס איז העכער פון נבראים; מצד איר כוונה,
וואס עס הערט זיך ווי זי איז בשביל עולם העשיה.

To unpack this idea: The ultimate purpose of the world
of atzilut is to aid the human project to draw G-dliness
into this world. This means that atzilut contains two
components: as it exists for itself, beyond creation; and
as it is cognizant of its purpose, to lead to the actions
of this world.

13

TAZRIA

Compassionate Condemnation

Love, Love, and Love Some More. Then Criticize

*Dedicated to **Rachelle Nedow** in appreciation of her friendship and partnership with JLI and her dedication to bringing the light of Torah to communities across the globe.*

PARSHA OVERVIEW
Tazria

The parsha *of Tazria continues the discussion of the laws of* tumah v'taharah, *ritual impurity and purity.*

A woman giving birth should undergo a process of purification, which includes immersing in a mikveh *(a naturally gathered pool of water) and bringing offerings to the Holy Temple. All male infants are to be circumcised on the eighth day of life.*

Tzaraat (often mistranslated as "leprosy") is a supranatural plague, which can afflict people as well as garments or homes. If white or pink patches appear on a person's skin (dark pink or dark green in garments or homes), a kohen *is summoned. Judging by various signs, such as an increase in size of the afflicted area after a seven-day quarantine, the* kohen *pronounces it* tamei *(impure) or* tahor *(pure).*

A person afflicted with tzaraat must dwell alone outside of the camp (or city) until he is healed. The afflicted area in a garment or home must be removed; if the tzaraat recurs, the entire garment or home must be destroyed.

Introduction

The Leper

TEXT 1

Vayikra (Leviticus) 13:1–3

וַיְדַבֵּר ה' אֶל מֹשֶׁה וְאֶל אַהֲרֹן לֵאמֹר:
אָדָם כִּי יִהְיֶה בְעוֹר בְּשָׂרוֹ שְׂאֵת אוֹ סַפַּחַת אוֹ בַהֶרֶת וְהָיָה בְעוֹר בְּשָׂרוֹ
לְנֶגַע צָרָעַת וְהוּבָא אֶל אַהֲרֹן הַכֹּהֵן אוֹ אֶל אַחַד מִבָּנָיו הַכֹּהֲנִים:
וְרָאָה הַכֹּהֵן אֶת הַנֶּגַע בְּעוֹר הַבָּשָׂר וְשֵׂעָר בַּנֶּגַע הָפַךְ לָבָן וּמַרְאֵה הַנֶּגַע
עָמֹק מֵעוֹר בְּשָׂרוֹ נֶגַע צָרַעַת הוּא וְרָאָהוּ הַכֹּהֵן וְטִמֵּא אֹתוֹ:

And G-d spoke to Moses and Aaron, saying:

If a man has a se'eith, a sapahath, or a bahereth on the skin of his flesh, and it forms a lesion of tzaraat on the skin of his flesh, he shall be brought to Aaron the kohen, or to one of his sons, the kohanim.

The kohen shall look at the lesion on the skin of his flesh, and [if] hair in the lesion has turned white and the appearance of the lesion is deeper than the skin of his flesh, it is a lesion of tzaraat. When the kohen sees this, he shall pronounce him unclean.

TEXT 2

Vayikra (Leviticus) 13:45–46

וְהַצָּרוּעַ אֲשֶׁר בּוֹ הַנֶּגַע בְּגָדָיו יִהְיוּ פְרֻמִים וְרֹאשׁוֹ יִהְיֶה פָרוּעַ וְעַל
שָׂפָם יַעְטֶה וְטָמֵא טָמֵא יִקְרָא:
כָּל יְמֵי אֲשֶׁר הַנֶּגַע בּוֹ יִטְמָא טָמֵא הוּא בָּדָד יֵשֵׁב מִחוּץ לַמַּחֲנֶה מוֹשָׁבוֹ:

And the person with tzaraat, *in whom there is the lesion, his garments shall be torn, his head shall be unshorn, he shall cover himself down to his mustache and call out, "Unclean! Unclean!"*

All the days the lesion is upon him, he shall remain unclean. He is unclean; he shall dwell isolated; his dwelling shall be outside the camp.

TEXT 3

Maimonides, Mishneh Torah, Laws of Tzaraat, 9:1

Rabbi Moshe ben Maimon
(Maimonides, Rambam)
1135–1204

Halachist, philosopher, author, and physician. Maimonides was born in Córdoba, Spain. After the conquest of Córdoba by the Almohads, he fled Spain and eventually settled in Cairo, Egypt. There, he became the leader of the Jewish community and served as court physician to the vizier of Egypt. He is most noted for authoring the *Mishneh Torah*, an encyclopedic arrangement of Jewish law, and for his philosophical work, *Guide for the Perplexed*. His rulings on Jewish law are integral to the formation of halachic consensus.

הכל כשירין לראות את הנגעים...

אך על פי שהכל כשירין לראות נגעים, הטומאה והטהרה תלויה בכהן. כיצד, כהן שאינו יודע לראות, החכם רואהו ואומר לו אמור טמא והכהן אומר טמא אמור טהור והכהן אומר טהור הסגירו והוא מסגירו שנאמר "ועל פיהם יהיה כל ריב וכל נגע". ואפילו היה הכהן קטן או שוטה החכם אומר לו והוא מחליט או פוטר או סוגר... ומצורע שנרפא בין מתוך הסגר בין מתוך החלט אפילו אחר כמה שנים הרי זה בטומאתו עד שיאמר לו כהן טהור אתה.

Anyone is acceptable to inspect blemishes. . . .

Despite the fact that everyone is acceptable to assess *blemishes, the designation of a person as impure or pure [namely, declaring him pure or impure] is dependent on a priest.*

What is implied? If there is a priest who does not know how to assess blemishes, a sage should observe them and instruct him, "Say, 'You are impure,'" and the priest says, "You are impure"; "Say, 'You are pure,'" and the priest says, "You are pure." "Isolate him," and he isolates him. The pronouncement must be made by a priest, because the verse states, "Their statements will determine every quarrel and every blemish." Even if a priest is a minor or intellectually or emotionally incapable, the sage instructs him, and he declares the person definitively impure, releases him from the inspection process, or isolates him. . . .

When a person who contacted tzaraat is healed, either after isolation or after having been deemed definitively impure, he remains impure even for several years, until a priest tells him, "You are pure."

Inner Cause and Cure

TEXT 4

Talmud Tractate Arachin, 15b

Babylonian Talmud

A literary work of monumental proportions that draws upon the legal, spiritual, intellectual, ethical, and historical traditions of Judaism. The 37 tractates of the Babylonian Talmud contain the teachings of the Jewish sages from the period after the destruction of the 2nd Temple through the 5th century CE. It has served as the primary vehicle for the transmission of the Oral Law and the education of Jews over the centuries; it is the entry point for all subsequent legal, ethical, and theological Jewish scholarship.

אמר רבי יוסי בן זימרא כל המספר לשון הרע נגעים באים עליו שנאמר "מלשני בסתר רעהו אותו אצמית", וכתיב התם "לצמיתות", ומתרגמינן "לחלוטין". ותנן: אין בין מצורע מוסגר למצורע מוחלט אלא פריעה ופרימה.

אמר ריש לקיש מאי דכתיב "זאת תהיה תורת המצורע"? –זאת תהיה תורתו של מוציא שם רע.

Further did Rabbi Johanan say in the name of Rabbi Joseph ben Zimra: Anyone who bears evil tales will be visited by the plague of leprosy, as it is said, "He who slanders his neighbor in secret, him azmith [will I destroy]," and there it is written "letzmituth," which is translated as "permanently." We have learned in a Mishnah, "The leper that is held in limbo differs from the leper that is certified tamei [Heb. 'chalutin—permanent'] only in respect of unkempt hair and rent garments."

Reish Lakish said: What is the meaning of the verse, "This shall be the law of the leper?" [It means,] "This shall be the law for him who brings up an evil name."

TEXT 5

Ibid., 16b

מה נשתנה מצורע שאמרה תורה "בדד ישב מחוץ למחנה מושבו"?
הוא הבדיל בין איש לאשתו בין איש לרעהו [שעל לשון הרע באו
נגעים עליו. –רש"י] לפיכך אמרה תורה "בדד ישב וגו'".

Why is the leper treated different such that about him the Torah prescribes, "He shall dwell alone; without the camp shall his dwelling be"?

He separated a husband from his wife, a man from his neighbor; therefore, says the Torah, "He shall dwell alone."

TEXT 6

Ibid.

אמר רבי יהודה בן לוי מה נשתנה מצורע שאמרה תורה יביא שתי
ציפרים לטהרתו אמר הקדוש ברוך הוא הוא עושה מעשה פטיט
לפיכך אמרה תורה יביא קרבן פטיט.

Rabbi Judah ben Levi said: Wherein is the leper differ- ent that the Torah said, "Two living clean birds [he should bring] so that he may become pure again"? The Holy One, blessed be He, said, "He did the work of a babbler; therefore, let him offer a babbler as a sacrifice."

TEXT 7A

Rabbi Shlomo Ephraim Luntshits, Keli Yakar to Vayikra (Leviticus) 13:2

Rabbi Shlomo Ephraim ben Aharon of Luntshits
1550–1619

After studying in the yeshiva of the Maharshal, Rabbi Shlomo Ephraim gained a reputation as a distinguished preacher and scholar. He traveled far and wide to deliver his fiery sermons, which were collected and published. He is primarily known today for his work *Keli Yakar*, and for his commentary on the Pentateuch, which was subsequently printed in many editions of the Bible.

על כן ראתה עיני להעמיד כל פרטי המעשים הנעשים במצורע על יסוד ג' אלה והם לשון הרע, וגסות רוח, וחמדת הממון... לכך נאמר "אדם כי יהיה בעור בשרו שאת". אין שאת אלא גבוהה ומין צרעת זה בא על גסות הרוח המתנשא לכל לראש. "או ספחת", אין ספחת אלא טפילה כו' והוא בא על החומד קנין הממון שהוא טפל אל האדם מבחוץ ואינו מתעצם באדם כלל כשאר המעלות, וכן כתב הרמב"ם בח' פרקיו כי כל הקנינים כחכמה וגבורה ומעלת המדות כולם מתעצמים עם האדם ודבוקים בו חוץ מן העושר כי הוא נטפל אל האדם מבחוץ ואינו דבק עמו כלל. "או בהרת" היינו לבנות, מין זה בא על המספר לשון הרע ומלבין פני חבירו ועושה בו חברבורות לבנות כי אזיל סומקא ואתי חיורא כמו שכתוב "לא עתה יבוש יעקב ולא עתה פניו יחוורו".

ובדרך זה הכרת פניו ענתה בו כי תוכו רצוף אהבת הממון, או הגסות, או לספר בגנות חבירו, ונגע זה מוציא רעתו לחוץ לגלות רעתו בקהל ועל שם זה נקרא מצורע מוציא רע, כדרך שנאמר "וירא משה את העם כי פרוע הוא" ואמרו רבותינו זכרונם לברכה שלקו בצרעת כדא אומר "וראשו יהיה פרוע" והוא לשון גילוי שתתגלה ותראה רעתו לעין כל והיינו ענין הצרעת.

Therefore I have decided to explain the procedure of the metzora *on the basis of the three sins of* lashon hara, *haughtiness, and lust for wealth.*

Thus it states, "A person who will have in his skin a se'eith." Se'eith *implies a raised lesion, which comes as a result of haughtiness.*

"Or a sapahath," which implies a peripheral *lesion. This is a punishment for greed, for monetary posses- sions are* peripheral *to a person and do not become internalized like a character trait. As the Rambam writes, acquisitions of wisdom or strength become one with man, as opposed to wealth which always remains peripheral.*

"Or a bahereth," which implies a whitish color. This arrives on one who slanders others and embarrasses (pales) the face of another, causing white splotches to appear among other red splotches on the victim's face. . . .

In this fashion, his face betrays his sin of lusting after wealth, haughtiness, or telling slander. The lesion draws out his sin to reveal it to others. This is why one who is afflicted with tzaraat *is called a "metzora" (מצורע), which can be read as, "motzi ra (מוציא רע)—ex- tracting and exposing evil." The idea behind this is akin to what is stated [regarding the Jews after they sinned with the golden calf], "And Moses saw the nation was 'paruah,'" and our sages explain that they were stricken with* tzaraat, *as it is stated, "And his face will be 'paruah (uncovered),'" which implies revelation, namely that his evil deeds are cast out in the open.*

TEXT 7B

Ibid.

"והובא אל הכהן". אין טהרתו כי אם על ידי כהן יען כי כל מי אשר הוא מזרע אהרן נמצאו בו ג' מדות טובות הפכיים לאלו.

כי חטא הלשון גורם כל ריב וכל נגע ובין אחים יפריד על כן יבא אהרן שאחז במדת השלום וירפא לזה כי הוא היה אוהב שלום ורודף שלום.

וכן חטא גסות הרוח ראוי שיתוקן על ידו כי הוא היה עניו ביותר כמאמר רבותינו זכרונם לברכה גדול מה שכתוב במשה ואהרן ממה שכתוב באברהם דאילו באברהם כתיב "ואנכי עפר ואפר" ובמשה ואהרן כתיב "ונחנו מה".

וכן חטא חמדת הממון לא היה גם כן באהרן יען כי הכהנים לא היה להם חלק ונחלה בארץ ולא היה להם יותר ממה שזכו משלחן גבוה על כן היו שלמים במדת ההסתפקות ולא היו בכלל צרי העין אשר כל מגמת פניהם לאסוף ולכנוס.

על כן מן הראוי שכל ג' מיני צרעת אלו לא יטהרו כי אם על ידי כהן.

"And he shall be brought before the kohen." *The purification is executed by the* kohen, *for all of Aaron's seed possess the opposite of these three attributes.*

The sin of slander causes discord between brothers; therefore, Aaron, who exemplifies the attribute of peace, shall come and heal him, for he loved peace and pursued peace.

Similarly, it is appropriate that he be the one to correct haughtiness, for he was extremely humble, as our sages have stated, "Greater is said regarding Moses and Aaron than what is said regarding Abraham. For by Abraham the verse states, 'I am dust and ashes,' whereas regarding Moses and Aaron it is stated, 'And what are we?'"

Likewise, Aaron did not desire money, for the kohanim *did not have a portion in the land and did not partake of more than they were given from on high. Therefore they were content with their lot, and they didn't busy themselves with gathering and amassing.*

For these reasons, these three forms of tzaraat *ought to be purified by the* kohen. *Inasmuch as the* kohanim *represented these three positive qualities, they were uniquely qualified to heal the* metzora.

TEXT 8

Ethics of the Fathers, 1:12, With Commentary of Rabbi Ovadiah of Bartenura

Rabbi Ovadiah of Bartenura
c. 1445–1524

Scholar and author. Born in Italy, Rabbi Ovadiah is commonly known as "the Bartenura," after the city in which he held the rabbinate. Arriving in Jerusalem in 1488, he quickly became an effective leader of the oppressed Jewish community, especially focusing his energies on the influx of Sephardic Jews to Jerusalem following the Spanish expulsion. His highly-acclaimed commentary on the Mishnah appears in almost every printed edition.

הלל ושמאי קבלו מהם. הלל אומר, הוי מתלמידיו של אהרן, אוהב שלום ורודף שלום, אוהב את הבריות ומקרבן לתורה.

"הוי מתלמידיו של אהרן, אוהב שלום ורודף שלום". פירשו באבות דר' נתן כיצד היה אהרון אוהב שלום?

כשהיה רואה שני בני אדם מתקוטטים, היה הולך לכל אחד מהם שלא מדעת חברו, ואומר לו, ראה חברך איך הוא מתחרט ומכה את עצמו על שחטא לך, והוא אומר לי שאבוא אליך שתמחול לו, ומתוך כך, כשהיו פוגעים זה בזה היו מנשקים זה את זה.

וכיצד היה מקרב הבריות לתורה? כשהיה יודע באדם שעבר
עבירה, היה מתחבר עמו ומראה לו פנים צהובות, והיה אותו אדם
מתבייש ואומר, אילו היה יודע צדיק זה מעשיי הרעים כמה היה
מתרחק ממני, ומתוך כך היה חוזר למוטב. הוא שהנביא מעיד עליו
"ובמישור הלך אתי ורבים השיב מעוון".

*Hillel and Shammai received from them. Hillel would
say, "Be of the disciples of Aaron—a lover of peace,
a pursuer of peace, one who loves the creatures and
draws them close to the Torah."*

*Bartenura: "Be of the disciples of Aaron: love peace
and pursue peace." In* Avot DeRabbi Natan *it explains
how Aaron loved peace:*

*When Aaron would observe two people fighting, he
would approach each one individually (without the
other's knowledge) and would tell him, "See how your
friend is remorseful and reproaching himself for sin-
ning against you, and he has told me that he will come
to you to ask forgiveness." As a result, when the two
would meet they would embrace each other.*

*How did he bring the people closer to Torah? When
he would become aware of a sin committed, he would
befriend the person and show him a gracious coun-
tenance. That person would become embarrassed,
saying to himself, "If that righteous one knew of my
misdeeds, how far would he distance himself from
me!" As a result, he would return to a good path. As
the prophet testifies, "In the straight path he went with
me, and he returned many from sin."*

Rebuke with Love

TEXT 9A

Vayikra (Leviticus) 13:46

כָּל יְמֵי אֲשֶׁר הַנֶּגַע בּוֹ יִטְמָא טָמֵא הוּא בָּדָד יֵשֵׁב מִחוּץ לַמַּחֲנֶה מוֹשָׁבוֹ"

All the days the lesion is upon him, he shall remain unclean. He is unclean; he shall dwell isolated; his dwelling shall be outside the camp.

TEXT 9B

Rashi, ad loc.

"בדד ישב". שלא יהיו שאר טמאים יושבים עמו ואמרו רבותינו מה נשתנה משאר טמאים לישב בדד הואיל והוא הבדיל בלשון הרע בין איש לאשתו ובין איש לרעהו אף הוא יבדל.
"מחוץ למחנה". חוץ לשלש מחנות.

"He shall dwell isolated": Other unclean people shall not abide with him. Our sages said, "Why is he different from other unclean people, that he must remain isolated? Since, with his slander, he caused a separation [i.e., a rift] between man and wife or between man and his fellow, he, too, shall be separated.

"Outside the camp." Outside the three camps.

Rabbi Shlomo Yitzchaki (Rashi)
1040–1105
Most noted biblical and Talmudic commentator. Born in Troyes, France, Rashi studied in the famed *yeshivot* of Mainz and Worms. His commentaries on the Pentateuch and the Talmud, which focus on the straightforward meaning of the text, appear in virtually every edition of the Talmud and Bible.

TEXT 10

The Rebbe, Rabbi Menachem Mendel Schneerson,
Likutei Sichot, vol. 27, pp. 89–90

Rabbi Menachem
Mendel Schneerson
1902–1994

The towering Jewish leader
of the 20th century, known
as "the Lubavitcher Rebbe,"
or simply as "the Rebbe."
Born in southern Ukraine,
the Rebbe escaped Nazi-
occupied Europe, arriving
in the U.S. in June 1941. The
Rebbe inspired and guided
the revival of traditional
Judaism after the European
devastation, impacting
virtually every Jewish
community the world over.
The Rebbe often emphasized
that the performance of
just one additional good
deed could usher in the era
of Mashiach. The Rebbe's
scholarly talks and writings
have been printed in more
than 200 volumes.

און אויף דעם זאגט תורה, אז וער קען פסק'נען אויף א צווייטן
איד אז ער איז כאילו אויסגעשלאסן ח"ו פון מחנה דקדושה—
בלויז א כהן :

א כהן איז ענינו "לברך את עמו ישראל באהבה" א כהן איז דער
"איש החסד" וואס בענטשט אידן, און באהבה [כידוע'ה אז דאס
איז א תנאי עיקרי אין ברכת כהנים אז עס מוז זיין באהבה, און
אויב דאס פעלט חס ושלום ביים כהן המברך, איז עס פאר אים א
סכנה]—און טאקע מהאי טעמא וואס דער כהן איז "איש החסד"
פארלאזט זיך תורה נאר אויף אים צו ארויסגעבן אויף א אידן אזא
"פסק" פון "מחוץ למחנה מושבו"...

אוודאי און אוודאי מוז דער פסק פון כהן זיין מיוסד בלויז אויף
תורה וואס דערפאר, איז לכל לראש מון זיין די ראיית הנגע דורך א
חכם בחכמת התורה און "בקי בכל הנגעים כו'" (און דערצו נאך אזא
חכם, וואס האט דאס מקבל געווען מפי רבו);

ווען עס קומט אבער צום אראפטראגן דעם פסק דין בפועל, מוז
דאס זיין דורך דעם כהן איש החסד. ווארום דוקא ער פילט דעם
פולן חומר פון ארויסגעבן אזא פסק דין אויף א צווייטן אידן און
דערפאר וועט ער ניט שפארן קיין יגיעה און גוט חוקר ודורש זיין
ביים חכם, בנוגע דעם פסק דין התורה ומעורר אויף ושפטו העדה-
והצילו העדה.

און אז נאך זיין יגיעה וחקירה ודרישה איז דער כהן איש החסד
מחליט און זאגט "טמא", איז מען זיכער אז דאס איז דער פסק
דין אמיתי פון תורה: ולאידך איז מען בטוח אז דער כהן וועט זיך
ארייגלייגן אין דעם בכל יכלתו אז דערנאך זאל זיין טהרת המצורע.

Regarding this, the Torah says that a kohen *is uniquely qualified to rule that a fellow Jew must leave the holy camp.*

A kohen's *function is to bless the nation of Israel with love. A* kohen *is a man of kindness who blesses us* with love *[as it is known that a main component of the blessing is the love, and if that love is lacking there can be negative outcomes]. Because a* kohen *is a person of love, the Torah relies on* him *to issue a ruling to expel another Jew from the camp. . . .*

Of course, the ruling of the kohen *is founded only on the Torah—which is why an expert who is well versed in all of the forms of* tzaraat *is needed (having studied under another rabbi). However, when it comes to actually carrying out the ruling, it must be in the hands of the* kohen, *the person of love. Only he appreciates the full implications of what this means, and he will not spare any effort to reexamine the case in order to find an alternate ruling. . . .*

And if, when all is said and done, the kohen *declares him impure, we can be sure that this is the true ruling of the Torah. At the same time, we can be assured that the* kohen *will do everything in his power to later declare him pure once again.*

TEXT 11

Siddur Tehilat Hashem, Liturgy for the Priestly Blessing

Siddur Tehilat Hashem
One of the prayer books
that follow the tradition of
the Arizal, as established
by Rabbi Shneur Zalman of
Liadi. It was first published
in New York in 1945.

בָּרוּךְ אַתָּה ה' אֱלֹקֵינוּ מֶלֶךְ הָעוֹלָם אֲשֶׁר קִדְּשָׁנוּ בִּקְדֻשָּׁתוֹ שֶׁל אַהֲרֹן וְצִוָּנוּ לְבָרֵךְ אֶת עַמּוֹ יִשְׂרָאֵל בְּאַהֲבָה.

Blessed are you, G-d, King of the universe, who has sanctified us with the holiness of Aaron, and has commanded us to bless His people, Israel, with love.

TEXT 12

Shulchan Aruch HaRav, Orach Chayim, 128:19

**Rabbi Shneur
Zalman of Liadi**
(Alter Rebbe)
1745–1812
Chasidic rebbe, halachic
authority, and founder of
the Chabad movement. The
Alter Rebbe was born in
Liozna, Belarus, and was
among the principal students
of the Magid of Mezeritch.
His numerous works include
the *Tanya*, an early classic
containing the fundamentals
of Chabad Chasidism, and
Shulchan Aruch HaRav,
an expanded and reworked
code of Jewish law.

כהן השונא את הצבור או הצבור שונאים אותו סכנה היא לכהן אם ישא את כפיו (ולכן יצא מבית הכנסת) ועל זה תקנו בברכה לברך את עמו ישראל באהבה.

[In the case of] a kohen who hates the congregation, or a congregation who hates him—it is a danger for that kohen to raise his hands [in blessing] (therefore he should leave the synagogue). Regarding this matter, the sages instituted the blessing with the language of, "To bless his people, Israel, with love."

TEXT 13

Rabbi Shneur Zalman of Liadi, Tanya, Likutei Amarim, ch. 50

> והנה כל בחינת ומדרגות אהבה הנ"ל הן מסטרא דימינא ובחינת
> כהן איש חסד.

Now, all of these abovementioned levels of love stem from the right side, the level of the *kohen*, person of love *[emphasis added]*.

Conclusion

TEXT 14A

The Rebbe, Rabbi Menachem Mendel Schneerson,
Hayom Yom, entry for 22 Elul

> תורת החסידות דורשת, כי תחלה להוכחה צריכים להסיר את
> הצפרנים, ניט שטעכען זיך, כי בטופרהא אחידן, יעדער שטאך איז
> קליפה וסטרא אחרא.

Chasidic doctrine demands that before reproving another, one must pare his own "fingernails" in order not to gash the other. "The forces of evil seize by the fingernails"; every stab is kelipah *and* sitra achra.

Hayom Yom

In 1942, Rabbi Yosef Y. Schneerson, the 6th rebbe of Chabad, gave his son-in-law, the future Rebbe, the task of compiling an anthology of Chasidic aphorisms and customs arranged according to the days of the year. In describing the completed product, Rabbi Yosef Yitzchak wrote that it is "a book that is small in format but bursting with pearls and diamonds of the choicest quality."

TEXT 14B

Ibid., entry for 24 Tishrei

הוכחה זו בעת ההתוועדות היא רק על דברים ועניינים שאין בהם
משום הלבנת פנים ולא כלום, כמו שהי' מאז ומקדם, אשר איש
את רעהו הוכיחו באהבה ובחיבת גדולה.

*Any reproving that occurs at a farbrengen should only
be for such matters that will not cause any embarrass-
ment whatsoever. This is the way it has always been,
from the very beginning: a person would only reprove
another with love and deep affection.*

14

PESACH

A Stranger to Passover

Developing a Taste for the Divine

*Dedicated in honor of **Rabbi Ahrele Loschak**, Managing Editor of Torah Studies, in appreciation for his leadership, dedication, and commitment to bringing the Torah Studies series to communities across the globe*

OVERVIEW
Pesach

Passover is celebrated in the early spring, from the fifteenth through the twenty-second of the Hebrew month of Nisan. It commemorates the emancipation of the Israelites from slavery in ancient Egypt. And, by following the rituals of Passover, we have the ability to relive and experience the true freedom that our ancestors gained.

After many decades of slavery to the Egyptian pharaohs, during which time the Israelites were subjected to backbreaking labor and unbearable horrors, G-d saw the people's distress and sent Moses to Pharaoh with a message: "Send forth My people, so that they may serve Me." But despite numerous warnings, Pharaoh refused to heed G-d's command. G-d then sent upon Egypt ten devastating plagues, afflicting them and destroying everything from their livestock to their crops.

At the stroke of midnight of 15 Nisan in the year 2448 from Creation (1313 BCE), G-d visited the last of the ten plagues on the Egyptians, killing all their firstborn. While doing so, G-d spared the Children of Israel, "passing over" their homes—hence the name of the holiday. Pharaoh's resistance was broken, and he virtually chased his former slaves out of the land. The Israelites left in such a hurry, in fact, that the bread they baked as provisions for the way did not have time to rise. Six hundred thousand adult males, plus many more women and children, left Egypt on that day and began the trek to Mount Sinai and their birth as G-d's chosen people.

Brother Daniel
and the Paschal
Sacrifice

Barred from the Paschal Lamb

TEXT 1A

Shemot (Exodus) 12:43

וַיֹּאמֶר ה' אֶל מֹשֶׁה וְאַהֲרֹן זֹאת חֻקַּת הַפָּסַח כָּל בֶּן נֵכָר לֹא יֹאכַל בּוֹ:

G-d said to Moses and Aaron, "This is the statute of the Passover sacrifice: no estranged one may partake of it."

TEXT 1B

Rashi, ad loc.

Rabbi Shlomo Yitzchaki
(Rashi)
1040–1105
Most noted biblical and
Talmudic commentator.
Born in Troyes, France,
Rashi studied in the famed
yeshivot of Mainz and
Worms. His commentaries
on the Pentateuch and
the Talmud, which focus
on the straightforward
meaning of the text, appear
in virtually every edition
of the Talmud and Bible.

"כל בן נכר": שנתנכרו מעשיו לאביו שבשמים. ואחד נכרי ואחד
ישראל משומד במשמע.

*"No estranged one": Whose deeds have become es-
tranged from his Father in heaven. Both a gentile and
an Israelite apostate are meant.*

Sin of the Golden Calf

TEXT 2

Midrash Shemot Rabah, 19:3

Shemot Rabah
An early rabbinic commentary
on the Book of Exodus.
Midrash is the designation of
a particular genre of rabbinic
literature usually forming
a running commentary on
specific books of the Bible.
Shemot Rabah, written
mostly in Hebrew, provides
textual exegeses, expounds
upon the biblical narrative,
and develops and illustrates
moral principles. It was first
printed in Constantinople in
1512 together with four other
Midrashic works on the other
four books of the Pentateuch.

אמרו רבותינו ג' דברים עשה משה והסכימה דעתו לדעת המקום...
הג', דרש בחקת הפסח, כשעשו ישראל את העגל, אמר: ומה אם
הפסח לשעה במצרים אמר לי: כל בן נכר לא יאכל בו, ישראל עבדו
עבודה זרה יכולין הן לקבל את התורה? מיד וישבר אותם תחת ההר.

*Our sages said: Moses initiated three things to which
G-d agreed. . . . The third is with regard to the laws of
Passover. When the Jews sinned with the golden calf,
Moses said, "The Paschal lamb was only performed
once in Egypt, and yet G-d instructed me that no
foreigner may partake of it; how, then, can the Jews
who have just served idolatry receive the entire Torah?" Immediately, Moses went ahead and shattered
the tablets.*

Question—Why the Exclusion?

TEXT 3

Talmud Tractate Sanhedrin, 44a

Babylonian Talmud
A literary work of monumental proportions that draws upon the legal, spiritual, intellectual, ethical, and historical traditions of Judaism. The 37 tractates of the Babylonian Talmud contain the teachings of the Jewish sages from the period after the destruction of the Second Temple through the 5th century CE. It has served as the primary vehicle for the transmission of the Oral Law and the education of Jews over the centuries; it is the entry point for all subsequent legal, ethical, and theological Jewish scholarship.

אמר רבי אבא בר זבדא אף על פי שחטא ישראל הוא.

Rabbi Aba bar Zavda stated: Though one has sinned, they remain a Jew.

TEXT 4

Talmud Tractate Berachot, 51a

מי שאכל שום וריחו נודף יחזור ויאכל שום אחר כדי שיהא ריחו נודף.

A person who ate garlic and his breath smells, should he continue eating garlic so that his breath smells even worse?

TEXT 5

Sefer Hachinuch, Mitzvah 13

Sefer Hachinuch

A work on the biblical commandments. Four aspects of every mitzvah are discussed in this work: the definition of the mitzvah; ethical lessons that can be deduced from the mitzvah; basic laws pertaining to the observance of the mitzvah; and who is obligated to perform the mitzvah, and when. The work was composed in the 13th century by an anonymous author who refers to himself as "the Levite of Barcelona." It has been widely thought that this referred to Rabbi Aharon Halevi of Barcelona (Re'ah); however, this view has been contested.

ראוי שלא יאכל בו משומד, אחר שאנו עושין אותו לאות ולזכרון שבאנו באותו הזמן לחסות תחת כנפי השכינה ונכנסנו בברית התורה והאמונה, אין ראוי שנאכיל ממנו למי שהוא הפך מזה שיצא מן הכלל וכפר באמונה. ועל כיוצא בזה נאמר בתלמוד לפעמים סברא הוא, כלומר ואין צריך ראיה אחרת.

It is not appropriate that an apostate partake of this sacrifice: The Paschal lamb is offered as a sign to commemorate how we were taken under the wings of the holy Shechinah *then, and entered the covenant of Torah and faith. Thus, it is improper to feed it to someone who represents opposite ideals—a man who defected from the community and renounced his faith.*

Regarding such matters, the Talmud will sometimes state, "It's only rational"; namely, the matter doesn't require further support.

Dialect of Distance and Involvement

The Wicked Son vs. the Wise Son

TEXT 6

Haggadah for Passover

Passover *Haggadah*

The Passover *Haggadah* was compiled during the Talmudic era. It incorporates verses from the Torah and Talmudic exegesis to tell the story of the Exodus. The *Haggadah*, which also establishes the structure of the seder, has been printed in thousands of editions and has spawned thousands of commentaries, making it one of the most popular books in the history of literature.

חכם, מה הוא אומר - "מה העדות, והחוקים והמשפטים, אשר ציווה ה' אלוקינו, אתכם". ואף אתה אמור לו כהלכת הפסח, אין מפטירין אחר הפסח אפיקומן.

רשע, מה הוא אומר - "מה העבודה הזאת, לכם". "לכם", ולא לו. ולפי שהוציא את עצמו מן הכלל כפר בעיקר. ואף אתה הקהה את שיניו ואמור לו: "בעבור זה, עשה ה' לי, בצאתי, ממצרים"-"לי", ולא לו; אילו היה שם, לא היה נגאל.

The wise one, what does he say? "What are the testimonies, the statutes, and the laws which the L-rd, our G-d, has commanded you?" You, in turn, shall instruct him in the laws of Passover, [until the law that] one is not to eat any dessert after the Paschal lamb.

The wicked one, what does he say? "What is this service to you?!" He says, "to you," but not to him! By thus excluding himself from the community, he has denied that which is fundamental. You, therefore, blunt his teeth and say to him: "Because of this, the L-rd did [this] for me when I went out of Egypt"; "for me"—but not for him! If he had been there, he would not have been redeemed!

TEXT 7A

Shemot (Exodus) 13:8

וְהִגַּדְתָּ לְבִנְךָ בַּיּוֹם הַהוּא לֵאמֹר בַּעֲבוּר זֶה עָשָׂה ה' לִי בְּצֵאתִי מִמִּצְרָיִם:

And you shall tell your son on that day, saying, "Because of this, the L-rd did [this] for me when I went out of Egypt."

TEXT 7B

Rashi, ad loc.

"בעבור זה". בעבור שאקיים מצותיו, כגון פסח מצה ומרור הללו.
"עשה ה' לי". רמז תשובה לבן רשע לומר, עשה ה' לי ולא לך, שאלו
היית שם לא היית כדאי ליגאל.

"Because of this." In order that I fulfill His commandments, such as the Passover sacrifice, matzah, and
bitter herbs.

"The L-rd did this for me." This alludes to the reply
given to the wicked son, to say, "The L-rd did this for
me," but not for you. Had you been there, you would
not have been worthy of being redeemed.

TEXT 8

Rabbi Yomtov Asevilli, Commentary of the Ritva to the Haggadah

Rabbi Yomtov Asevilli
(Ritva)
c. 1250–1330
Spanish rabbi and Talmudist.
Ritva was born in Seville.
He is mostly known for his
Talmudic commentary, which
is extremely clear, and,
to this day, remains most
frequently quoted and used.

אף אתה הקהה את שיניו הרוצה ללעוס ולאכול בהם ואמור לו
בעבור זה עשה ה' לי בצאתי ממצרים לי ולא לו.

"You shall blunt his teeth": He wishes to chew and eat
with his teeth, so tell him, "It is because of this that G-d
did this for me when I went out of Egypt"—for me but
not for you.

Appreciating the Taste of G-dliness

TEXT 9

Rabbi Mordechai Yosef of Izbitz, Mei Shiloach, Parshat Bo, p. 26

Rabbi Mordechai Yosef Leiner of Ishbitze
1801–1854
Born in Tomashov, Poland, Rabbi Leiner was a disciple of Rabbis Simchah Bunim of Peshischa and Menachem Mendel of Kotzk. He eventually moved to Ishbitze, where he founded his own Chasidic court. He authored *Mei Shiloach*, considered a groundbreaking work in Chasidic thought, and is popular in many communities to this day.

מי שהוא נכרי מדברי תורה לא יבין ולא ירגיש הטעם. כי באמת טעם הפסח היא, שהאדם ירגיש טעם צאתו לחירות, וירגיש שטוב יותר משהיה נכנע תחת שעבוד ועול טובות עולם הזה, כי במצרים היה עיקר השעבוד כדאיתא שאין עבד היה יכול לברוח ממצרים, לפי שהיתה משופעת בחמדות עולם הזה, כמו שנאמר "כגן ה' כארץ מצרים, והיה נוח לו להיות עבד במצרים מלהיות שר בארץ אחרת.

והוציאנו השם יתברך ממצרים שנקבל עלינו עול תורה ומצות, ואז מבין האדם שכל אלו החמדות המה הבלים ואין בהם שורש חיים כלל. אבל מי שהוא נכרי מדברי תורה אינו מבין טובת יציאת מצרים, אף שעל הגוון יקיים גם כן מצות הפסח, לא ירגיש בו טעם כלל, למשל מי שיש לו בן משכיל וטוב וכששומע אביו שמהללים אותו אז יתענג מאוד, אבל איש נכרי אין לו שום תענוג מזה, וזה כל בן נכר לא יאכל בו.

Someone who is a "stranger" to the words of Torah will not understand or feel the "taste/reason." For, in truth, the reason for the Paschal lamb is that one should feel the taste of freedom, freedom from being enslaved to worldly pleasures. Egypt was the epitome of hedonistic desires, as the Mechilta states, "No slave was able to escape from Egypt." This was because they were under the influence of its materialistic pleasures.

(It was more desirable to be a slave in Egypt than a nobleman in another country.)

G-d took us out of Egypt so that we may accept the yoke of Torah and mitzvot. For then a person can appreciate that all physical pleasures are empty and fleeting without any vitality.

One who is a stranger to the Torah, however, can't comprehend the goodness of the Exodus from Egypt. Superficially, he too may be keeping the mitzvah of the Passover [sacrifice], but he won't feel its taste at all.

This is the reason for "no stranger may eat from it."

Don't Be a Stranger

Taste It, for It Is Good!

TEXT 10

The Rebbe, Rabbi Menachem Mendel Schneerson,
Torat Menachem, vol. 9 (5713, vol. 3), p. 65–66

פעם אחת הגיע אדמו"ר הזקן לשקלאָב, בתקופה שבה סבלו
החסידים רבות מרדיפותיהם של המתנגדים, וכאשר עלה על
בימת בית-הכנסת כדי להשיב על הטענות והשאלות שהכינו עבורו,
אמר תורה קצרה – כפי שנהג בתקופה ההיא לומר תורות קצרות,
וכדרכו—בניגון: "טעמו וראו כי טוב הוי', פאַרזוכט און זעהט אַז
דער אויבערשטער איז גוט"...
וכשירד מהבימה, רצו אחריו כמה מנינים של אברכים, אשר במשך
הזמן נעשו מעמודי החסידות!

Rabbi Menachem Mendel Schneerson
1902–1994
The towering Jewish leader of the 20th century, known as "the Lubavitcher Rebbe," or simply as "the Rebbe." Born in southern Ukraine, the Rebbe escaped Nazi-occupied Europe, arriving in the U.S. in June 1941. The Rebbe inspired and guided the revival of traditional Judaism after the European devastation, impacting virtually every Jewish community the world over. The Rebbe often emphasized that the performance of just one additional good deed could usher in the era of Mashiach. The Rebbe's scholarly talks and writings have been printed in more than 200 volumes.

The Alter Rebbe one time arrived in the city of Shklov, during the period when the Chasidim were suffering tremendously at the hands of the mitnagdim. *When the Rebbe walked up to the* bimah *to respond to all of the questions that had been prepared for him, he said a short "Torah"—as was his custom then to deliver short ideas—in his trademark singsong: The verse states, "Taste and see that G-d is good!" [The Rebbe proceeded to sing the Yiddish translation of these words,] "Varzucht veht ir zehn az der Aibishter iz gut!" . . .*

When he alighted from the bimah, *tens of young schol-ars followed after him and eventually became some of the founding members of his Chasidim!*

TEXT 11

The Rebbe, Rabbi Menachem Mendel Schneerson,
Torat Menachem 5742, vol. 2, p. 992

דברתי פעם עם יהודי אודות ענין זה, ובראותי שהדברים הנ"ל
אינם פועלים עליו כל כך—לא היתה לי ברירה אלא להביא דוגמא
פשוטה ביותר:

עסקו של יהודי הנ"ל היה—ליטוש יהלומים. וכאשר שאלתי אותו
כיצד קובעים את ערכם (המחיר והיוקר) של "יהלומים", אמר לי,
שהדבר נקבע בהתחשב עם האיכות והכמות של ה"יהלומים":
"איכות"—מראה ויופי האבן, גוונה, העדר הפגימה וכו', ו"כמות" -
משקל האבן, היינו, יהלום שמשקלו ו"קאראט" אחד מחירו כך וכך,
ויהלום שמשקלו מאה "קאראט", מחירו מאה פעמים ככה.

שאלתי אותו: הרי כאשר מדובר אודות יהלום שמשקלו מאה
"קאראט" צריכים להתייגע בנשיאת ה"יהלום" מאה פעמים ככה
מאשר היגיעה בנשיאת אבן שמשקלה "קאראט" אחד בלבד—
ואם כן, מדוע מחירה רב כל כך?!

(כ"ק אדמו"ר שליט"א חייך, ואמר:) כאשר יהודי הנ"ל שמע את
השאלה, אמר לי: "בטלנות" כזו לא ציפיתי לראות אפילו אצלכם
("אויף אזא א "בטלנות" האב איך זיך ניט גערעכט אפילו בא אייך"):
הלוואי שיתנו לי "יהלומים" לא רק במשקל של מאה "קאראט",
אלא במשקל של אלף "קאראט", מאה אלף "קאראט", ועוד יותר,
עד שאין הפה יכול לספור, ומקבל אני על עצמי את כל הטורח
והיגיעה שבנשיאת משא זה לד' אמותי!

והמשכתי לשאול ולהקשות: הרי צריכים להתייגע ולהזיע כדי לשאת משא כבד כזה?!

וענה לי שוב: יש גבול ל"בטלנות" ("וויפל איז א שיעור צו בטלנות")!—הרי מדובר אודות נשיאת "יהלומים", ולכן, כדאי להתייגע ולשאת ריבוי "יהלומים" (כולל ריבוי מלשון "ריבוא"), ואדרבה: נשיאת משא זה אינו נחשב בלי יגיעה כלל, אלא זהו תענוג הכי גדול!!

ומזה מובן בנוגע לכללות העבודה בעניני התורה ומצות—שהם ה"אבנים טובות ומרגליות" האמיתיים—שעבודה זו נחשבת לתענוג הכי גדול, ולכן, מחפש ומשתדל כל יהודי למצוא עוד ענין ועוד פעולה שיכול להוסיף בכללות העבודה דקיום התורה ומצות.

I once spoke with a certain Jew on this topic, and when I saw that my words were not having any real impact, I had no choice other than to cite a simple analogy:

This particular Jew was a diamond polisher. I asked him how the price of a diamond is determined, and he explained to me the matter is determined based on the quality and volume of the stone. The quality refers to the general appearance, color, cleanliness, etc. Volume refers to its weight, namely a stone of one carat will have a certain price, and a stone of a hundred carats will be worth a hundred times more.

So I asked him whether, to carry a hundred carat diamond, one needs to exert one hundred times the amount of energy; why, then, should it fetch such a high price?

[The Rebbe smiled and said:] When this Jew heard my question, he exclaimed, "I didn't expect such lazy questions even from you! I wish I could have a diamond that weighs a hundred carats, why not a thousand, or even a hundred thousand—and I would happily take the effort to carry that stone into my possession!"

I persisted, "But you have to work so hard to carry such a heavy weight!"

He replied, "There's a limit to the ignorance here! We're talking about diamonds! It's worth every ounce of energy to lift a diamond, and what's more—it's not really even considered 'effort' at all; on the contrary, it's the greatest pleasure!"

So it is with our overall religious experiences: They are true "precious stones," and, as such, our duties are indeed the greatest pleasure to be had! In that spirit, a Jew only seeks to increase his or her observance, looking for another thing to add to his or her religious pleasure.

"Befriending" G-d

TEXT 12

Rabbi Mendel of Kotzk, Ohel Torah, p. 76

"לא יהיה בך אל זר", אל - לא יהיה בך זה.

"No strange god shall be within you"—Do not let G-d be strange or foreign to you, neither to your heart nor to your soul.

Rabbi Menachem Mendel Morgenstern
1787–1859
Chasidic rabbi and leader. Born near Lublin, Poland, Rabbi Menachem Mendel went on to succeed the Chozeh (Seer) of Lublin and Rabbi Simchah Bunim of Peshischa as a Chasidic rebbe in Kotzk. His teachings, some of which are gathered in *Ohel Torah* and *Emet Ve'emunah*, are well-known in the Chasidic world for their sharpness.

TEXT 13

The Rebbe, Rabbi Menachem Mendel Schneerson,
Torat Menachem 5749, vol. 1, p. 218

"אתה" ("דו")—מורה על היחס של יהודי (כל אחד ואחד מישראל, האנשים והנשים והטף) עם הקדוש ברוך הוא באופן שפונה אליו בלשון נוכח, ועד שמראה באצבע ואומר "אתה" ("דו").

כלומר, היחס של יהודי עם הקדוש ברוך הוא אינו באופן שהקדוש ברוך הוא נמצא למעלה בשמים, ברקיע השביעי, והיהודי נמצא למטה בארץ, ומבקש מהקדוש ברוך הוא שישלח לו משם (מן השמים לארץ) המצטרך לו—יהודי אינו חפץ ורוצה יחס כזה, והעיקר, שיחס כזה אינו מתאים ושייך למעמדו ומצבו ודרגתו של יהודי—כי אם, שהקדוש ברוך הוא נמצא יחד עמו ממש, שלכן, פונה אליו בלשון נוכח, "אתה".

Using the term "You" expresses the close relationship a Jew has with G-d.

In other words: The association of a Jew with G-d isn't of such nature that G-d is above in the heavens and the Jew is below on earth, and he requests from G-d to send his needs from the Heavens. No—a Jew doesn't want or desire such a relationship! Rather, G-d is here with him (literally), and thus, he can refer to G-d as "You."

JLI
JEWISH LEARNING INSTITUTE

THE ROHR
Jewish Learning Institute

822 Eastern Parkway, Brooklyn, New York 11213

An affiliate of
Merkos L'Inyonei Chinuch
The Educational Arm of the Worldwide
Chabad Lubavitch Movement

MERKOS L'INYONEI CHINUCH

JEWISH LEARNING INSTITUTE

THE JEWISH LEARNING MULTIPLEX
Brought to you by the Rohr Jewish Learning Institute

In fulfillment of the mandate of the Lubavitcher Rebbe, of blessed memory,
whose leadership guides every step of our work,
the mission of the Rohr Jewish Learning Institute is to transform
Jewish life and the greater community through the study of Torah,
connecting each Jew to our shared heritage of Jewish learning.

While our flagship program remains the cornerstone of our organization,
JLI is proud to feature additional divisions catering to specific populations,
in order to meet a wide array of educational needs.

THE ROHR JEWISH LEARNING INSTITUTE,
a subsidiary of *Merkos L'Inyonei Chinuch,*
is the adult education arm of the Chabad-Lubavitch Movement.

TORAH STUDIES

Torah Studies provides a rich and nuanced
encounter with the weekly Torah reading.

MYSHIUR
TALMUD LEARNING INITIATIVE

MyShiur courses are designed to assist students in developing
the skills needed to study Talmud independently.

SINAI SCHOLARS SOCIETY
IN PARTNERSHIP WITH CHABAD ON CAMPUS

This rigorous fellowship program invites select college
students to explore the fundamentals of Judaism.

JLI TEENS
YOUNG SMART JEWISH
IN PARTNERSHIP WITH CTEEN: CHABAD TEEN NETWORK

Jewish teens forge their identity as they engage in
Torah study, social interaction, and serious fun.

ROSHCHODESH society

The Rosh Chodesh Society gathers Jewish women
together once a month for intensive textual study.

TORAHCafé

TorahCafe.com provides an exclusive selection
of top-rated Jewish educational videos.

National JEWISH RETREAT

This yearly event rejuvenates mind, body, and spirit with
a powerful synthesis of Jewish learning and community.

the LAND & the SPIRIT
ISRAEL EXPERIENCE

Mission participants delve into our nation's rich past while
exploring the Holy Land's relevance and meaning today.

JLI ACADEMY

Select affiliates are invited to partner with peers and noted
professionals, as leaders of innovation and excellence.

מכון שמואל

THE SAMI ROHR
RESEARCH INSTITUTE

Machon Shmuel is an institute providing Torah
research in the service of educators worldwide.